THOMAS MORAN

WATERCOLORS OF THE AMERICAN WEST

TEXT AND CATALOGUE RAISONNÉ BY CAROL CLARK

PUBLISHED FOR THE AMON CARTER MUSEUM OF WESTERN ART
BY THE UNIVERSITY OF TEXAS PRESS, AUSTIN AND LONDON

FRONTISPIECE: ***Looking up the Trail at Bright Angel, Grand Canyon of Arizona*** 1901
Cooper-Hewitt Museum, The Smithsonian Institution's National Museum of Design
Gift of the artist (1917.17.83); catalogue no. 126

Copyright © 1980 by the Amon Carter
Museum of Western Art
All rights reserved
Printed in the United States of America

The Amon Carter Museum was established in 1961 under the will of the late
Amon G. Carter for the study and documentation of westering North America.
The program of the museum, expressed
in permanent collections, exhibitions,
publications, and special events, reflects
many aspects of American culture, both
historic and contemporary.

LIBRARY OF CONGRESS
CATALOGING IN PUBLICATION DATA

Clark, Carol.
  Thomas Moran.

  Issued on the occasion of an exhibition to
be held May 23–July 13, 1980 at Amon
Carter Museum of Western Art, Fort Worth,
Tex., Aug. 5–Oct. 5, 1980 at Cleveland
Museum of Art, and Oct. 23, 1980–Jan. 4,
1981 at Yale University Art Gallery.
  "Catalogue raisonne": p.
  Bibliography: p.
  Includes index.
  1. Moran, Thomas, 1837–1926—
Exhibitions. 2. The West in art—
Exhibitions. I. Moran, Thomas, 1837–
1926. II. Amon Carter Museum of Western
Art, Fort Worth, Tex. III. Cleveland
Museum of Art. IV. Yale University. Art
Gallery. V. Title.
  ND1839.M84A4 1980   759.13   80-13459
  ISBN 0-292-75059-5

This book accompanies an exhibition titled
"The Most Remarkable Scenery": Thomas Moran's Watercolors of the American West

May 23–July 13, 1980	Amon Carter Museum, Fort Worth
August 5–October 5, 1980	The Cleveland Museum of Art, Cleveland
October 23, 1980–January 4, 1981	Yale University Art Gallery, New Haven

AMON CARTER MUSEUM
OF WESTERN ART
BOARD OF TRUSTEES

FOR JON CLARK

Mrs. Carter Johnson, Chairman
Mrs. Adelyn D. Breeskin
Bradford R. Breuer
Mrs. Amon G. Carter, Jr.
Amon G. Carter, Jr.
Mrs. Katrine Deakins
Richard M. Drew
Eldridge C. Hanes
Sherman E. Lee
Richard W. Moncrief
Charles Parkhurst
Walter D. Scott

Jan Keene Muhlert, Director

Tower Falls and Sulfur Rock, Yellowstone ca. 1874–1875
Private Collection
catalogue no. 57

Contents

List of Illustrations

PHOTOGRAPHS

LENDERS TO THE EXHIBITION

Addison Gallery of American Art, Phillips Academy, Andover,
    Massachusetts
American Heritage Center, University of Wyoming at Laramie
Amon Carter Museum of Western Art, Fort Worth, Texas
The Art Institute of Chicago
The Bancroft Library, University of California at Berkeley
Mr. and Mrs. William Belknap
Mr. and Mrs. William H. Bertsche
The Chrysler Museum, Norfolk, Virginia
The Cleveland Museum of Art
Mr. and Mrs. Michael Coleman
Colorado Springs Fine Arts Center
Cooper-Hewitt Museum, The Smithsonian Institution's National Museum
    of Design
Carl Schaefer Dentzel
The Dietrich Corporation, Philadelphia, Pennsylvania
East Hampton Free Library, East Hampton, New York
Grand Teton National Park, Moose, Wyoming
J. V. Hawn
Jefferson National Expansion Memorial, St. Louis, Missouri
Kennedy Galleries, Inc., New York
Robert H. Levis II
Christopher T. May, Sterling A. May, Meredith May, and Laura May
Mead Art Museum, Amherst College, Amherst, Massachusetts
Mills College, Oakland, California
Museum of Fine Arts, Boston
National Collection of Fine Arts, Smithsonian Institution, Washington, D.C.
The Parrish Art Museum, Southampton, New York
Peabody Museum of Archaeology and Ethnology, Harvard University,
    Cambridge, Massachusetts
The Pennsylvania State University, Ogontz Campus, Abington,
    Pennsylvania
Mr. and Mrs. Gerald P. Peters
Phelan Collection
Philbrook Art Center, Tulsa, Oklahoma
Reynolda House Museum of American Art, Winston-Salem, North
    Carolina
Charlotte Moran Rich
Schweitzer Gallery, New York
Trinity College, Hartford, Connecticut
and Anonymous Lenders

ACKNOWLEDGMENTS

A research project of this scope is never done individually, and therefore I am greatly indebted to the many people who generously gave their assistance. Within the museum and library profession, I would especially like to thank Janet Flint, Curator of Prints and Drawings, National Collection of Fine Arts; Sinclair Hitchings, Keeper of Prints, Boston Public Library; Dorothy T. King, Librarian, Long Island Collection, East Hampton Free Library; Martin E. Petersen, Curator of Painting, San Diego Museum of Art; Sue Reed, Assistant Curator of Prints and Drawings, Museum of Fine Arts, Boston; and Helen Schreider, National Park Service, Harper's Ferry, West Virginia. Alfred Bush, Curator, Princeton Collection of Western Americana, Princeton University, provided his large collection of photographs of Moran's paintings. Fred A. Myers, Director, and Anne R. Roden, Curator of Art, opened for research the vast Moran collection of the Thomas Gilcrease Institute of American History and Art, which had been unavailable to scholars under the previous administration. Helen Cooper, Associate Curator of American Painting, Yale University Art Gallery, and William S. Talbot, Associate Curator of Paintings, The Cleveland Museum of Art, supported the exhibition and kindly made arrangements for it to travel to New Haven and Cleveland.

The very beautiful field watercolors at Yellowstone National Park were not available for this exhibition, because, at long last, they are on view in the park at the Horace M. Albright Visitor Center. The problem of contacting owners of Moran watercolors and of tracing provenance was facilitated by the help of dealers, notably Warren Adelson, Coe Kerr Gallery, Inc., New York; Stuart P. Feld, Hirschl & Adler Galleries, New York; Jim Fowler, Scottsdale, Arizona; Michael Frost, J. N. Bartfield, Inc., New York; James Maroney, New York; M. R. Schweitzer, New York; and Rudolf P. Wunderlich, Kennedy Galleries, Inc., New York.

Many watercolors belong to private collectors who graciously permitted me to study their paintings and who shared with me information about how they acquired them. Almost all generously agreed to lend to the exhibition. Several discussed their friendship with Thomas Moran and his daughter, Ruth: Horace M. Albright, Sherman Oaks, California; Mrs. William Belknap; and F. M. Fryxell, Rock Island, Illinois.

The library at the Amon Carter Museum is the ideal place to conduct research in the art of the American West. My special thanks to Nancy Graves Wynne, Librarian, and Milan Hughston, Assistant Librarian, for their excellent help. Marni Sandweiss, Curator of Photographs, assisted with materials by W. H. Jackson and John K. Hillers in the museum's collection. Karen Dewees Reynolds, Research Assistant; Ron Tyler, Curator of History; and Mark Thistlethwaite, Assistant Professor of Art History, Texas Christian University, each read and offered suggestions which improved the manuscript. Suzanne M. Studdard and Margaret L. Booher typed the manuscript and handled correspondence. Anne Adams, Registrar, and Carol Roark, Assistant Registrar, managed the details of shipping and insuring the watercolors.

This exhibition and catalogue are the products of an opportunity provided me several years ago by Mitchell A. Wilder, the late Director of the Amon Carter Museum. Each exhibition that he undertook benefited from Mitch Wilder's vision, challenge, and support. I hope this project, of which he was so much a part, will continue in that tradition.

Carol Clark
Curator of Paintings

Thomas Moran: Watercolors of the American West

Summit of the Sierras, Nevada 1874
The Art Institute of Chicago
Gift of Mrs. Byron Harvey (1965.852); catalogue no. 98

Introduction

"Coloured sketches, taken directly from nature, are the only means by which the artist, on his return, may reproduce the character of distant regions in the more elaborately finished pictures." [1] So Alexander von Humboldt wrote in 1849, and while he referred specifically to exploration in South America, his words carried meaning for artists seeking imagery in the exotic lands west of the Mississippi River. Traditionally, exploration artists strove to produce large oil paintings or series of paintings from their experiences, and Humboldt reflects this attitude by suggesting that the colored field sketches might be used as *aide-memoire* for "finished pictures." These small field sketches, however, and the more highly finished watercolors developed later in the artist's studio from the sketches, are valued today as greatly as the large oil paintings that appealed to nineteenth-century sensibilities. They seem fresher, closer, both to their natural inspiration and to the spirit of the artist's initial vision. Indeed, these watercolors fascinated a group of nineteenth-century patrons to whom they were particularly suited—fellow artists, explorers, and scientists who valued their spontaneity and literalism. Because Thomas Moran traveled with government expeditions, for magazines, and on his own to record and interpret "the most remarkable scenery" [2] of western America, he was in a position to fulfill the demands of both kinds of western art patron—the more traditional collector who cherished large oils and the explorer-scientist who sought watercolor sketches.

Unfortunately, the first major government-sponsored expedition (led by Meriwether Lewis and William Clark) included no artist, but thereafter artists accompanied most important publicly and privately supported exploration parties. These artists were often well-trained professionals, such as Karl Bodmer, who accompanied Prince Maximilian of Wied-Neuwied, and Alfred Jacob Miller, who traveled with Sir William Drummond Stewart. Bodmer and Miller, both in the West during the 1830s, practiced the well-established European tradition of working in watercolor while in the field. Watercolor was the medium of eighteenth-century English topographical artists for travel and discovery of rural and sometimes wild northern country. Although the advent of the collapsible tube for oils in the 1850s facilitated transport to the field, Moran and other exploration artists chose to work in the traditional watercolor medium. Watercolor was particularly suited to painting the western lands, because, in addition to its

---

1.   Alexander von Humboldt, *Cosmos: A Sketch of a Physical Description of the Universe*, p. 452, cited in Theodore E. Stebbins, Jr., *Close Observation: Selected Oil Sketches by Frederic E. Church*, p. 23.
2.   "The Hayden Expedition," *Rocky Mountain News* [Denver], May 20, 1873, p. [4], col. 2.

ease of transport and use, it made possible the quick execution of sketches while the intensity of color was fresh in the artist's mind.

Moran is heir to British watercolorists, especially J. M. W. Turner, who painted the countryside in watercolor for an urban audience increasingly confined to London. The American public of the nineteenth century was not far different. Few families could support themselves on the land, and many of their children by necessity sought a living in urban areas. These new city dwellers were nostalgic for country views and contributed to the success of the so-called Hudson River School artists during the 1830s, 1840s, and 1850s. Demand grew for scenes more exotic than the Hudson, Schuylkill, and Allegheny Rivers provided, and artists like Frederic Church accommodated patrons (as well as their own urge for exploration) by going farther into the northeastern wilderness and eventually to South America, while others like Albert Bierstadt and Thomas Moran chose to travel through and paint the American West.

Between 1871 and 1892, Moran made eight trips to the trans-Mississippi West, three with official government expeditions. The first journey, with Ferdinand V. Hayden to the Yellowstone region, saw the production of a major body of work in watercolor. Following this trip, Moran established his reputation with large canvases and "finished" watercolors developed from his pencil and watercolor field sketches. Impressed by Moran's watercolors (immediately transformed into engravings for *Scribner's Monthly* and for Hayden's report to the Congress) and William Henry Jackson's photographs, Congress declared the Yellowstone area the first national park. These journeys were part of the last great era of exploration in the American West, and in 1890, two years before Moran's last major trip, the Census Bureau declared the frontier officially closed. In an 1893 speech before the American Historical Association meeting at the Chicago World's Fair, historian Frederick Jackson Turner heralded the passage of exploration of the vast western lands into history.

This essay will consider Moran's position as primary artist of the final decades of exploration; assess the impact of his work on an eastern audience whose scientific, nationalistic, and overriding romantic interest in the West was at a peak; and attempt to explain his stylistic development. Moran's choice of the watercolor medium will be central to each of these discussions. Color (something photographers could not supply) was crucial to many collectors' admiration of western landscapes, and the patrons of Moran's oils and watercolors sought out the artist because of his vivid interpretations. Moran's ability to convey a scientific and romantic sense of investigation of the western landscape gives particular importance to the place of these watercolors in the history of American art during the last quarter of the nineteenth century.

The most important research to date on Thomas Moran is chiefly biographical, attempting to link his few letters and diaries and the notations inscribed on field drawings to his extensive travel. Ruth B. Moran, his devoted daughter, aided in this task, especially assisting Fritiof M. Fryxell in his early gathering of material on Moran. In 1963, William H. Gerdts, assisted by Louise Nelson and Samuel Sachs II, organized a small, important exhibition at the University of California at Riverside, based in part on Mr. Sachs's master's thesis devoted to the artist. In 1969, Thurman Wilkins published *Thomas Moran: Artist of the Mountains*, bringing new historic information to the growing biography and contributing the most substantive body of work on Moran. More recently, Thomas Fern and William Truettner have written about Moran's watercolors, especially those of the 1871 Yellowstone trip. Now that such groundwork exists, a more critical interpretation of the watercolors is needed, evaluating their position, importance, and quality within the historic context of late nineteenth-century painting and exploration.

Approximately two-thirds of the almost three hundred watercolors listed in the *catalogue raisonné* have been located. It is hoped that its publication will bring to light the remaining watercolors and produce additional forgotten works of art. Thomas Moran probably would not be surprised at the attention given to his small sketches, for as highly as he valued his large oils (the marks of a successful nineteenth-century artist), he reserved praise for his watercolors. Referring to a group of watercolors he did for William Blackmore, he wrote to Ferdinand V. Hayden, ". . . they were considered here to be a very fine and remarkable lot of subjects."[3] A modest man, he wrote again to Hayden that he would send the watercolors for exhibition in Washington, D.C., adding, "It will attract attention, I think."[4] Moran's watercolors still deserve that attention today.

3.   Thomas Moran to Ferdinand V. Hayden, November 24, 1872, U.S. National Archives, U.S. Geological Survey Records, Record Group 57.
4.   Ibid., January 28, 1873.

Thomas Moran fishing while on Dr. Ferdinand V. Hayden's survey of the Yellowstone country, 1871
Photograph by William Henry Jackson; courtesy National Park Service, Grand Teton National Park

1. TRAINING AND EARLY CAREER

It may be that Moran's English heritage rather than his brief American training more greatly influenced his chosen career. The artist's early life parallels that of Thomas Cole, for although Moran was only seven years old when he emigrated with his family, and Cole seventeen, each came from an urban, industrialized, ugly section of England. The striking difference between childhood in such surroundings and adolescence in Philadelphia, where picturesque rivers and hills of the Schuylkill and Wissahickon valleys were close by and ripe for the sketchbook, undoubtedly affected the sensibilities of the growing artist. That Moran would follow Cole as a devoted and successful landscapist, shifting between real and idealized subjects, comes as less of a surprise when seen against their similar backgrounds.

Thomas Moran's father, Thomas, Sr., was an artisan, a weaver by trade, and probably passed his artistic talents to his children. Although none practiced his father's trade for long, each of the four sons who grew to adulthood became an artist: Edward, Thomas, and Peter were painters, and John was a photographer. Frances Benson reported that Edward did not believe in artistic inheritance: "In spite of the artistic trend of the family, Edward Moran, the leader and teacher of them all, does not believe in heredity; he claims it is all due to circumstances. Back of him, so far as anybody knows, there wasn't even a sign painter."[1]

The elder Moran arrived in America in 1843, sent for his family the following year, and settled them in Baltimore. They subsequently moved to Philadelphia, where Thomas, Sr., gained citizenship for them all in 1849. It was a fortuitous move for the Moran boys, because at mid-century Philadelphia rivaled New York as the nation's artistic capital.[2] Exhibitions at the Pennsylvania Academy of the Fine Arts, and nearby galleries, and the proximity of practicing and teaching artists would not escape the young Thomas Moran's attention.

Edward Moran, the eldest son, began his artistic career almost immediately upon arrival in Philadelphia, though he continued for a time as a weaver. Thomas finished grammar school and apprenticed to the engraving

1. Frances M. Benson, "The Moran Family, *Quarterly Illustrator* 1, no. 2 (April–June 1893): 69.
2. John's version of his family history credited Edward with the impetus for the move, although, for unknown reasons, Thomas Moran's daughter Ruth vehemently denied this, positive that it was her grandparents' search for better public schooling that drew them to Philadelphia. See "Artist-Life in New York," *Art Journal* 4 (1880): 59–60; and marginalia to Benson, "The Moran Family," pp. 67–84, at East Hampton Free Library, Thomas Moran Biographical Collection, cited in Thurman Wilkins, *Thomas Moran, Artist of the Mountains*, pp. 13–15.

firm of Scattergood and Telfer, where his drawing talents assured that he would spend most of his time designing rather than cutting wood blocks. Such an entry into the art world was the most typical for young Americans at the time. Few could support themselves exclusively as "fine" artists, and most made their way in the commercial market for part if not all of their careers. The discipline and precision of wood engraving suited perfectly the demand for carefully observed and rendered paintings, and Thomas Moran benefited from his brief association with the industry. Even after he turned to painting in watercolor and oil, Moran continued to supply drawings for use as illustrations, as well as to execute original etchings and lithographs. By such means, his imagery and reputation spread to a much larger audience.

During his apprenticeship, Moran began to sell his watercolors, usually to local bookstores, often in trade for their books. This modest success encouraged him to abandon the apprenticeship to try his hand as an independent artist, and he joined his brother Edward in a small studio. Although never his student, Moran profited from the advice of James Hamilton, who had taught and encouraged Edward. A reliable biographer, S. G. W. Benjamin, credited Hamilton with financial as well as artistic support of the younger brother: "Not only did he [Hamilton] aid him with wholesome advice, but out of his scanty purse he sometimes purchased some of the young artist's watercolors; for after leaving the engraver, Mr. Moran had devoted himself to water-colour painting, and with such success that he was soon able to find a rapid sale for his sketches."[3] Moran, writing in the third person, singled out Hamilton's help: "After two years at engraving, he left it to begin the practice of Art without a master, and had the skill to succeed. He picked up instruction from the painters of his acquaintance in Philadelphia; especially from James Hamilton, who well suited the boy's imaginative temperament."[4] James Hamilton was not only a watercolorist, but also one devoted to Turner. Having studied the master's work in England, he was often referred to as "the American Turner,"[5] and he provided a perfect model for the impressionable young Moran.

Moran's early practice of watercolor very likely drew him to the series of exhibitions of English watercolors that began in the late 1850s at

3. Samuel G. W. Benjamin, "A Pioneer of the Palette: Thomas Moran," *Magazine of Art* (5 February 1882): 90.
4. Thomas Moran, unpublished autobiography, 1910, Office of the Architect of the Capitol, p. 1.
5. The Brooklyn Museum, *James Hamilton, 1819–1878: American Marine Painter*, text by Arlene Jacobowitz (March 28–May 22, 1966), p. 23.

the Pennsylvania Academy,[6] though surprisingly he does not mention them in later autobiographies. His interest in scenery more spectacular than that of eastern Pennsylvania led him on his first American journey to the Pictured Rocks of Lake Superior in the summer of 1860. The dramatic rock formations, water spills, and forested hills whetted the young man's appetite for travel, and he would venture twice to Europe before returning to the American West eleven years later. He drew while on this summer trip and washed his pencil drawings to achieve a sense of form and atmosphere, but he used very little color. The few canvases resulting from his Michigan trip tend to be dark, almost grisaille, appropriate to the color of the area.

He did not let another summer pass without traveling beyond Philadelphia; in 1861 he went to England with Edward. The primary purpose of the trip was to study the original works of Turner, whose etchings of paintings Moran had known in the *Liber Studiorum* from his first days as an artist. Moran spent months at the National Gallery in London absorbing the English artist's masterful sense of color in oil, and especially in watercolor, and dramatic interpretations of nature. Moran held Turner's early, topographical paintings in much higher esteem than his later, more purely aesthetic ones. In an interview published about twenty years later, Moran summarized his admiration for the British painter:

Turner is a great artist, but he is not understood, because both painters and the public look upon his pictures as transcriptions of Nature. He certainly did not so regard them. All that he asked of a scene was simply how good a medium it was for making a picture; he cared nothing for the scene itself. Literally speaking, his landscapes are false; but they contain his impressions of Nature, and so many natural characteristics as were necessary adequately to convey that impression to others. The public does not estimate the quality of his works by his best paintings, but by his latest and crazier ones, in which realism is entirely thrown overboard.[7]

Moran also devoted the summers of 1861 and 1862 to travel in England and Scotland, sometimes following in Turner's path, always relishing the beauty of the English countryside and its picturesque ruins. The best evidence of this pleasure is in the many drawings and watercolors that Moran

---

6. Samuel Sachs II, "Thomas Moran—Drawings and Watercolors," Master's thesis, New York University, 1963, p. 8.
7. G. W. Sheldon, *American Painters*, p. 123.

completed while traveling in the British Isles. The sketching techniques mastered in England would be useful on the many American trips to come. After a year of travel and study, he returned to Philadelphia richer for his sketches and acquired memories of his native land.

Immediately upon his return in 1862, Thomas Moran married Mary Nimmo, a Scottish woman he had known for several years, and set out to achieve a successful artistic career. In 1866 and 1867, Thomas and Mary Moran traveled to England, France, and Italy, making the "grand tour" essential to the development of any American artist of the mid-nineteenth century. But Moran remained true to his British artistic heritage, renouncing in particular the French Barbizon style that was gaining a great following in Boston.

By 1870, Moran was on his way to becoming a competent landscape painter in the manner of the so-called Hudson River School and descendant of this unofficial, unaffiliated group of artists who painted the wilderness of the eastern United States. But two events intervened to redirect his career: an illustration commission and a subsequent offer to accompany the government's exploration party to the area of the Yellowstone River in Wyoming Territory.

Although Moran was selling pictures, he needed to supplement his income to support his wife and growing family (a son, Paul Nimmo, was born in 1864; a daughter, Mary Scott, in 1867 or 1868; and another daughter, Ruth Bedford, in 1870). He taught painting and continued to provide illustrations for magazines and books. An early friendship with Richard Watson Gilder, an editor of the newly founded *Scribner's Monthly*, led to his first assignment with that magazine and, soon after, to one involving the Yellowstone.

2. THE YELLOWSTONE

Nathaniel P. Langford, of Helena, Montana Territory, wrote two articles for *Scribner's Monthly*, recounting a journey he took into the uncharted Yellowstone country in the summer of 1870.[1] The Yellowstone was among America's last great natural wonders accessible to travelers. Although fur trappers had long known of its rich wildlife and unusual geography, easterners and westerners alike largely discounted the fantastic stories of men like John Colter, George Drouillard, and Jim Bridger. The Yellowstone was mysterious country, difficult to penetrate and navigate within and reportedly rife with hostile Indians. Such a land perfectly suited the romantic sensibilities of nineteenth-century American artists, and it was Thomas Moran's luck to be the first artist to see and paint its remarkable beauty. He later wrote of the effect the Yellowstone had on him in 1871 ". . . the impression then made upon me by the stupendous & remarkable manifestations of nature's forces will remain with me as long as memory lasts."[2]

Langford's trip was not one of pure exploratory pleasure, and he ended his *Scribner's* articles with an exaltation of Yellowstone's marvelous, picturesque beauty, noting that it was a perfect area for future tourism: "By means of the Northern Pacific Railroad, which will doubtless be completed within the next three years, the traveler will be able to make the trip to Montana from the Atlantic seaboard in three days, and thousands of tourists will be attracted to both Montana and Wyoming in order to behold with their own eyes the wonders here described."[3] The optimistic, resourceful nineteenth-century mind found *use* for an area that the government or private enterprise might otherwise not exploit. This was certainly not the first seed planted for the establishment of a national park, but it was one that quickly took root in Congress during the next two years. George Catlin was the first artist to suggest such a national park, as part of his effort to persuade Congress to purchase his Indian Gallery and preserve the Indian in his natural habitat. Thirty years later, when Congress unanimously voted the establishment of the first national park, American opinion could not have been further from Catlin's ideal of preserving the land's native inhabitants.[4] It is not a coincidence that Langford and F. V. Hayden each mentioned Jay Cooke's Northern Pacific Railroad, the biggest busi-

---

1. Nathaniel P. Langford, "The Wonders of the Yellowstone," *Scribner's Monthly* 2, nos. 1–2 (May–June 1871): 1–17, 113–128.
2. Moran papers, Gilcrease Institute.
3. Langford, "Wonders of the Yellowstone," p. 128.
4. William H. Truettner, *The Natural Man Observed: A Study of Catlin's Indian Gallery*, pp. 43, 59, 80.

ness venture of the early 1870s, and stressed the tourism potential of Yellowstone.[5]

A military escort, led by Lieutenant Gustavus C. Doane, accompanied Langford and General Henry D. Washburn into the Yellowstone in August 1870. No artists traveled with the combined civilian and military group of nineteen men, but one soldier, Private Charles Moore, and one civilian, Walter Trumbull, drew primitive, rough pictures of the sights.[6] The leaders of this expedition wanted a visual record at least partially to substantiate the verbal and written reports they planned to make.[7] Langford recognized the importance of such representations: "The solemn grandeur of the scene surpasses description. It must be seen to be felt."[8]

Scribner's planned to publish Langford's articles (which were part of a writing and lecture campaign to open the nation's eyes to the region's potential) but could not use the expedition's pencil sketches. Here, Thomas Moran's experience and skill as a wood-engraving draftsman introduced him to Yellowstone and the West. Although the artist had never been farther west than Michigan, Gilder chose Moran to make sketches from Moore's and Trumbull's drawings and Langford's account. By the time the engravings appeared in the May and June 1871 issues of *Scribner's*, Moran was well on his way to see the landscape he had only imagined for the wood block. This time the expedition to the Yellowstone was under official governmental supervision, specifically the aegis of the Department of the Interior's United States Geological Survey of the Territories, founded in 1869. The survey's chief, Dr. Ferdinand Vandiveer Hayden, led the Yellowstone expedition of 1871, the largest and most important to enter the region. Simultaneously, the army (which would vie with the Interior Department for supremacy in territorial exploration) fielded a Yellowstone party led by Captain J. W. Barlow and including photographer Thomas J. Hines.[9] Unfortunately, the work of this lesser-known group (reports, maps, and photographs) was consumed in the terrible Chicago fire of 1871. William Henry Jackson, Hayden's photographer, lightly referred to

---

5. Ferdinand V. Hayden, "The Wonders of the West—II: More about the Yellowstone," *Scribner's Monthly* 3, no. 4 (February 1872): 390–391.
6. These sketches are preserved at Yellowstone National Park.
7. A good, brief description of this expedition is contained in William H. Goetzmann, *Exploration and Empire: The Explorer and the Scientist in the Winning of the American West*, pp. 401–406.
8. Langford, "Wonders of the Yellowstone," p. 12.
9. Goetzmann, *Exploration and Empire*, pp. 406–409.

his luck: "And so the fact that my pictures were the only ones published that year is something for which I have to thank Mrs. O'Leary's cow." [10]

F. V. Hayden was one of western exploration's most interesting characters. Trained as a physician, Hayden preferred geological field work and managed to secure government funding to pursue his career. Unlike the Langford-Washburn-Doane expedition, Hayden made sure that professional artists accompanied him, although he usually had no money to pay them. His 1869, 1870, and 1871 surveys included Henry W. Elliott as the official artist for topographical studies. During the summer of 1869, Hayden met William Henry Jackson, then on a photographic commission for the Union Pacific Railroad in Wyoming, and later saw his photographs in Jackson's Omaha studio. Hayden offered Jackson a position on his 1870 survey, and the photographer quickly accepted, though the geologist made it clear that he could not pay him. As Jackson recalled, Hayden could offer "only a summer of hard work—and the satisfaction I think you would find in contributing your art to science." [11] Like Moran, Jackson later remembered his first Hayden trip as a turning point in his career: "For Dr. Hayden and the veterans it was more or less routine, and nothing of striking value was unearthed. But for me the expedition was priceless—it gave me a career." [12]

Jackson certainly began an important career in exploration photography, and he accompanied Hayden a total of eight times between 1870 and 1878 (never again unpaid!). He left the field only after the reorganization of the United States Geological Survey and opened his own photography business in Denver. Artists Henry W. Elliott and Sanford Robinson Gifford joined Jackson on Hayden's 1870 survey in Wyoming and Utah, and the photographer began an artistic collaboration with one artist, Gifford, that would continue in his close relationship with another, Thomas Moran, the following summer. [13]

---

10. William Henry Jackson, *Time Exposure: The Autobiography of William Henry Jackson*, p. 203.
11. Ibid., p. 187.
12. Ibid., pp. 190–191.
13. Hayden met Gifford in August 1870, while the artist was traveling in the West with Worthington Whittredge and John F. Kensett. See Ila Joyce Solomon Weiss, "Sanford Robinson Gifford, 1823–1880," Ph.D. dissertation, Columbia University, 1968, p. 131.

    W. H. Jackson's photograph of S. R. Gifford on the Hayden Survey, 1870, in the collection of the Academy of Natural Sciences, Philadelphia, shows Gifford painting a small landscape, *Valley of the Chugwater, Wyoming Ter.*, August 9, 1870 (oil on canvas, 8¼ × 13⅜ inches), now in the collection of the Amon Carter Museum. Jackson also wrote in his unpublished "Diary" (August 1–November 1, 1870), New York Public Library: "He [Gifford] had been a constant companion on all our photographic side trips" (cited in Weiss, "Sanford Robinson Gifford," p. 132).

Hayden had two of the finest landscape artists on his survey of 1871. He recognized Jackson's untapped potential as a landscape photographer and wisely accepted Moran's request to accompany the group. Gifford's temperament and style better suited beautiful than sublime scenery, and he seemed to dislike working in the West. Worthington Whittredge recalled the circumstances of Gifford's joining the survey: "When he accompanied Kensett and myself to the Rocky Mountains he started fully equipped for work, but when he arrived there, where distances were deceptive, he became an easy prey to Col. Hayden, who offered him a hovel. He left us and his sketch box in cold blood in the midst of inspiring scenery. We neither saw or heard from him for several months. . . . He had done literally nothing in the way of work during a whole summer spent in a picturesque region."[14] Only eight small paintings survive from Gifford's summer, suggesting that he worked very little, and on his next western trip four years later he did not sketch at all, preferring only to tour and fish.[15] Few artists were as suited to western travel as Moran.

Hayden was not displeased with Gifford, for he wrote that the artist "rendered us most efficient aid, and by his genial nature endeared himself to all,"[16] but if the explorer asked him to accompany the survey in 1871, the artist chose not to go. Albert Bierstadt, who had first traveled in the West with Frederick W. Lander in 1859, also was to have gone on Hayden's 1871 trip,[17] but instead traveled in California that summer and joined Clarence King's Fortieth Parallel Survey the next.[18] Thus, Hayden did not have an artist other than Elliott, so he must have been amenable to Thomas Moran's request to accompany the expedition. Hayden's concession was based, at least in part, on self-interest, for he would not have permitted an extra, useless member of his party. As Goetzmann observed, "In the main, Hayden was interested in using whatever artistic means he could to convey the complex reality of the West."[19] His choice was excellent. Thomas Moran turned out to be a faithful artist-explorer and a powerful force in bringing the image of Yellowstone back to an eastern audience.

14. Worthington Whittredge, *Gifford Memorial Meeting of the Century Association* (New York, October 29, 1880), p. 45, cited in Weiss, "Sanford Robinson Gifford," p. 331.
15. Weiss, "Sanford Robinson Gifford," p. 337.
16. F. V. Hayden to Hon. Columbus Delano, Secretary of the Interior, published in *The Preliminary Report of the U.S. Geological Survey of Wyoming and Portions of Contiguous Territories* (Washington, D.C.: Government Printing Office, 1871), cited in Weiss, "Sanford Robinson Gifford," p. 332.
17. Nina Spalding Stevens, unpublished biographical sketch of Thomas Moran, Gilcrease Institute.
18. Gordon Hendricks, *Albert Bierstadt, Painter of the American West*, pp. 217–220.
19. Goetzmann, *Exploration and Empire*, p. 500.

The *Scribner's* assignment had awakened Moran's interest in the Yellowstone. Through Langford, he learned of Hayden's 1871 expedition and obtained a letter of introduction from General A. B. Nettleson, who worked for Jay Cooke. The artist borrowed money from the magazine in addition to $500 from Jay Cooke, of the Northern Pacific Railroad, to finance his trip. He left a canvas with each and promised to complete a dozen watercolors of the region for Cooke upon his return.[20] A good businessman, Jay Cooke saw an opportunity to publicize tourism along his northern rail route, and *Scribner's* saw a chance to publish more Yellowstone stories and illustrations and, of course, sell more magazines. American enterprise provided Moran his first trip West.

The thirty-four–year–old artist joined the Hayden camp outside Virginia City, Montana, having traveled by rail to Green River (where he painted his first western sketch, *Green River, Wyoming, First Sketch Made in the West* (Gilcrease Institute, catalogue no. 289), and by stagecoach the rest of the way. He was green but adventurous, and Jackson aptly described his new friend: ". . . despite his lack of horsemanship, he made a picturesque appearance when mounted. The jaunty tilt of his sombrero, long yellowish beard, and portfolio under his arm marked the artistic type, with something of local color imparted by a rifle hung from saddle horn."[21] Later, Jackson remembered Moran: "Prior to 1871 Moran had never known a true wilderness, and he was as poorly equipped for rough life as anyone I have ever known. . . . Never had he mounted a horse before we left the Botelers'. And then he did so with a pillow tucked in over the cantle of his saddle. Frail, almost cadaverous, he seemed incapable of surviving the rigors of camp life and camp food. . . . He astonished every member of the party."[22]

They set out about July 4 with Moran's watercolors, sketchbook, and paper and Jackson's bulky photographic equipment, accompanied by photographer J. Crissman and artist Henry Elliott, as part of Hayden's party of forty. They passed through Beaver Head Canyon of the Madison River, which Moran sketched on the trail and later finished in watercolor in camp (*Beaver Head Cañon, Montana*, Museum of Fine Arts, Boston, catalogue no. 1), through the Gallatin Valley, and on to Fort Ellis. Moran kept a brief diary of the Yellowstone trip, with entries typically decreasing in length and detail as time passed. His longest passage described the land they

20.   Wilkins, *Thomas Moran*, pp. 58–59; and Stevens, Moran biographical sketch.
21.   William Henry Jackson, "With Moran in Yellowstone," *Appalachia* 21, no. 82 (December 1936): 149–158, reprinted in *Thomas Moran: Explorer in Search of Beauty*, ed. Fritiof M. Fryxell, p. 54.
22.   Jackson, *Time Exposure*, p. 200.

traversed before reaching Fort Ellis; he wrote: "Sketched but little but worked hard with the photographer selecting prints to be taken,"[23] suggesting that Moran may have had an idea how useful those photographs would be to him back in his Philadelphia studio. Here they had their first good view of the Yellowstone mountains, which impressed even Hayden: "For beauty and symmetry of outline I have never seen this range equalled in the Far West." But he could not resist comparing them to better-known geography, since he was writing for an audience who probably had never glimpsed an American mountain: ". . . several members of the party, who were familiar with the mountains of Central Europe, were struck at once with the resemblance to the Alps."[24] This sight affected Moran as well, for he painted a beautiful, panoramic view of the range (*The Yellowstone Range from Near Fort Ellis*, July 12, 1871, Yellowstone National Park, catalogue no. 27) and recorded in his diary: "The view from the mountains south east of our Camp and on the road to the lake looking toward the Yellowstone Country [is] glorious, and I do not expect to see any finer general view of the Rocky Mountains."[25]

On July 15 they left Fort Ellis and traveled thirty miles due east to the valley of the Yellowstone River, then ten miles farther south through the valley, arriving two days later at Boteler's Ranch, where they established a base camp. Leaving Boteler's on July 19, the party traveled through Middle Canyon to their first impressive wonder of the Yellowstone, Devil's Slide on Cinnabar Mountain, which Moran sketched (*Cinnabar Mountain, Yellowstone River*, July 20, 1871, and *The Devil's Slide, Yellowstone*, July 21, 1871, Yellowstone National Park, catalogue nos. 3 and 5).

Mammoth Hot Springs superseded that sight the next day, as the party, the first white men to see it, reached the junction of Gardiner's River.[26] Jackson photographed Moran that day, showing the artist examining the spring's formation (*Mammoth Hot Springs*, photograph, July 21, 1871, Yellowstone National Park). Moran only briefly recorded their stay in his diary, but his watercolors of the area show an obvious delight in "those bubbling caldrons of nature."[27] He painted two overviews of the springs, *Hot Springs of Gardiner's River, Yellowstone* (Yellowstone National Park, catalogue no. 11) and *Extinct Craters, Gardiner's River* (Yellowstone National Park, catalogue no. 6), which revealed the power and flux evident in the swelling ground and hollow craters. He wrote on *Extinct Craters*,

---

23.   Moran diary, entry dated July 13, 1871, Jefferson National Expansion Memorial.
24.   Hayden, "The Wonders of the West—II," p. 388.
25.   Moran diary, entry dated July 13, 1871.
26.   Jackson, *Time Exposure*, p. 198.
27.   Ibid.

"Showing manner of formation," and placed the viewer thousands of years in the past when a great turmoil created the Yellowstone. Here, indeed, was a legendary land suited to the nineteenth-century artist who sought dramatic natural history to paint. This watercolor makes almost no reference to human scale or foreground motifs, throwing the viewer immediately into geology's chaotic remains. Moran never achieved the strength of *Extinct Craters* in any of his oils.

Hayden's group remained in the area of the Hot Springs for three days, gathering information and naming the sights they discovered, such as the extinct crater "Liberty Cap." Moran painted these newly found formations: *Gardiner River* and *Liberty Cap and Clematis Gulch* (Yellowstone National Park, catalogue nos. 7 and 15). Hayden must have appreciated Moran's watercolors and Jackson's photographs (which often show Moran as the lone explorer included as a scale reference), for he recognized the importance of visual material, writing: "The scenery in the vicinity of these hot springs is varied and beautiful beyond description."[28]

The next important stop was Tower Creek and Tower Falls, the first of a series of spectacular falls the Yellowstone affords its visitors ascending the river. They remained only two days, but Jackson faced and resolved a logistical challenge: "At the point where that stream [Tower Creek] drops into the gorge the view is magnificent—but recording it on a glass plate from the bed beneath turned out to be my biggest photographic problem of the year."[29] Jackson solved the problem by carrying wet plates quickly up and down the canyon. To judge from Moran's work those two brief days, and from the number of times he repeated the motif later in his career, Tower Falls was a special place. He painted the creek and showed the distinctive rock formation of Devil's Hoof (*Tower Creek*, Yellowstone National Park, catalogue no. 20), a keynote in future pictures of the towers and an indication of the underworld terminology the nineteenth century found suitable to Yellowstone. Moran's giant, looming towers suited Hayden's description: "On either side the somber brecciated columns stand like gloomy sentinels."[30] Interested in the scientific aspects of Hayden's survey, Moran inscribed the verso of *Tower Falls and Sulphur Mountain, Yellowstone National Park* (unlocated, catalogue no. 56): "It is certainly [one] of the most weird and impressive scene[s] in the [Yellowstone] park. The Sulphur Mountain lies across the Yellowstone river which flows at its base. The snowy dome of the Mountain is supported upon a base of colum-

---

28. Hayden, "The Wonders of the West—II," p. 391.
29. Jackson, *Time Exposure*, p. 199.
30. Hayden, "The Wonders of the West—II," p. 392.

nar basalt of great regularity and formation. The columns of which are about 40 feet in height. Beneath these columns lies a strata of calcerous deposit intermixed with sulphur and iron given the most delicate and beautiful tints of red and yellow. This is again supported upon another mass of columnar structure."[31]

Beyond Tower Creek begins the Grand Canyon of the Yellowstone, which continues for thirty miles to the Great Falls and which Moran would later choose as the subject for an enormous canvas. Although the party remained around the falls for four days, and although Moran's diary reveals nothing more illuminating than "sketching and photographing," "photographing and sketching,"[32] Jackson later judged the area as "pictorially the climax of the expedition."[33] Hayden described it: "In some respects this cañon is the greatest wonder of all . . . the striking feature of this remarkable view is the effect of colors derived from the hot spring deposits, which have a brilliancy like the most delicate of our aniline dyes. None but an artist with a most delicate perception of colors could do justice to the picture. The well-known landscape painter, Thomas Moran, who is justly celebrated for his exquisite taste as a colorist, exclaimed, with a sort of regretful enthusiasm, that these beautiful tints were beyond the reach of human art."[34] Yet Moran strove to do what he told Hayden was impossible, and he painted the canyon on scales varying from 2 × 3 inches (*Lower Falls, Yellowstone*, Mr. and Mrs. Horace Marden Albright, catalogue no. 17) to 86 × 141 inches (*Grand Canyon of the Yellowstone*, 1872, oil on canvas, United States Department of the Interior, Washington, D.C.). Moran recorded the same sense of powerful creation that he had observed at the extinct craters of Gardiner's River, and he again dazzled his viewer with the representation of white mineral deposits by taking full advantage of playing off transparent and opaque white watercolor (*Yellowstone from above the Lower Fall, Yellowstone Cañon*, and *Yellowstone Cañon*, August 3, 1871, Yellowstone National Park, catalogue nos. 25, 23, and 24).

Moran continued on to the Upper Falls, where he was particularly impressed by the fishing[35] (W. H. Jackson, *Thomas Moran in the Yellowstone Country*, photograph, 4½ × 7 inches, Grand Teton National Park) and the relative intimacy of this fall compared to the overpowering Lower

---

31. New York, Kennedy Galleries, Inc., *Kennedy Quarterly* 3, no. 2 (October 1962): no. 106.
32. Moran diary, entries dated July 28 and July 29, 1871.
33. Jackson, *Time Exposure*, p. 199.
34. Hayden, "The Wonders of the West—II," p. 392.
35. Inscription on verso of *Upper Falls, Yellowstone*, Philbrook Art Center.

Falls. The Yellowstone provided the scenic variety every landscape painter wanted, and it exemplified the aesthetic categories developed during the eighteenth and nineteenth centuries in England by Edmund Burke, William Gilpin, Richard Alison, and Richard Payne Knight, among others, to explain the range of responses to nature and their pictorial expression. The falls represented the sublime; Yellowstone Lake, the beautiful; and the forthcoming geysers, the picturesque. Hayden perceived the richness of the land's variety: "If below the Falls this river surpasses all others in the West for its rugged grandeur, above the Falls it excells in picturesque beauty."[36] The artists took advantage of the boat that the expedition's members had carried and assembled for collecting scientific data on the river. Although Moran reported their difficulty in maneuvering it,[37] they expanded their viewpoints by its use. Moran's most delicate, idyllic water-colors of the trip showed Yellowstone Lake (*Yellowstone Lake*, Jefferson National Expansion Memorial, catalogue no. 26, and *Springs on the Border of Yellowstone Lake*, July 28, 1871, Yellowstone National Park, catalogue no. 19).

On August 7, Moran was ready to return home in the company of an escort from Fort Ellis, for he wrote: ". . . as the Wonders of the Yellowstone had been seen I concluded to return."[38] He also had tired of the food and closed the entry for that day with "4 Biscuits a day for the last 5 dayes."[39] He and Jackson left the group with Lieutenant Gustavus Doane and headed for the geyser basins of Fire Hole River (largest tributary of the Madison River), where they observed Castle Geyser in eruption and saw Old Faithful, so named by the Langford party the year before. These geysers would become the mainstays of Moran's later Yellowstone watercolor series, though he would paint the most famous, Old Faithful, for only one patron, probably Jay Cooke (*Old Faithful*, 1873, Phelan Collection, catalogue no. 52).

On the face of *The Great Spring on the Firehole River* (Yellowstone National Park, catalogue no. 9), Moran included "color notes," or references to remind himself of special effects he could only suggest in the watercolor itself. On *The Great Blue Spring of the Lower Geyser Basin of Fire Hole River, Yellowstone* (1871, unlocated, catalogue no. 8), he noted: "The Basins graduate from White to yellow to Brown to Orange to Red to Gray / Water in Great Spring pure Blue." Moran wanted to remember the varied colors of the springs of Gardiner's and Fire Hole Rivers because he

---

36.   Hayden, "The Wonders of the West—II," p. 393.
37.   Moran diary, entry dated August 4, 1871.
38.   Ibid., August 7, 1871.
39.   Ibid.

made similar notes to himself on *Hot Springs of Gardiner's River, Yellowstone* (Yellowstone National Park, catalogue no. 11), following a mode of notation used by English painter Edward Lear and by American Thomas Cole. These spectacular geysers and springs, still favorites of tourists today, perfectly capped a month-long stay in the remarkable area of the Yellowstone. Moran and the party left the region through the Madison Valley, and he painted two beautiful views of the canyon, *Lower Entrance to Madison Cañon, Yellowstone* (August 8, 1871, Jefferson National Expansion Memorial, catalogue no. 16) and *In Lower Madison Cañon* (August 8, 1871, Gilcrease Institute, catalogue no. 12). They then went south to Fort Hall, Idaho, while Moran sketched *Pocatello Station, Idaho, Port Neuf Cañon, Idaho*, and two views of the Tetons (Mr. and Mrs. Horace Marden Albright, catalogue nos. 171, 172, 175, and 182) as his final field watercolors of the season.[40]

Moran had learned a great deal about the West and about his own art and had forged a fruitful working relationship with Jackson, who recalled that "Moran became greatly interested in photography, and it was my good fortune to have him at my side during all that season to help me solve many problems of composition. While learning a little from me, he was constantly putting in more than he took out."[41] Like Jackson, Moran had made his career—as a western painter with a Yellowstone specialty. His friends on the expedition called him "T. Yellowstone Moran,"[42] and later that year he began signing his name in a colophon incorporating a "Y" into his own initials.

Hayden's party left the field with important scientific data and a mission for future use of the land. His description of the sights summarized the journey: "We pass with rapid transition from one remarkable vision to another, each unique of its kind and surpassing all others in the known world. The intelligent American will one day point on the map to this remarkable district with the conscious pride that it has not its parallel on the face of the globe."[43]

Moran had good reason to rush home. A devoted husband and father, he faithfully wrote to his wife, affectionately called Mollie, until her death in 1899. (Regrettably, no letters from the 1871 trip survive, possibly because the Morans moved to Newark immediately upon his return to Philadelphia that fall.) He also carried a portfolio stuffed with pencil sketches

40. The Albright watercolors are clearly dated 1871. If these dates are accurate, Moran must have seen the Tetons after leaving the area of the Yellowstone. It is possible that Moran misdated the watercolors and that they are from his 1879 Teton trip.
41. Jackson, *Time Exposure*, p. 201.
42. Fritiof M. Fryxell, ed., *The Thomas Moran Art Collection of the National Parks*, 1:2.
43. Hayden, "The Wonders of the West—II," p. 396.

and watercolors, since he had commissions waiting and debts to repay. He must have had in mind as well a monumental canvas of the Yellowstone, for which he stored mental imagery of the area and which he began several months later. But first he made sketches for the *Scribner's* article, which Hayden wrote, and began the series of Yellowstone watercolors for Jay Cooke and William Blackmore, a British industrialist.

Jackson was in Washington, D.C., during the winter of 1871–1872, in the employ of the United States Geological Survey, to help sort through Hayden's material and prepare a lobbying effort to persuade Congress to establish the first national park. Hayden recognized the importance of Moran's field watercolors as propaganda for congressmen and requested that the artist send them to Washington during hearings on the Yellowstone bill.[44] Hayden quietly distributed Jackson's photographs and Moran's watercolors among the senators.[45] Jackson, modestly omitting his own name, boasted that the survey's photographs and Moran's watercolors "were the most important exhibits brought before the [Congressional] Committee."[46] The exhibits may indeed have swayed the congressmen, for many easterners of the 1870s would more readily accept pictures than verbal or written reports. Reviewing Hayden's book, *The Yellowstone National Park*, and Moran's chromolithographic illustrations, one critic wrote: "The colors will be thought too brilliant by those who have not visited the region, and perhaps in one or two cases the artist has allowed his feelings in that exhilarating atmosphere to influence in some degree his brush . . . but [sometimes] the colors even fall short of reality."[47]

Moran impressed his family with the importance of the Yellowstone to him. Although his daughter Ruth was only a toddler when he first went to the Yellowstone, she grew up with her father's stories of his journey, later recalling: "Every artist of genius experiences during his life a great spiritual revelation and upheaval. This revelation came to Thomas Moran as he journeyed on horseback through an almost unbelievable wilderness. To him it was all grandeur, beauty, color and light—nothing of man at all, but nature, virgin, unspoiled and lovely. In the Yellowstone country he found fairy-like color and form that his dreams could not rival."[48]

The American West yielded the perfect landscape for the expansionistic, scientific, patriotic, and romantic nineteenth-century mind embodied in Thomas Moran.

44. Ruth Moran's notes for biography of her father, Gilcrease Institute.
45. Richard A. Bartlett, *Nature's Yellowstone: The Story of an American Wilderness That Became Yellowstone National Park in 1872*, p. 208.
46. Jackson, "With Moran in Yellowstone," reprinted in *Thomas Moran*, ed. Fryxell, p. 59.
47. *American Journal of Science and Arts* 13, no. 75 (March 1877): 229.
48. Cited in Fryxell, ed., *Thomas Moran*, p. 9.

Thomas Moran at Mammoth Hot Springs, Yellowstone, 1871
Photograph by William Henry Jackson; courtesy National Park Service, Yellowstone National
Park

3. MORAN AND NINETEENTH-CENTURY WATERCOLOR AESTHETICS

If Thomas Moran's field sketches were privately available to congressmen in the winter of 1871–1872, the New York press heralded the appearance of his finished Yellowstone watercolors at Goupil's Gallery the following autumn.[1] Although, according to a contemporary review, these watercolors were "not, strictly speaking, on exhibition,"[2] many people must have viewed them before they were shipped to their purchaser, William Blackmore, in England. Real public acclaim and financial success came that winter with the exhibition in New York and Washington, D.C., of Moran's huge oil painting, *Grand Canyon of the Yellowstone*. One critic, however, after seeing the Yellowstone canvas, preferred the Blackmore watercolors: "They are abundantly finer works than the painting we have been admiring. They are rapid, racy, powerful, romantic specimens of water-color sketching, showing in each example faculties any artist ought to glory in."[3] The *Scribner's* reporter declared them "the most brilliant and poetic pictures that have been done in America thus far."[4]

It is significant that Moran did not exhibit or sell his summer's work of field sketches. Presumably he needed them for later reference, and the possibility of exhibiting and selling them probably never crossed his mind. Watercolors themselves had only recently been accorded attention in America. In 1865, an exhibition of foreign, chiefly English, watercolors in New York alerted a number of artists to the benefits of organization,[5] and the American Society of Painters in Water-Colors (later the American Water-Color Society) began to exhibit at the National Academy of Design. The society's first exhibition impressed critic S. S. Conant, who wrote: "The most striking Art feature of the Fall and Winter, is the great interest suddenly manifested by the New York public in watercolors. Heretofore this beautiful art has been under a cloud in America. . . . [The watercolors'] qualities of tone and color were so admirable and attractive, that the oil paintings in the exhibition were quite neglected in their favor."[6]

---

1. It has been published previously (William H. Truettner, "'Scenes of Majesty and Enduring Interest': Thomas Moran Goes West," *Art Bulletin* 58, no. 2 [June 1976]: 244) that the *Nation* (September 5, 1872) and *Scribner's* (5, no. 3 [January 1873]) critics were reviewing Moran's field sketches exhibited at Goupil's. A close reading of these and other reviews, however, shows that the watercolors were those "finished" paintings sold to William Blackmore and that the field sketches were probably only seen by members of Congress as part of the lobby effort for Yellowstone National Park.
2. "Thomas Moran's Water-Color Drawings," *Scribner's Monthly* 5, no. 3 (January 1873): 394.
3. "Fine Arts: The Yellowstone Landscape at Washington," *Nation*, September 5, 1872, p. 158.
4. "Thomas Moran's Water-Color Drawings," p. 394.
5. Samuel G. W. Benjamin, *Our American Artists, 1879*, p. 40.
6. S. S. Conant, "Fine Arts," *Putnam's Magazine* n.s. 1, no. 1 (January 1868): 132.

Yet, sixty years later, around the time of Moran's death, when there were a dozen exhibitions exclusively devoted to his watercolors, the thought of preferring watercolors to oils was still suspect. Reviewing a 1925 exhibition in Santa Barbara, Laura Bride Powers wrote of his Grand Canyon watercolors: "Sketches though they be—studies for larger work— there are many nice persons who would be as happy at the possession of one of the sketches as of the canvas it inspired. Heretical, but true. These ring with directness, spontaneity and terseness, and sing with a beauty of color."[7] Although the Santa Barbara exhibition contained some finished watercolors, most were field sketches, many with penciled color notes, including a few of the Yellowstone studies. Mrs. Powers made it clear that, as late as 1925, critics recognized these watercolors as studies, intended to inspire a larger work.

A market for watercolors existed during the 1870s and 1880s, and we are beginning to have a better idea of its impetus and supporting patronage, echoed in part by contemporary criticism. The Society of Painters in Water-Colors exhibited as a group at the nation's centennial celebration in Philadelphia. By 1880, the society's members presented as many as eight hundred watercolors at their annual exhibition. Yet controversy still clung to the medium, fed by its amateur status, by comparison to contemporary English watercolors, and by the sketch-finish dispute central to the history of nineteenth-century landscape painting. Moran's position as a Western watercolorist must be viewed against this background.

The Hudson River artists were the first well-known Americans to take sketchbooks and paints into the countryside, but they usually chose oils rather than watercolors for such jaunts. Though accomplished watercolorists were certainly practicing in America with some success throughout the nineteenth century, the medium was widely regarded as one for amateurs. Oil was held much the preferable medium for serious artists, and many more chose it.[8] As late as 1868 one critic felt compelled to correct a generally held assumption: ". . . another erroneous impression . . . is that working in water-colors injures the eye for working in oils."[9]

Mid-nineteenth-century watercolor artists recognized the medium's unique advantages for landscape painting, and pamphlets on watercolor instruction appeared, one of which observed: "The masters of water color,

7. Laura Bride Powers, "Early Art of Thomas Moran Shown in Art Club Exhibit," *Santa Barbara Morning Press*, June 16, 1925.
8. James Jackson Jarves, *Art Thoughts*, p. 198, cited as *The Art Idea*, 1869, p. 198, in Darryl Patrick, "The Iconographical Significance in Selected Western Subjects Painted by Thomas Moran," Ph.D. dissertation, North Texas State University, 1978, p. 20 n. 28.
9. Conant, "Fine Arts," p. 132.

however, maintain, with some reason, that for certain luminous qualities, for purity of tint and tone, for delicate gradation especially in skies and distance, their favorite style of painting has decided advantages over oil."[10]

The English first exploited landscape as raw material for the most inventive use of watercolor. The medium enabled the artist to record changing atmospheric conditions and, after Winsor and Newton introduced tubes for moist colors about 1846, to carry colors easily into the field.[11] Moran looked to his birthplace for inspiration, admiring Turner at an early age and choosing that country for his first artistic voyage of discovery in 1861 and 1862. English watercolors were available for Americans to study at mid-nineteenth-century exhibitions, primarily in New York, and it was from these artists that Moran and other American watercolorists learned. Watercolor manuals of English origin, some adapted for American use, became widely available in the 1850s[12] and, with the English exhibitions, assured the supremacy of that country's style and technique for thirty years.

British watercolorists, however, practiced their art as more than a vehicle for *plein air* sketching. The carefully composed and highly detailed finished watercolor appealed to British patrons, who looked upon them as substitutes for oil paintings and regarded them that much more highly because of their close association with the more accepted oil medium.[13] Moran's finished watercolors of the 1870s resemble their British antecedents in carefully prepared surfaces, pencil underdrawings, jewellike application of opaque colors, especially white, and delicate playing-off of transparent passages. Although none of Moran's paintings retains a gold mat, contemporaries like Winslow Homer's dealer, Doll and Richards, preferred them, suggesting that Moran may have, too.

Moran's style in these watercolors is different from that of his oils, in which he conveys a grand conception of the West in sweeping brushwork on a large scale. In the more limited scale of watercolor (usually 9 × 14 inches, and the largest about 20 × 28), Moran pulls the viewer into a

10. *Water Color Painting, Some Facts and Authorities in Relation to Its Durability* (New York, 1868), cited in Ralph Fabri, *History of the American Watercolor Society: The First Hundred Years*, p. 14.

11. Majorie B. Cohn, in *Wash and Gouache: A Study of the Development of the Materials of Watercolor* (pp. 13, 55), points out that, for outdoor sketching, English artists generally preferred moist colors in pans or squeezed onto a palette to those in metal tubes. The latter, however, allowed the application of color at full saturation and the attainment of the appearance of oil painting in watercolor.

12. Theodore E. Stebbins, Jr., *American Master Drawings and Watercolors*, p. 146.

13. University of Maryland, College Park, Art Gallery, *From Delacroix to Cézanne: French Watercolor Landscapes of the Nineteenth Century*, text by Alain de Leiris (October 26–December 4, 1977), p. 33.

miniature world of suggested immensity. That which is overwhelming in person or by description becomes comprehensible through carefully controlled line, definite form, and deep, clear color. The richness of color is the material vehicle of the painting, as well as the introduction to the American West's atmosphere, which permits the perception of such color. Moran achieves this color by superimposed transparent washes and judicious use of gouache, or opaque color, to highlight or suggest shimmering geological formations. The paintings' small scale and delicacy of color and brushwork are strangely appropriate to comprehending vast distances and remarkable geography.

Nineteenth-century American critics were divided in appreciation of the finished watercolor. For some, oil and watercolor effects could become too similar, and they cautioned artists not to carry imitation too far. One critic, C. Howard Dudley, denounced the fad of "a use of the [watercolor] medium for which the [American Water-Color] Society stands pledged by its very name to be a representative in such a way as to suggest oil" and the "reprehensible use of body color [opaque color] as though it were oil, thus giving a dull, lack-luster, opaque effect foreign alike to both media."[14] As early as 1880, S. G. W. Benjamin, a pioneering watercolor critic, called for pure transparent watercolor, without the use of opaque color.[15]

Watercolors could stray too far from finish, however, and in the eyes of many become sketchy, unfinished, and unpleasant. Reaction to Winslow Homer's changing watercolor technique, in which he generally worked from greater opacity to greater transparency, is typical of the nineteenth-century regard for finish.[16] He adopted a more carefully composed and highly detailed style during his British sojourn of 1881–1882 and received approval from the critics, one of whom stated that the watercolors were, "to begin with, *pictures* in the truest sense and not mere studies or sketches like most of his earlier aquarelles."[17]

Moran knew the opinion of most critics on the position of sketches and did not regard them as finished, exhibitable works of art, but rather as

14.   C. Howard Dudley, "Exhibition of the American Water-Color Society," *Brush and Pencil* 10, no. 3 (June 1902): 140, 148.
15.   Samuel G. W. Benjamin, "American Water-Colour Society: Thirteenth Annual Exhibition," *Art Journal* 6 (1880): 91. The opinions of Dudley and Benjamin are the dominant ones of the period and are also expressed in "Current Opinion on Landscapes and Water-Colours," *Art Journal* 4 (1878): 94.
16.   My thanks to Helen Cooper, who shared her research on Winslow Homer's watercolors.
17.   M. C. Van Rensselaer, *Century Illustrated Monthly Magazine* 27 (November 1883): 16–17, cited in Hereward Lester Cooke, "The Development of Winslow Homer's Water-Color Technique," *Art Quarterly* 24, no. 2 (Summer 1961): 178.

studies of nature, in the French academic meaning of the word *study*.[18] They were pleasurable reminders of profound visual experiences and were tools for creating other watercolors and oil paintings. The sketches were not his only tools, however, for the artist relied on memory and imaginative invention, as well as the more literal photograph.

Like most artists trained as illustrators, Moran could translate the sketches and photographs of others into drawings or watercolors for reproduction. This was part of his early profession and a method employed by his mentor James Hamilton, who used Solomon Carvalho's photographs from the Frémont expeditions as sources for his own paintings and engravings.[19] Moran's use of photographs is easy to see and somewhat difficult to document. His fruitful collaboration with Jackson in 1871 and later is described in Moran's journal and Jackson's autobiography and is evident in the similarity of the photographs and watercolors from the Hayden expedition and the Mount of the Holy Cross. Yet Moran does not simply *use* Jackson's compositions in his watercolors. The photographer said that he and Moran together chose the sights for photographing and sketching. Moran did quote directly from John K. Hillers' photographs of the Grand Canyon for illustrations of the same subject, yet he limited their use to illustrations and not watercolors or oil paintings. Like Bierstadt, Moran had a brother, John, practicing as a professional photographer, and, although there is no evidence that he took his own photographs, a list of his personal possessions included fifty photographs of the West.[20] Moran infrequently expressed opinions about his fellow artists and photographers, yet he wrote to Hayden about the photographs taken by William A. Bell on the 1872 Wheeler expedition: "I saw Wheeler's photos from the Grand Canon of the Colorado today. They are poor and Jackson will knock spots out of them."[21] Bell's unusual compositions of sharp juxtapositions and great variation in light and shade did not appeal to an artist who looked for geological truth rather than artifice in photographs.

Moran's field sketches were his most important sources, and he kept the Yellowstone portfolio all his life. They were still in his studio, in use as *aide-memoire*, when William H. Simpson saw them there about 1909. Simpson expressed an interest in a "little book, now crumpled and soiled

18. See Albert Boime, *The Academy and French Painting in the Nineteenth Century*, passim, for a thorough and provocative discussion of this subject.
19. Elizabeth M. Cock, "The Influence of Photography on American Landscape Painting, 1839–1880," Ph.D. dissertation, New York University, 1967, pp. 52–56.
20. Undated document, Gilcrease Institute Library.
21. Moran to Hayden, May 12, 1873, National Archives, Records of the Territorial Surveys, Record Group 57.

and worn, containing copious pencil sketches and a few color notes made when he first visited the Far West. One of the paintings now underway was based on a motive taken from that old book."[22] Simpson was a very useful observer, because he was in charge of a Santa Fe Railroad trip to the Grand Canyon in 1901 that included Moran. On that trip he noted that the artist "sketched scarcely at all, contenting himself with pencil memoranda of a few rock forms, and making no color notes whatever. He depended entirely upon keen powers of observation and a well-trained memory for the rich tones which perhaps a year later were to reappear on canvas."[23] In thirty years Moran had completely changed his method of working in the West and, significantly, he painted few watercolors, *en plein air* or in the studio, in the twentieth century.

Moran's most prolific sketching period was between 1871 and 1892, when summer after summer he filled notebooks and paper with impressions of the West. Some western areas affected him more than others, and he was especially active sketching *en plein air* in 1871, 1879, 1883, and 1892. These sketches vary in their degree of completeness. Some are quick pencil underdrawings with color notes and one or two color washes added for their own effect and to create form. In others, Moran exploited the chance effects of dripping paint, absorbent paper, and blotted areas to enhance his impressions of the landscape. Moran never completely fills the paper, and its white surface acts as important formal elements in many instances. The rigors of western travel are evident in these watercolors, some of which he painted on precarious perches chosen for the view they availed. Varying degrees of completeness can be explained by Moran's practice of starting a watercolor in the field and then either leaving it alone or working further on it in camp or during his stops at frontier towns along the way. Moran's field technique is close to that of Alfred Jacob Miller, who worked in pencil and watercolor at the site, including color notes then, and later adding to them after returning to camp.

Moran's working method contrasts with that of Frederic E. Church, who used oil almost exclusively for painting out-of-doors.[24] Moran's sketches are generally more highly finished than Church's, who preferred to paint effects of light and atmosphere rather than vignettes of scenic or geological wonder. The two artists, however, admired Turner, respected

22. William H. Simpson, "Thomas Moran—The Man," *Fine Arts Journal* 20, no. 1 (January 1909): 21.
23. Ibid., p. 25.
24. The discussion of Church is based on Theodore E. Stebbins, Jr., *Close Observation: Selected Oil Sketches by Frederic E. Church*, and David C. Huntington, *The Landscapes of Frederic Edwin Church: Vision of an American Era*.

finish in art, chose literary sources for inspiration of paintings done before actual travel to an exotic site, and regarded their sketches as improper for public display and discussion. It is coincidental that Moran and Church both donated their sketches to the Cooper Union School, yet each artist wanted them available for future art students rather than as exhibition pieces. That these paintings are subjects of current exhibition interest is indicative of changing tastes and attitudes.

Moran never entered into America's sketch-finish controversy. Even though critic S. S. Conant claimed that "a sketch is often more interesting than a finished picture, especially a sketch in watercolors,"[25] or that "there is a certain charm about a master's sketch which no finished picture has— a freshness and vividness of idea, and a truth to nature, often left out of the work elaborated with art and science in the studio,"[26] Moran continued to prefer his finished watercolors as exhibition pieces. He would have agreed with Conant's judgment of a fine, finished watercolor as "an admirable specimen of what a highly-finished water-color should be, pure and transparent in tone, yet not wanting in depth, texture, and solidity where these characteristics are in place."[27]

Thus, sketch vs. finish, a major controversy of nineteenth-century French and, to a lesser extent, American landscape painting, never seems to have affected Moran. The revolution of Impressionism and the "unfinished" picture, deeply rooted in the academic tradition of studies and sketches, had no meaning for an American artist who planned to make a career on large "machines," or canvases of historic value. At the time of Moran's first success, the group of artists derogatorily dubbed "Impressionists" were exhibiting in Paris to a scandalous reception. Moran had little use for contemporary French painting, dismissing even the Barbizon artists who were achieving great success in Boston.[28] He wrote: "I am an impressionist, but I do not belong to the accepted school of impressionism. . . . The school of impressionism is false to the very thing it pretends to imitate, and is therefore a mere pretension, and not real art."[29]

Moran's opinion of Impressionism reflected the language of John Ruskin, who stressed the difference between truth and imitation. Ruskin wrote that truth "has reference to statements both of the qualities of mate-

25.   S. S. Conant, "Fine Arts," *Putnam's Magazine* n.s. 3, no. 15 (March 1869): 378.
26.   S. S. Conant, "Fine Arts: The Winter Exhibition," *Putnam's Magazine* n.s. 3, no. 13 (January 1869): 121.
27.   Conant, "Fine Arts," (March 1869): 378.
28.   Sheldon, *American Painters*, pp. 126–127.
29.   Thomas Moran, "Knowledge a Prime Requisite in Art," *Brush and Pencil* 12, no. 1 (April 1903): 16.

rial things, and of emotions, impressions, and thoughts."[30] Ruskin addressed himself to the problems of finish as well: "Now both the finish and incomplete are right where they are the signs of passion or of thought, and both are wrong . . . when they cease to be so."[31]

Moran made his most often quoted aesthetic statement in Ruskinian terms. G. W. Sheldon reported that the artist told him: "I place no value upon literal transcripts from Nature. My general scope is not realistic, all my tendencies are toward idealization. . . . Topography in art is valueless . . . while I desired to tell truly of Nature, I did not wish to realize the scene [*Grand Canyon of the Yellowstone*] literally, but to preserve and to convey its true impression."[32] Here Moran does not belie his attempts to authenticate his scenes with the help of geologists, as he did with the Yellowstone and Grand Canyon watercolors and oils of the 1870s. He may have overstated the sentiment in an attempt to justify his position as a "fine" artist rather than illustrator or photographer, either of whom could convey "literal transcripts from Nature." Yet the artist clearly differentiated between the "truth" of a completed picture and the "truth" of sketches and subsequent details of a painting which he admitted "are so carefully drawn that a geologist could determine their precise nature."[33]

Moran was just one of many American artists committed to Ruskin's thought. *The Crayon* (1855–1861) and *The New Path* (1863–1865) heralded this ideology to a society convinced of the unity of nature, religion, and art. Harvard professor Charles Eliot Norton spread Ruskin's word in Boston, and one geologist-explorer, Clarence King, became a devoted follower and founding member of the Society for the Advancement of Truth in Art. He wrote of his experiences in the Sierra Nevada and his desire to discover an artist equal to Ruskin's ideal. Although he admired Frederic Church, he hated what he viewed as Bierstadt's distortions of mountain scenery. "Thus I came to Ruskin," he wrote, "wishing I might see the work of his idol, and after that longing for some equal artist who should arise and choose to paint our Sierras as they are, with all their color-glory, power of innumerable pine and countless pinnacle."[34] Unable to find such an artist in America, King created Hank G. Smith, "California-born and

30.   John Ruskin, *Modern Painters*, 1:95.
31.   Ibid., p. 167.
32.   Sheldon, *American Painters*, p. 125.
33.   Ibid., p. 126.
34.   Clarence King, *Mountaineering in the Sierra Nevada* (Boston: James R. Osgood and Company, 1872), p. 207, cited in David Howard Dickason, *The Daring Young Men: The Story of the American Pre-Raphaelites*, p. 93.

mountain raised,"[35] to paint the West as he and Ruskin wanted. Thus, America was ready for an artist who might know the western landscape and paint its appearance as well as its higher symbolic and artistic truth. Thomas Moran proved to be such an artist.

It was mountain scenery that could so move explorer, author, and artist alike. The Alps were a favorite stop for artists touring Europe in the nineteenth century, yet many artists found them lacking in comparison to their New World counterparts. "Must I tell you that neither the Alps nor the Apennines, no, nor even Aetna itself, have dimmed in my eyes the beauty of our own Catskills?" wrote Thomas Cole upon his return from Italy in 1842.[36] Ruskin's chapters entitled "Mountain Gloom" and "Mountain Glory" afforded aesthetic guides for readers of the 1856 American edition of *Modern Painters* and reinforced the need for exploration of America's mountainous West. For Ruskin and his followers, bringing mountain scenery out of "gloom" and into "glory" by painting it provided the means of spiritual and emotional uplift. Mountains were the gauge of quality in artistic endeavor, the highest attainment possible for an artist. Ruskin wrote: "Connected with this love of liberty we find a singular manifestation of love of mountains, and see our painters traversing the wildest places of the globe in order to obtain subjects with craggy foregrounds and purple distances. Some few of them remain content with pollards and flat land; but these are always men of third-rate order; and the leading masters, while they do not reject the beauty of the low grounds, reserve their highest powers to paint Alpine peaks or Italian promontories."[37] Ruskin's views rarely were wholly consistent and he later chided Moran for his bombastic painting.

Ruskin and Moran enjoyed a brief friendship during Moran's stay in London in 1882, and Ruskin later corresponded with the artist. The Englishman purchased a set of Prang's chromolithographs of Moran's watercolors, as well as several of Thomas and Mary Nimmo Moran's works. Yet Ruskin felt he could help Moran: ". . . please do mind what I said, about a severer and simpler severity of study," he wrote.[38] And later: ". . . I *do* wish with my whole heart you would give up—for a while all that flaring and

35. Ibid., p. 209.
36. Louis Le Grande Noble, *The Life and Works of Thomas Cole* (New York, 1853), p. 333, cited in University of Kansas at Lawrence, Museum of Art, *The Arcadian Landscape: Nineteenth Century American Painters in Italy*, text by Charles C. Eldridge (November 4–December 3, 1972), p. xiv.
37. Ruskin, *Modern Painters*, vol. 3, pt. 4, p. 263, cited in Marjorie Hope Nicholson, *Mountain Gloom and Mountain Glory: The Development of the Aesthetics of the Infinite*, p. 6.
38. Ruskin to Moran, undated letter, typescript, Gilcrease Institute.

glaring and splashing and roaring triumph—and *paint*, not etch—some quiet things like that little tree landscape absolutely from nature."[39] As closely as Moran followed English watercolor precedent and admired John Ruskin, Turner's early champion and Britain's chief aesthetic theorist, he rarely followed the critic's advice, and he continued to paint dramatic and quiet landscapes throughout his career.

Ruskin seems, in his published works and his letters to Thomas Moran, to recognize the necessity of a varied artistic and aesthetic vocabulary. Whether Ruskin realized it or not, Moran painted western scenery in its sublimity, beauty, and picturesqueness, if he, like most Americans of his generation, preferred the most dramatic and sublime imagery. Thus Moran, lucky to have accompanied an expedition into the West's most varied landscape, had as a scientific guide Ferdinand Hayden, whose own reactions heightened the artist's aesthetic appreciation. American artists and their public had found one answer to the nineteenth-century search for exotic and affecting experiences in an unexplored land rife with national and religious meaning and capable of being described in Ruskinian language. This exoticism paralleled that of other distant lands for Romantic artists, like the Arctic or South America for Frederic Church. Moran's studio in East Hampton was filled with exotic objects from around the world, much as Frederic Church's Olana was. Yet the West was special for Moran precisely because it was American and thus fulfilled his national *and* his exotic expectations.

Present historians link Moran with other Western artists of the last three decades of the century as "Second Generation Hudson River School," or the more poetic "Rocky Mountain School." Among these artists are several who preceded Moran into the territories: John F. Kensett, Sanford Robinson Gifford, and Worthington Whittredge. These artists preferred the simple, pastoral offerings of the West, the broad plain framed by cottonwoods and quiet streams or the vignette of interesting geological formations. Their styles hardly changed from those employed on dissimilar eastern scenery, assuring them the same reception for their western canvases as they had had for those of eastern subjects. Even Albert Bierstadt, whose interpretation of the West is closer to Moran's than any of his contemporaries, continued a style developed in Düsseldorf and practiced in the Alps in the years prior to his western experiences.

Thomas Moran, alone of America's western artists, arrived there at a formative moment in his career, skilled as a draftsman, somewhat experienced as a watercolorist, and tuned by some European travel. In this way

---

39.   Ibid., December 27, 1882.

he was able to compose new views as he developed his own style, and thus his work is associated most closely with its inspirational source. This is not to say, however, that Moran arrived without prior assumptions (primarily those of Turner and English watercolorists), but his relative freshness, association with scientists and photographers, and desire to interpret anew afforded him a high position as an artist-explorer.

Moran rarely wrote about his fellow artists and never about Bierstadt, an obvious rival. However, he consistently praised Frederic Church in his interviews and articles. In one published interview he said: "The old Hudson River school, so called, F. E. Church, Kensett, and the Harts—these were purely American, and they were an honor to our land. Perhaps Church was the greatest landscape painter we have ever produced."[40] Moran admired Church because he was "purely American." He went on: "I want to voice myself as being opposed to the foreign subject in painting when we have every phase of landscape and subject at home. America is richer in material for the true artist working along the lines of individual development than any country in the world."[41] Gustave Buek, author and close friend of the artist, recalled Moran's words: "I decided very early that I would be an American painter. I'll paint as an American, on an American basis, and American only. I traveled the country over and the West appealed to me. I like the comparatively flat land of Eastern Long Island, such as I have near my studio at East Hampton and Montauk; and then I like the rugged mountains of the Rockies."[42]

In this statement of Moran's nationalism is a seed of the artist's awareness of the eighteenth- and nineteenth-century aesthetic categories of the sublime, the beautiful, and the picturesque. The critics well recognized this aspect of Moran's paintings. One wrote in 1900: "With his keen sense of the beautiful is also linked an equally clear appreciation of grandeur and sublimity, and one finds these qualities betraying themselves even in his simplest canvases."[43] Another wrote the next year: ". . . and I think me there is no better exponent of God's own architecture. From the base to the pinnacle the volcanic upheaval and descendant stand in sullenness and pride, dignified and morose, yielding nothing but a diversified quality and quantity, unintelligible, unconquered, but brought nearer

---

40. Moran, "Knowledge a Prime Requisite in Art," p. 16.
41. Ibid.
42. Gustave H. Buek, "Thomas Moran, N.A.—The Grand Old Man of American Art," *Mentor* 12, no. 7 (August 1924): 34.
43. Frederick W. Morton, "Thomas Moran, Painter-Etcher," *Brush and Pencil* 7, no. 1 (October 1900): 2.

home by Mr. Moran than by any other artist throughout the length and breadth of the land."[44]

Moran rarely spoke or wrote of any religious inspiration behind his art, but his daughter often repeated that her father found spiritual sustenance in the landscapes he painted, especially the western ones. It was a religious era, and most mid-nineteenth-century men infused their writing and painting with a spiritual presence, however vague. Although the Civil War brought much of the explicit nature of this spiritualism to an end and ushered in a period of greater secularization and scientific investigation,[45] the older aesthetic categories continued in the language. An artist could achieve sublimity only by idealizing nature, by selecting and painting scenes of great dramatic potential. Beauty came from balance, harmony, and grace, and he could achieve the picturesque by choosing that which had the most variety and irregularity.[46] In choosing scenes for his watercolors, Moran adhered to these aesthetic categories and to Ruskin's opinions on mountain views.

Illustrations for Nathaniel P. Langford's *Scribner's* articles provided Moran's first touch with the West and Yellowstone. Much more so than in Hayden's article a year later, Langford's language was that of sublimity. He admired the variety of Yellowstone's falls; the Lower was "a sheer, compact, solid, perpendicular sheet, faultless in all the elements of grandeur and picturesque beauty," and he described the Upper Falls: "What this cataract lacks in sublimity is more than compensated by picturesqueness."[47] The Grand Canyon of the Yellowstone inspired Langford's most emotional prose:

The brain reels as we gaze into this profound and solemn solitude. We shrink from the dizzy verge appalled, glad to feel the solid earth under our feet. . . . The stillness is horrible. . . . The sense of danger with which it impresses you is harrowing in the extreme. . . . If you could see a luring tree in the depth beneath you . . . you would rise from your prostrate condition and thank God that he had permitted you to gaze, unharmed, upon this majestic display of natural architecture. As it is, sympathizing

44.   W. P. Lockington, "Philadelphia Water-Color Exhibition," *Brush and Pencil* 8, no. 2 (May 1901): 68.

45.   See David C. Huntington's essay in University of Michigan at Ann Arbor, Museum of Art, *Art and the Excited Spirit: America in the Romantic Period*, (March 19–May 14, 1972), for a discussion of this subject.

46.   Although written about fifty years ago, these books remain the most interesting on this topic: Christopher Hussey, *The Picturesque: Studies in a Point of View*, and Samuel H. Monk, *The Sublime: A Study of Critical Theories in XVIII-Century England*.

47.   Langford, "Wonders of the Yellowstone," p. 13.

in spirit with the deep gloom of the scene, you crawl from the dreadful
verge, scared lest the firm rock give way beneath and precipitate you into
the horrid gulf.[48]

As ably as Langford seemed to describe the Yellowstone's impression, he stressed that "the solemn grandeur of the scene surpasses description. It must be seen to be felt,"[49] making Moran's sketches, illustrations, and paintings crucial ingredients in the public's comprehension of the West.

Moran's western canvases and watercolors depicted areas of great significance to the American public; they conferred historical legitimacy to a land lacking human associations and presented a stage for the unfolding drama of a nation's future. Moran's American landscape could also rise in status by association with historical themes. As America viewed her land, especially the West, as part of a natural historic past destined to determine a great future, Americans began to accept landscape painting in oil and watercolor as an integral and formative element of this destiny.

---

48. Ibid., p. 12.
49. Ibid.

Thomas Moran en route to the Yellowstone, 1871
Photograph by William Henry Jackson (retouched by Moran); courtesy National Park Service,
Grand Teton National Park

4. MORAN'S WATERCOLOR PATRONS

Patronage of American artists and subject matter is only one aspect of the increased awareness and support of art that marked the last quarter of the nineteenth century in the United States. Attempts to democratize connoisseurship paralleled the rise of Jacksonian democracy in the 1840s, signaled an increase in the number of patrons, and provided a new range of popular subjects. Landscape and genre subjects benefited most artists, and native rivaled foreign themes in the marketplace. Business, a guiding force in American society, discovered the art marketplace as a new arena for its activity.

Thomas Moran participated in Louis Prang's chromolithography business, the greatest and most successful experiment in the democratization of art, though he was critical of Prang's business practices and generally suspicious of the availability of multiple images. James Jackson Jarves, a major critical voice in the nineteenth century, disapproved of the American middle-class approach to art and its purchase, judged it too brash and commercial, and compared it unfavorably to its European counterpart. He wrote: "Commissions are called 'orders,' as in trade, and art is mainly ordered as one orders a style of calico of a cotton factory. . . . An increasing number of persons engage in art for no sincere purpose except to speedily become rich; their credit, like that of merchants, being based on the amount of business they do."[1]

Few artists of Moran's generation would have agreed with Jarves's estimation of the profit potential of art. Yet in almost every instance Moran agreed with Jarves's condemnation of the American business of art. Moran was not a good businessman, and his daughter reported that he often accepted a lower price for a painting simply to get the bargain seeker out of his studio so that he could return to work.[2] He ignored his record books, or brought them up to date periodically from memory, and he gave quite a few paintings away to friends and visitors. Although Moran supported his family quite well with earnings from his art, he consistently supplemented his income with commercial illustration commissions. And in 1886 he found it necessary to sell much of his work at auction in order to finance a European trip. Upon his death in 1926, critics hailed him as the grand old master of American art and recounted his successes, yet he left very little to support his devoted and dependent daughter Ruth. She lived twenty-two years longer, trying simultaneously to stretch out the sales of his studio collection to support herself and also to assure her

---

1.   Jarves, *Art Thoughts*, p. 293.
2.   Ruth B. Moran, "Thomas Moran: An Impression," *Mentor* 12, no. 7 (August 1924): 38–39.

father's place in the pantheon of American artists. In many instances before her death, family friends assisted in emergencies when Ruth was too proud to ask for help for needed food and fuel.

Moran did not experience the wide swings between success and failure of Albert Bierstadt. During the 1860s, Bierstadt was by far the most popular and successful western artist, yet by the end of the decade criticism of his work was widespread, and he never recovered his former position.[3] Moran's success was more modest but steadier, even if the public acclaim seemed at its height at the beginning of his western career when Congress purchased *Grand Canyon of the Yellowstone* and *The Chasm of the Colorado* (1873, oil on canvas, 84 × 144 inches, United States Department of the Interior, Washington, D.C.).

Moran expressed distinct opinions about artistic support to G. W. Sheldon, who reported the artist's statement:

My life, so far, has been a series of experiments, and I suppose, will be until I die. I never painted a picture that was not the representation of a distinct impression from nature. It seems to me that the bane of American art is that our artists paint for money, and repeat themselves, so that in many instances you can tell the parentage of a picture the moment you look at it. It is not true that the public require such a repetition on the part of the artist. Men who are constantly rehashing themselves do so from sheer inability to do otherwise. . . . If a man's studio is simply a manufactory of paintings, which shall tickle the ignorant in art; if he is continually repeating himself in order to sell his pictures more rapidly or easily, this fact will convey itself to every intelligent mind. The pleasure a man feels will go into his work, and he cannot have pleasure in being a mere copyist of himself—in producing paintings which are not the offspring of his own glowing impressions of Nature.[4]

Moran's statement to Sheldon is unusually defensive, for the artist willingly made replicas of his own work on commission. He might have been defending his practice by claiming that nature, not another picture, was always his source.

The repetition of themes is not unique to Moran. Duplicating a picture for a patron was an accepted practice in nineteenth-century America, and duplicated sets of paintings were even more common in western art, possibly because there were relatively few artists who had seen the sights

3.   See Hendricks, *Albert Bierstadt*, pp. 177 ff.
4.   Sheldon, *American Painters*, pp. 124–125.

in demand. Catlin adopted this practice, and Alfred Jacob Miller may have gotten it from him.[5] Whether or not Moran was aware of the precedent, he quickly adapted his methods to produce sets, the most important of which were Yellowstone scenes for William Blackmore, Jay Cooke, and Louis Prang.

Alfred Jacob Miller had supportive patrons, including Scotsman Sir William Drummond Stewart, his first sponsor in the West, and William T. Walters, one of several Maryland collectors who commissioned duplicates of Miller's on-the-spot sketches.[6] Yet until the post–Civil War period when the government began to constantly employ expedition artists, it was unusual for a western artist to find adequate patronage in the land he painted. Bodmer was in North America only long enough to accompany Prince Maximilian, and Miller spent over a year working at Murthly Castle, Stewart's home in Scotland. George Catlin's critical success at touring his Indian Gallery portraits was not matched by support from the government or any significant portion of the private sphere, causing the artist to take the collection on an extended European tour in 1839. Despite royal French patronage (interrupted by the revolution of 1848) and good receptions in European capitals, Catlin never achieved financial success, or even stability. Jailed, plagued by creditors, and fraught with family problems, he pursued the dream of government purchase and display for his vast collection.[7] In 1872, the year of Catlin's death, Congress passed the bill creating the first national park and purchased Moran's landscape *Grand Canyon of the Yellowstone*, for $10,000. Response to western painting had changed, and Catlin's previously romantic subjects no longer had even critical support, as Indians seemed to impede the last burst of American territorial expansion.

Ferdinand Hayden, Moran's first western sponsor (spiritually if not financially), admired the artist's watercolors for more than their potential political value in Congress. He commissioned several in the winter of 1872–1873, when Moran had just finished his *Grand Canyon of the Yellowstone* and the watercolors for William Blackmore. Moran wrote to Hayden about his hectic but welcome schedule: "The four drawings that I was to make for you are not all finished as yet, but I can complete them by the end of this week. The main reason why they are not all finished, was because I lately finished a very large drawing of the Hot Springs (20 × 30

5. Marvin C. Ross, *The West of Alfred Jacob Miller*, p. xxv.
6. Ibid., p. xxiv.
7. Information on Catlin comes from an excellent critical and historic account: Truettner, *The Natural Man Observed*.

inches) which will be exhibited in New York in a couple of weeks. I also have an order from Jay Cooke for 16 watercolor drawings and many other parties."[8] Moran worked continually and quickly, finishing the large *Hot Springs of Gardiner's River, Yellowstone National Park, Wyoming Territory* (Reynolda House, catalogue no. 46) just four days after beginning it.[9] Yet still he could not keep up with the orders. Hayden must have been anxious for his watercolors, because Moran wrote again two months later, describing his full schedule: "I am hard at work again upon watercolor drawings and I shall be hard pressed to get through my work by the time of departure next summer."[10] They corresponded twice again about the commission, and Moran did not enter Hayden's payment in his receipt book until October 15, 1873, almost a year after he had promised the watercolors. Hayden encouraged Moran with kind words as well as commissions. He had written to the artist from the Madison Valley during the summer of 1872, the year Moran did not accompany Hayden: "There is no doubt that your reputation is made. Still you must do much to nurse it. . . . It will not be difficult for you to see all this country [the Tetons] next year in a few weeks and make all the sketches you wish. . . . Put in your best strokes this summer so as to be ready for a big campaign next summer."[11]

Ferdinand Hayden was but one of many supporters and patrons of the relatively new watercolor medium. Two totally different kinds of patrons demanded Moran's work after his return from the Yellowstone. His best known patron was the government, whose involvement in the arts had been (and would continue to be) sporadic and frustrating to artists. Congressional enthusiasm over the establishment of Yellowstone as the first national park on March 1, 1872, precipitated a bill passed on June 10 to purchase Moran's huge canvas of the Yellowstone for the government. That this was the first landscape to enter the national collection did not escape the notice of one reviewer: "In fact, if the national patronage were to be in future dispensed according to this precedent, and our Capitol to be adorned with the pictorial bulletins of our civil engineers, the public as well as the academician would be obliged to change ideas with an alacrity quite charactistic of the period."[12] The review continued with a discussion of government art patronage in America and abroad, which generally sup-

8.   Moran to Hayden, November 24, 1872, U.S. National Archives, U.S. Geological Survey Records, Record Group 57.
9.   Moran's notebook, Gilcrease Institute.
10.   Moran to Hayden, January 28, 1873, U.S. National Archives, U.S. Geological Survey Records, Record Group 57.
11.   Hayden to Moran, August 29, 1872, Gilcrease Institute.
12.   "Fine Arts: The Yellowstone Landscape at Washington," p. 157.

ported familiar themes, long esteemed by the public. The purchase of Moran's painting for the Capitol collection was entirely new because it conferred importance on an event and place known only through the painting. "It is confusing to be asked to displace the verdicts of history by the sketches of the reporter,"[13] the critic concluded. His words suggest that American landscape had taken its place as natural history painting, but that many members of the public still suspected its proper position in the hierarchy of American art. More specifically, the public feared as much as anticipated the unknown and exotic West.

The patrons of Moran's watercolors shared an important attribute— they were all adventurers. Some were actual western explorers, others were armchair travelers, and a few were fellow artists. These collectors had seen the land Moran painted, or wished they had, and did not desire huge canvases as decorative attributes for a new wealth. They were sometimes, but not always, less moneyed than patrons of oil paintings, and they were attracted to the lower prices of watercolors. Moran's most famous watercolor patron was William Blackmore, a British industrialist who saw his Yellowstone field sketches when they circulated in Washington during the winter of 1871.[14] Blackmore accompanied Hayden's 1872 Yellowstone expedition and his wife tragically died on the journey. Hayden wrote to Moran that Blackmore was anxious to receive the previously commissioned watercolors: "I think you ought to try hard to complete Blackmore's pictures. It was a sad event, the death of his wife, now he wishes to have them as a sort of monument to her memory."[15] They were indeed a fitting monument of beauty and remained in Blackmore's possession until his death, after which they descended through his family until 1934. At that time they were returned to the United States and offered for sale through the Newhouse Galleries in New York. In December 1934, they went on view for the first time since their brief stay at Goupil's in 1872. William Henry Jackson saw the sixteen watercolors at Newhouse: "It was with a wonderful thrill that I turned from one picture to another, all reminiscent of the glorious days of '71. They are as fresh in tone and color as the day each picture was completed with the date of 1872."[16] These finished, commissioned watercolors differed significantly from the field sketches on which they were loosely based. Moran chose to carefully complete each outline, leave no part of the paper exposed, and to use opaque colors spar-

13. Ibid.
14. Ruth B. Moran's notes for biography of her father, Gilcrease Institute.
15. Hayden to Moran, August 29, 1872, Gilcrease Institute.
16. *December at Erich-Newhouse, Inc.* 1, no. 1 (December 1934): 10.

ingly and skillfully to highlight the brilliant whites of mountain tops and spring deposits. It is fortuitous that all sixteen of Blackmore's watercolors remained together, sold first to George Hormel and then passing through M. Knoedler and Company to Thomas Gilcrease of Tulsa, Oklahoma. Gilcrease's purchase of the Blackmore watercolors, as well as the estate of Ruth B. Moran in 1948, assured that the institution founded in his name by the people of Tulsa would have the foremost collection of Moran drawings and watercolors, supplemented by major paintings.

The fate of Jay Cooke's commission is not as clear. Moran probably began work on this watercolor set shortly after his return from the Yellowstone, for he needed to repay his debt for Cooke's financial support of the trip. Only a few clues exist as to the identification and present location of these watercolors. Moran logged them into his notebook only as "Jay Cooke's Drawings / about 10 × 12,"[17] apparently completed after the Blackmore commission. However, further along in the notebook, amid records of sales and gifts to Hayden, Alexander W. Drake, and so on, is a notation: "Hot Springs of Gardiners River. Same as the large drawing—to Nettleton then to Cooke."[18] This watercolor is now known as *Minerva Terrace, Yellowstone National Park, Wyoming Territory* (private collection, catalogue no. 51), and the larger version to which he refers is *Hot Springs of Gardiner's River, Yellowstone National Park, Wyoming Territory* (Reynolda House, catalogue no. 46). The Reynolda House watercolor is one that Moran completed in four days in November 1872; it remained in his possession until about 1880, when he sent it to England and, with A. G. Renshaw, presented it to the Geological Society of London.[19] Thus, it was in his studio and available for replica, or inspiration as Moran would have preferred. The smaller watercolor evidently passed through the hands of General A. B. Nettleson of Jay Cooke and Company, a man instrumental in securing Moran a position with Hayden's party in 1871.

The other watercolor clearly identified with Jay Cooke is *Tower Creek, Yellowstone* (catalogue no. 53), which just recently came to light in the attic of the Pennsylvania State University, Ogontz Campus in Abington, Pennsylvania.[20] That campus was at one time the Ogontz School

17. Thomas Moran notebook, Gilcrease Institute.
18. Ibid.
19. Ibid.: "Lg wc drwg of the Hot Springs of Gardiner's River 22 × 29 made in 4 days Nov 8th 1872. Exhibited at Shaw's & in Washington & it is there yet Feb 28. 1874/have it still 1878." And another document in the Gilcrease Institute records: "Hot Springs Yellowstone Water Color 20 × 30 Now at Phila. Ex Nov 1879/Still in Eng 1882."
20. John P. Driscoll, "Moran Watercolor Found in University Attic," *American Art Journal* 10, no. 1 (May 1978): 111–112.

for Girls, which from 1883 until 1917 resided in Jay Cooke's mansion, Ogontz, and retained some of his collection of Moran paintings. *Tower Creek, Yellowstone* probably came to Pennsylvania State from Jay Cooke through the Ogontz School for Girls.[21]

If this watercolor remained in Cooke's possession, what happened to the others? No doubt the financier's losses in the disastrous venture with the Northern Pacific Railroad bonds and the ensuing Panic of 1873 caused him to limit his art interests and perhaps even sell paintings. There are seven additional Yellowstone watercolors, dated 1872 and 1873, that very possibly once belonged to Jay Cooke.[22] Only one of them can definitely be traced back before 1900.

Jay Cooke, William Blackmore, and Ferdinand Hayden were not Moran's only watercolor patrons during the 1870s. He painted about fifty watercolors between 1872 and 1874 for various patrons, including Alexander W. Drake, art editor for *Scribner's*; Richard Watson Gilder, Moran's friend and *Scribner's* editor; James Stevenson, officer on Hayden's 1871 expedition who was also with Moran when he saw the Mount of the Holy Cross in 1879; Mrs. George Franklin Edmunds, wife of the senator from Vermont who advocated passage of the Yellowstone bill; Russell Sturgis, American architect and author; and William Henry Jackson. William Henry Holmes, who accompanied Hayden's expeditions in 1872 and following years, also purchased and commissioned Moran's watercolors. Holmes was a geologist, anthropologist, noted mountaineer, and artist who became director of the National Gallery of Art. A great admirer of Moran's works, he was instrumental in acquiring paintings for the gallery, as well as the gift of his own collection of Moran drawings and watercolors. He purchased a watercolor of the Hot Springs as early as October 14, 1873,[23] and corresponded with Moran about other orders. About 1892, Moran wrote to Holmes that he had just finished his two drawings, but they were delayed because "I am indeed 'awfully' busy. . . . I have now over a hundred drawings to make for various parties."[24]

Of all Moran's watercolor patrons during his lifetime and after, none had more public impact than Louis Prang. His patronage offered new op-

21. Richard Porter, Registrar, Museum of Art, Pennsylvania State University, University Park; Dr. Robert Bernoff, Director, Ogontz Campus; and Terrie Smith, Public Relations, Ogontz Campus, each kindly assisted in obtaining this information from the university's files and in calling my attention to Abby Sutherland, *One Hundred Years of Ogontz*.

22. Catalogue nos. 29, 31, 36, 39, 49, 52, 65.

23. Moran's notebook, Gilcrease Institute.

24. Moran to William Henry Holmes, undated [probably 1892], Bushnell Collection, Peabody Museum.

portunities for the public to see Moran's original watercolors, but through Prang's chromolithographic reproductions one thousand copies of fifteen watercolors were printed and sold. This blatant marketing of culture embodied James Jackson Jarves's feared commercialism in art, and in the opinion of the *Nation* the term "chromo" was synonymous with declining American morality.[25]

Louis Prang was an aggressive and successful entrepreneur who built an enormous lithographic business. Much of his production was commercial, yet Prang sustained an ideal of reproducing oil and watercolor paintings, to which he turned in 1865.[26] His first successful chromos reproduced paintings of sentimental and historic interest, but by 1873 he was anxious to undertake an ambitious project involving the increasingly popular American West. With this intention he tried to commission Thomas Moran to paint "12 or more water color pictures of the Yellowstone country."[27] Moran was wary of Prang because of a previous unsatisfactory arrangement between the two, and he referred to this in a letter of December 22, 1873: ". . . your declining to pay for the pictures you had ordered, was, to put it in the mildest form, taking a most unfair advantage of me."[28] Moran proceeded to outline his conditions for the project (an unusually businesslike procedure for the otherwise impractical artist) and requested $100 per watercolor and half the payment in advance. Edward Moran must have been involved in the former misunderstanding between his brother and Prang, because, in response to Prang, Thomas apologized for his outburst, blaming the business on Edward's "unfortunate faculty of muddling everything that he transacts for other people . . . ," closing with a plea that "should you desire to reopen the matter of the drawings of the Yellowstone region please let me know at your convenience."[29] Moran must have accepted the commission, for he wrote to Prang a month later with the promise that he would begin the series soon.[30] The commission was on Prang's terms, however, with payment only after the artist delivered each drawing. Moran's records show the first payment for three watercolors on March 3, 1874.[31]

25. Peter C. Marzio, *Chromolithography, 1840–1900: The Democratic Art; Pictures for a 19th-Century America*, chap. 1.
26. Ibid., p. 98.
27. Moran to Prang, December 22, 1873, Hallmark Historical Collection.
28. Ibid.
29. Ibid., January 8, 1874.
30. Ibid., February 7, 1874.
31. Moran's Receipt Book, Gilcrease Institute.

Moran collaborated with Prang on the selection of subjects, sketching suggested designs in the margins of his letters, and asking, "Shall I give you a geyser? The most pictorial one is the 'Castle,' but the 'Giant' is the largest."[32] As a lithographer, experienced in the printing trade, Moran knew well how Prang's artists and printers would use his watercolors for making chromolithographs. His highly finished watercolors, with distinct outlines and delicate but clear colors, suited their methods of reproduction, and Moran did not change his style for this commission. In all, he made twenty-four paintings for Prang, of which the printer used fifteen for *The Yellowstone National Park, and the Mountain Regions of Portions of Idaho, Nevada, Colorado and Utah*, published in 1876 with text by F. V. Hayden.[33]

The series was enthusiastically received and reviewed, even in the weekly *Nation*, which had previously condemned chromos because "good color, that is, delicately gradated color, is not to be produced by the printing press."[34] In 1877 the *Nation*'s fine arts column reported the publication of *The Yellowstone National Park*: ". . . commend[ing] that Mr. Prang was willing to undertake so costly an enterprise, the copying of such watercolors as these being one of the things that lithography is undeniably fitted to effect, and, indeed, its chief reason for existence. Having seen several of the original aquarelles prepared by Mr. Moran, we are prepared to testify to the remarkable accuracy of the rendering into chromolithographs, an accuracy which we do not think could have been surpassed in any country."[35] Praise was not limited to the chromos, and those who saw Moran's watercolors admired the artist's ability: "Concerning Mr. Moran's artistic qualifications, we can cheerfully say that we think he is at his best when working on paper instead of canvas. . . . the boldness and facility of the drawing are really impressive. . . . On the whole, the untravelled world is under vast obligation for these vivid reports of regions we shall not all live to see in any other form."[36]

Regrettably, Moran's most public watercolor patron did not keep his collection intact. Prang's Yellowstone watercolors were among more than 440 paintings auctioned at the American Art Galleries, New York, in 1892.

32.   Moran to Prang, April 6, 1874, Hallmark Historical Collection.
33.   Moran's notebook, Gilcrease Institute, states: ". . . in all made 24 drwgs for Prang for his chromos of Yellowstone—used 15—Mr. Kirkpatrick of Newark later bought 2 of them . . . ," and he records $100 for each of at least twenty-one watercolors.
34.   "Fine Arts: Color Printing from Wood and from Stone," *Nation*, January 10, 1867, pp. 36–37, cited in Marzio, *Chromolithography*, p. 105.
35.   "Fine Arts," *Nation*, February 15, 1877, p. 107.
36.   Ibid.

Several of these watercolors have been lost, but many have passed to public and private collections.[37] Perhaps the best known, *Lower Yellowstone Range* (catalogue no. 48) is in the National Museum of History and Technology, a gift from L. Prang and Company in 1883 to the Smithsonian Institution, where visitors can still compare it to its chromolithographic reproduction.

Although the 1870s were Moran's most productive years as a watercolorist, he also painted a large body of work in that medium in the 1880s, much of which was the result of his 1883 trip through Mexico, and in the 1890s, from his "grand tour" of 1892. His watercolor patronage is not as clearly known from these years, although he exhibited and sold watercolors all during this period. Among Moran's late patrons were Charles F. Lummis, founder of the Southwest Museum; Goelet Gallatin of New York and Wyoming; and Gustave H. Buek, artist and author of works on Moran.

We have seen that Moran's watercolors for Blackmore were favorably reviewed when they were shown at Goupil's Gallery in 1873. Subsequently, Moran exhibited western watercolors at annual exhibitions of the American Water-Color Society and the Philadelphia Art Club, as well as at the nation's Centennial Exhibition in Philadelphia. Concurrent with Moran's 1882 trip to England, Thomas Bromley's Art Gallery in Bolton (the artist's birthplace) exhibited twenty-two oils and one hundred watercolors and subsequently traveled the works to London.[38] The attendant publicity stressed that the watercolors were all of western subjects, something which greatly impressed the English.[39] The warm reception of Moran's watercolors in England might be expected of a country long associated with the medium, but Moran's English birth, his travels in England, Blackmore's patronage, and his acquaintance with John Ruskin all helped.

The year 1886 saw the largest exhibition of Moran's watercolors to that date. In an attempt to raise money for a forthcoming trip to Venice, the artist sold paintings, watercolors, and prints at the Galleries of Messrs.

37. The watercolors prepared for Prang's Yellowstone series that can now be located are *Lower Yellowstone Range*, catalogue no. 48 (Division of Graphic Arts, National Museum of History and Technology); *Summit of the Sierras*, catalogue no. 98 (The Art Institute of Chicago); *Tower Falls and Sulfur Rock, Yellowstone*, catalogue no. 57 (private collection); *Mammoth Hot Springs (Hot Springs of Gardiner's River)*, catalogue no. 49 (Robert H. Levis II); *Great Blue Spring of the Lower Geyser Basin, Yellowstone*, catalogue no. 40 (private collection); *Mosquito Trail, Rocky Mountains of Colorado*, catalogue no. 149 (private collection); and *Shoshone Falls, Snake River, Idaho*, catalogue no. 176 (The Chrysler Museum).

38. Unidentified clipping from a Bolton newspaper, East Hampton Free Library, cited in Wilkins, *Thomas Moran*, p. 161 n. 9.

39. "Exhibition of Paintings in Bolton," *Bolton Weekly Guardian*, June 9, 1882.

Ortgies and Company, New York, under the auspices of the American Art Association. The sale netted him $10,321 for sixty-four paintings, and he expressed disappointment at the low sum.[40] The watercolors derived chiefly from his recent Mexican trip, and most were priced at about $50, the most expensive at $150. Six years later, the Denver Art League hosted a large Moran show comprising seventy-five watercolors from all of his western journeys, including the most recent trip of 1892. The late-nineteenth-century West was proud of its heritage and wanted to exhibit its imagery. The last Moran watercolor exhibition of the nineteenth century presented Louis Prang's chromolithographs, and the watercolors on which they were based, at the World's Columbian Exposition in Chicago in 1893.

After Moran's death his watercolors gained increasing attention, and interest was not limited to the finished paintings that critics had long admired. In December 1926, just four months after the artist's death, the Milch Galleries in New York organized a memorial exhibition of sixty-five western watercolors, including a nucleus of the sketches he had made on his first trip to the Yellowstone. Critics who knew Moran's oil paintings responded to the watercolors with greater enthusiasm, as one New York writer observed: "Because they are more straight-forward and have a more direct reaction to nature, they are, in the majority of cases, better painting than the rainbow-misted canvases which won him his reputation."[41] Another review echoed such praise: "In the mass they present a charm of delicate color that is almost ethereal. In their details, as single pictures, they reveal qualities of craftsmanship of which his oils give only a faint foreshadowing."[42] Robert Allerton Parker's review, in particular, stands among the best articles on Moran. He wrote:

Admitting that those vast "official" canvases of Thomas Moran, canvases covering acres of wall space in public buildings, are a bit tiresome to contemporary eyes accustomed to the spice and jazz of modernity, one was surprised and delighted to find here the intimate Moran, an artist exquisite in sensibility and a veritable master in his analysis of the scattered heterogeneous elements of a vast expanse of wild nature into its essential elements, and the re-creation of these elements into a significant unit. "Color-notes" they might be called; and yet, after half a century, they live undimmed by the passage of time.[43]

40. Wilkins, *Thomas Moran*, p. 186.
41. "Thomas Moran Memorial," *Brooklyn Eagle*, December 26, 1926.
42. "Thomas Moran Art in Milch Galleries an Amazing Record," *New York American*, December 26, 1926.
43. Robert Allerton Parker, "The Water-Colors of Thomas Moran," *International Studio* 86 (March 1927): 66.

James Stevenson's party on a trip to the Mount of the Holy Cross, 1874 (Moran is seated fourth from the left, and James Stevenson is standing third from the left)
Photograph by William Henry Jackson; courtesy National Park Service, Jefferson National Expansion Memorial

As a result of the Milch exhibition, seventeen of Moran's 1871 Yellowstone sketches were returned to the site of their inspiration. Stephen Tyng Mather, first director of the National Park Service, persuaded George D. Pratt, John D. Rockefeller, Jr., Mrs. Henry Strong, and Colonel Herbert J. Slocum to buy the watercolors for $4,000 and, following their first public view, the watercolors were made available to visitors to Yellowstone National Park. Ruth B. Moran generously gave three hundred of her father's drawings, watercolors, oils, and prints to the Park Service in 1935, and in 1979 selected Yellowstone material of both gifts was put on display in the Horace Marden Albright Visitor Center at the park. Moran might have been perplexed by the stir his small watercolors caused, but he could not have been anything but pleased.

5. LATER WESTERN TRIPS

Yosemite

Thomas Moran's first western journey, to the Yellowstone in 1871, had the most profound effect on his style, his choice of subject matter, and his career. As we have seen, by the winter of 1871–1872 the public associated his name with Yellowstone, and his patrons had commissioned enough works to keep him occupied for more than a year. So, the summer of 1872 presented a problem for the artist. Hayden was anxious for Moran to accompany his second Yellowstone survey that summer, and John Wesley Powell had asked him to join his survey of the Grand Canyon of the Colorado. Moran declined the invitations, writing to Powell that he had too much work to complete from the previous summer's journey.[1] These work habits were not unusual for a western artist; Catlin followed the pattern of remaining in his studio every other summer.[2]

Dedication to his work and patrons could not contain Moran's restless urge to travel, and at the end of the summer he recorded in his diary: "Left home for the Yo-Semite / Aug 24th 1872." This was not the artist's first contact with that area, which the governor of California had designated a state recreation area in 1864. As with Yellowstone, a *Scribner's* illustration commission first introduced Moran to the Yosemite. Though the trees of Yosemite usually impressed visitors, neither Moran's 1871 *Scribner's* illustrations nor his sketches the following summer convey the awe they inspire in others. Isaac Bromley wrote of the Yosemite trees: "... the idea of its vastness took full possession of me, and for the first time I grasped its greatness. . . . And though one looks with profoundest wonder at the vast size of these monsters, it is, afterall, the suggestion they give of their far reach backward into time that most impresses the beholder."[3] By comparison, Moran's illustration design for a tree, *Study of Conifers in Yosemite* (August 1871, private collection, catalogue no. 97), is delicately brushed and washed, showing interest in the botany of the tree rather than its setting and grandeur. Moran recorded his production on that brief trip as follows: "Mrs. M. & I went to Yosemite in August 1872 & made a number of pencil & ink sketches & 4 sketches in water colors."[4] How different this was from the bulging portfolio he had brought out of the Yellowstone the previous summer. In the midst of painting the hot,

1. Moran to Powell, June 24, 1872, National Archives, cited in Amy O. Bassford and Fritiof Fryxell, *Home Thoughts from Afar: Letters of Thomas Moran to Mary Nimmo Moran*, p. 132.
2. Truettner, *The Natural Man Observed*, p. 26.
3. Isaac H. Bromley, "The Wonders of the West—I: The Big Trees and the Yosemite," *Scribner's Monthly* 3, no. 3 (January 1872): 267.
4. Moran notebook, Gilcrease Institute.

brilliant colors of Yellowstone, the cool tonality of Yosemite must have seemed subdued and almost dull. No grand vistas inspired him to record them in paint, and no bubbling caldrons or eerie geysers provided delight. His few watercolors, *The Sentinel, Yosemite Valley* (unlocated, catalogue no. 92) and *South Dome, Yosemite Valley* (Jefferson National Expansion Memorial, catalogue no. 95), and wash drawings, *Falls of Yosemite from the Merced* (Cooper-Hewitt Museum) and *Cascade of Vernal Falls* (Jefferson National Expansion Memorial), are vague and not well realized, showing no evidence of an artist delighting in their execution. His only beautiful Yosemite watercolor is one he may have begun in the field that summer and finished in the studio the following year. *South Dome, Yosemite* (Cooper-Hewitt Museum, catalogue no. 94) focuses on the brilliant white of the dome bulging out of the landscape distinctive to the area, but it is reminiscent of the Wyoming mountain tops that Moran preferred to paint. Another possible reason for Moran's cool reaction to Yosemite was the association of that place with Albert Bierstadt. Bierstadt's name is as closely tied to Yosemite as Moran's is to Yellowstone, and Moran may have seen no future in focusing on that California landscape. The first of Bierstadt's many trips to Yosemite was in 1863, but he only visited Yellowstone for the first time in 1881. Without any agreement or conscious rivalry, Moran and Bierstadt each chose and stayed with painting the scenery that best suited him. Whatever Moran's reasons for indifference to Yosemite, his wife, Mollie, did not take well to western travel. She accompanied him on future European sojourns but never again journeyed west.

Canyons of the Colorado River

After two years' devotion to painting Yellowstone, Moran decided to seek out new scenery in the West. When, in 1873, Hayden's plans called for a summer in Colorado, Moran declined his invitation and accepted that of Major John Wesley Powell. With this decision, Moran assured his association with two of the four great post–Civil War explorers and broadened his experiences more than just geographically. The summer of 1873 saw the continuation of Powell's survey of the Colorado River's plunge through Utah and Arizona. In previous seasons, artist Frederick Dellenbaugh and photographers E. O. Beaman, James Fennemore, and John K. Hillers (one of the survey's boatmen who assumed the position of photographer in 1872) had accompanied Powell, but in 1873 the explorer succeeded in securing Moran's services as expedition artist.

Like Hayden, Powell needed visual images to supplement his written reports. Years later he declined to describe the view of the Grand Canyon he had shared with Moran: "The landscape is too vast, too complex, too grand for verbal description."[5] Moran's traveling companion during the summer of 1873 was writer J. E. Colburn, with whom he shared a commission for a chapter of William Cullen Bryant's *Picturesque America*. By July 5, Moran and Jack Colburn headed out of Omaha on the rails, bound to meet Powell in Salt Lake City. The major was in that city to confer with Indian delegations concerning the plight of the Southern Paiutes living in Utah. As a result of these meetings, Powell received instructions from the government and funding from the Bureau of Indian Affairs to investigate and report on the condition of the Indians.[6] Moran and Colburn met Powell in Salt Lake City and visited Brigham Young. Moran wrote to Mollie about the Mormons he had met: "They are very much like the rest of mankind and all smart fellows."[7] But, like many of his contemporaries, he had little patience with the religion. "Mormonism is a beastly institution and ought to be wiped out," he later wrote to Mollie.[8] Moran also noted in this letter that Powell would be gone for three weeks "as he goes off to make treaties with the Indians."[9]

If Moran kept a diary that summer, it does not survive, and details of his journey must be gathered from the letters to his wife; the diaries of Powell and his chief assistant, Almon Harris Thompson; later accounts of the Powell survey; and dated notations in Moran's own sketchbook (catalogue no. 106) and on field watercolors. Powell left the party at Fillmore, Utah, and Moran, preferring canyon scenery to painting the Indians, continued on with Colburn to join Thompson at Powell's camp at Kanab, Utah. They passed through the Zion Valley, where Moran painted *The Gate Keeper, Zion Valley* (Gilcrease Institute, catalogue no. 108), foretelling the spectacular canyons he would soon see. Along their route, Moran found a landscape more suited to his brilliant palette and topographic abilities than anything he had seen since the Yellowstone. His 1875 watercolor *Canyon of the Rio Virgin, Utah* (private collection, catalogue no. 102), intended for Louis Prang but sold to a collector in Newark, New Jersey, portrayed the depth of the canyon. The spectacular and colorful cliffs of the Rio Virgin inspired his best watercolors of the region (Cooper-

5.   John Wesley Powell, *Canyons of the Colorado*, p. 331.
6.   See Wallace E. Stegner, *Beyond the Hundredth Meridian: John Wesley Powell and the Second Opening of the West*, for a discussion of Powell's survey. Stegner's account of Moran's journey in the summer of 1873 before joining Powell is, however, apocryphal.
7.   Moran to Mary Nimmo Moran, July 9, 1873, East Hampton Free Library, cited in Bassford and Fryxell, *Home Thoughts*, p. 29.
8.   Ibid., July 17, 1873, p. 33.
9.   Ibid., July 9, 1873, p. 29.

Hewitt Museum, catalogue nos. 101 and 103). Not one to poetically extol the sights along his route, Powell nevertheless wrote of the cliffs near the Rio Virgin, which he named "Vermilion Cliffs": "I look back and see the morning sun shining in splendor on their painted faces; the salient angles are on fire, and the retreating angles are buried in shade, and I gaze on them until my vision dreams and the cliffs appear a long bank of purple clouds piled from the horizon high into the heavens."[10]

A. H. Thompson had received a message from Powell as early as July 4 that Moran and Colburn would join him in camp. The two new members of the survey finally arrived on July 30.[11] Their first trip out of camp was to a fork of the Rio Virgin on August 1 and 2 with Thompson and Jack Hillers. On August 5, the same party traveled to the brink of the Grand Canyon of the Colorado at To-Ro-Weap. Moran wrote to Mollie: "On reaching the brink the whole gorge for miles lay beneath us and it was by far the most awfully grand and impressive scene that I have ever yet seen."[12] Moran also detailed the work he undertook at the canyon: "I made an outline and did a little color work but had not time nor was it worth while to make a detailed study in color. We made several photos which will give me all the details I want if I conclude to paint the view."[13] When the party returned to camp, they found that Powell had arrived and planned to visit lakes near the Rio Virgin and to view the Grand Canyon from the Kai Bab Plateau, a site which Moran would portray in his next large oil painting.

If the Yosemite had proved disappointing the year before, Moran now had sketches, Hillers's photographs, and the memory of spectacular scenery to occupy him for the next year. He enthusiastically closed his last letter to Mollie from Kanab with details of the drawing commissions he had "beside the water colors and oil pictures."[14]

From this journey, Moran established a lasting friendship with John Wesley Powell and would provide illustrations for four of Powell's most important reports, as well as articles. While he did not form the same kind of friendship with photographer Jack Hillers that he had with W. H. Jackson two years earlier, he was even more dependent on Hillers's photographs for the many illustration commissions he had to complete. Few of

10. Powell, *Canyons of the Colorado*, p. 299.
11. See "Diary of Almon Harris Thompson," *Utah Historical Quarterly* 7, nos. 1, 2, 3 (January, April, July 1939).
12. Moran to Mary Nimmo Moran, August 13, 1873, East Hampton Free Library, cited in Bassford and Fryxell, *Home Thoughts*, p. 39.
13. Ibid., p. 40.
14. Ibid., p. 42.

Moran's pen and watercolor designs for these reports survive, but the illustrations are hard and uninspired, quite obviously based on another source, Hillers's photographs. Moran's real achievement for the summer was the field sketches and subsequent watercolor commissions. The best known result of the trip is his huge canvas *The Chasm of the Colorado* (oil on canvas, 7 × 12 feet, United States Department of the Interior), which the government purchased for $10,000 as a pendant to his *Grand Canyon of the Yellowstone*.

Mount of the Holy Cross

The Mount of the Holy Cross was a symbolic wonder to nineteenth-century religious sensibility, heightened by its difficult access. Again, Moran's introduction to a site he would later visit came through a commission, this time for Appleton and Company. His illustrations for William H. Rideing's Rocky Mountain article in *Picturesque America* were based on W. H. Jackson's photographs from the 1873 Hayden survey of the Colorado Territory. Jackson's view of the huge, perpetually snowy cross formed by two deep ravines fascinated Moran, and the artist determined to see the phenomenon for himself. He joined James Stevenson, of Hayden's party, for a trip there in August 1874.

Moran recounted the perilous ascent in letters to his wife. His first good view was on the east ridge before Holy Cross Creek: "When we got to the top the view was perfectly magnificent. 2,000 feet below us lay the *Moutonnée Valley* with the Holy Cross Creek rushing through it & at the head of the valley the splendid peak of the Holy Cross, with the range continuing to the left of us."[15] Later, they climbed part way up the mountain but became tired and did not press on to the height they had intended to achieve. Moran's method of working in the field differed greatly from that in the Yellowstone, where he seemed to sketch continually. "I have not done much sketching, but have done a good deal of looking,"[16] he wrote to Mollie, but he evidently had a planned picture well in mind. "In the Valley is one of the most picturesque waterfalls that I have ever seen. I shall use it in the foreground of the picture."[17]

Moran painted a beautiful watercolor, *The Mountain of the Holy Cross* (private collection, catalogue no. 152), just after his return to Newark. Its cathedral-top format was one which he had used before but which seemed especially appropriate for this religiously suggestive natural mar-

---

15. Ibid., August 24, 1874, p. 53.
16. Ibid., p. 57.
17. Ibid., p. 55.

vel. This watercolor became the possession of W. H. Jackson, who admired it more than he did Moran's canvas of the subject. The artist also chose this scene for chromolithographic reproduction by Louis Prang, and his large oil, *The Mountain of the Holy Cross* (1875, 82¾ × 64¾ inches, National Cowboy Hall of Fame, Oklahoma City), won a gold medal at the Centennial Exposition in Philadelphia. Moran exhibited the canvas at the Royal Academy in London, where William A. Bell purchased it for his home in Colorado. The artist later painted another watercolor of the mountain (great grand-daughter of William A. Bell, catalogue no. 153), full of chiaroscuro and dramatic movement, which he gave as a wedding present to William Bell's eldest daughter. Though the sketches from this trip are scarce, Moran again had found a subject suitable to his oil and watercolor palettes.

The Tetons

Following several years of summer travel in the West, Moran remained at home in 1875 and 1876, preoccupied with preparation for the Centennial Exhibition in Philadelphia. He only traveled briefly to Madison, Wisconsin, to complete a commission for the Women's Centennial Committee of that state. In 1877 he made the first of several trips to Florida, perhaps because his wife, who was not suited to the rigors of western travel, could accompany him. The artist spent that winter at St. Augustine and Fort George Island. Although Florida was not a typical or popular spot with American painters, Moran was not the only artist to succumb to that colorful, lush landscape. Martin Johnson Heade succeeded in finding a patron in St. Augustine, where he developed characteristic subjects of tropical landscapes and magnolias. Moran's subjects were less exotic and tended more toward the historical, such as the story of Ponce de León.

Yet Moran did not forsake the West. After a five-year absence, he accepted a commission from the Union Pacific Railroad in 1879 and set out West with his brother Peter. They spent most of the month of August in Nevada, Utah, and Idaho, and completed the journey with a view of the Teton Range. Moran had long wanted to see the three Tetons, the most impressive of which Hayden had named Mount Moran in his honor in 1872. The artist had planned to accompany Hayden there in 1873, but changes in the expedition's plans and Moran's desire to see the Colorado canyons with Powell precluded the trip. In 1879, Moran would not be denied his one and only opportunity to see and sketch the Tetons.

Before departing for the Tetons, he and Peter spent more than two weeks in Nevada and Utah. They went through the Donner Pass and saw

Lake Tahoe, then continued on through the valley of the Humboldt to Elko. In depicting Lake Tahoe (Gilcrease Institute, catalogue no. 88), a settled area unusual among his western sketches, Thomas Moran developed an approach that would prove useful in his 1883 trip to Mexico. On August 8, he executed one of the most beautiful watercolors of the journey, *The Ruby Range, Nevada* (The Cleveland Museum of Art, catalogue no. 191), which offered a stark horizontal site for Moran's pencil and brush. The watercolor divides into three sections: foreground (without the comfort of *repoussoir* details), middle ground of massed mountains showing high reliefs, and a luminous sky above. The deep, rich colors and rugged plasticity of the range perfectly suited the artist's sensibilities. The brothers pressed on to Cottonwood Canyon in the Wasatch Range, Utah, where Thomas again composed simple, bold watercolors rich in their surface texture. Notable among these are *The Upper End of Little Cottonwood Cañon* (Cooper-Hewitt Museum, catalogue no. 195), and four watercolors at the Gilcrease Institute (catalogue nos. 187, 190, 193, and 192). The last of these, *Toledo Mine, Cottonwood Cañon, Utah*, signaled Moran's fascination with the mining industry and its landscape, which he would use to greatest effect in Mexico four years later.

A few days before August 21, the Moran brothers reached Fort Hall, Idaho, where they planned to secure a military escort to the Tetons. Captain Augustus H. Bainbridge obliged them, leaving the fort for a twelve-day trek to the mountains. Moran painted the fort in its hilly setting, *Fort Hall, Idaho* (Grand Teton National Park, catalogue no. 165). Upon departure from Fort Hall on August 21, Moran began a diary which he kept until August 30.[18] He recorded the difficult conditions of the trip through potentially hostile Indian country that was dry, dusty, windy, and rife with fires. "Desolation" and "abomination" were two prominent descriptive words in his first entry.[19] They had their first glimpse of the Tetons, some twenty miles in the distance, on August 22. Despite the smoke and mist that partially obscured them from view, Moran described the colors of that range and a closer one: ". . . an intervening ridge dividing us from the Teton Basin stretches for miles to the north of a beautiful pinkish yellow with delicate shades of pale cobalt while the distant range is of an exquisite Blue with but little definition of forms on their surfaces."[20] By

18.   The diary is at Grand Teton National Park, Wyoming. Fritiof M. Fryxell published it: "Thomas Moran's journey to the Tetons in 1879," *Augustana Historical Society Publications*, no. 2 (1932), pp. 3–12.
19.   Moran's 1879 diary, entry for August 21, Grand Teton National Park.
20.   Ibid., August 23.

August 25, they had reached the Teton Basin, and Moran wrote: "The Tetons here loomed up grandly against the sky & from this point it is perhaps the finest pictorial range in the United States or even in N. America."[21] Even from this distance Moran found the range difficult to sketch: "This afternoon we made sketches of the Teton Range but the distance 20 miles is rather too far to distinguish the details especially as it is very smoky from fires in the mountains on e[a]ch side of the peaks."[22] *The Three Tetons, Idaho, 18 Miles Distant* (Grand Teton National Park, catalogue no. 183) defines the party's view at just this point.

Final approach to the mountains proved as difficult as the early part of the trip. It was hot during the day and cold at night as rain and violent thunderstorms marked the end of their journey. Although on August 27 he could spend "some 3 hours sketching,"[23] Moran's entry for August 26 better characterized the possibilities for artistic production on the trip: "It is very hot this Afternoon & so very smoky that the Teton peaks can scarcely be seen & at times are entirely obscured so that sketching is out of the question & we spend our time working up some of our sketches made previously."[24]

August concluded a productive month for Thomas Moran. He had a portfolio of beautiful sketches of Cottonwood Canyon and other sights along the way to the Tetons. The artist also managed a few watercolor sketches, *The Tetons, 1879* (Grand Teton National Park, catalogue no. 180), *The Tetons* (Yellowstone National Park, catalogue no. 179), and *The Tetons, Idaho* (Cooper-Hewitt Museum, catalogue no. 181), each of which emphasizes the dark, forbidding, and mysterious character of the range Moran for so long had wanted to see.

Thomas and Peter crossed the Green River on their way home in September, and Thomas painted about a dozen watercolors of the colorful cliffs he had admired and sketched on his first trip. They proved to be a lasting motif, one with imagery freshly renewed on almost every western journey. Their similarity provided a basis around which the artist painted the variety of atmospheric and coloristic effects the scenery offered. They became for Moran a rite of passage to the West he would visit less and less as an explorer as the century drew to a close.

---

21. Ibid., August 25.
22. Ibid.
23. Ibid., August 27.
24. Ibid., August 26.

Mexico

Between the Teton journey of 1879 and the Mexican trip of 1883, Moran's travels were varied, but distinctly un-western. He and Mollie spent the summer of 1880 in East Hampton, where they had first come in 1878. Each was preoccupied with the newly popular print medium of etching and found the flatlands of eastern Long Island perfect subjects for this technique. Moran may have needed a time away from the sublime grandeur of the West, and two of his travel choices of the 1880s—Mexico and England—were more suitable to his picturesque mode. Certainly he enjoyed the quiet summer of 1880, spent with his wife and children in the charming rural village of East Hampton.

But the next summer found Moran again combining the sublime and the picturesque, with a commission to paint Niagara Falls and then a trip on the Baltimore and Ohio Railroad to illustrate a book planned by its publicity department. He traveled with writer J. G. Pangborn to Baltimore and Washington, D.C., and on through the countryside of Virginia, West Virginia, and Ohio to Chicago.

Moran did not end his trip there, however, but set off to the West in order to meet W. H. Jackson in Denver. Together, the artist, the photographer, and author Ernest Ingersoll journeyed through Colorado and New Mexico, visiting potential tourist areas (Moran was on commission for the *Colorado Tourist*) and gathering material for Ingersoll's book, *Crest of the Continent*, published the following year. The silver mines that Moran saw at San Juan persuaded him to invest two years later but, more importantly, readied him for the dramatic mining country he would encounter in Mexico.

Moran's Mexican trip began in January 1883, and Cuba provided its prelude. The artist sketched in Havana and completed a watercolor exhibited the following year at the Water-Color Society in New York.[25] He steamed on to Vera Cruz, then took the train, stagecoach, and mule-drawn buckboard west and north in a great arc through Mexico. No fully adequate diary of Moran's trip survives, but one can partially reconstruct the journey by reference to two diary fragments (at the Gilcrease Institute and the East Hampton Free Library), letters written to his wife (East Hampton Free Library), and notations on his drawings and watercolors (primarily at the Gilcrease Institute).

25. The sketches of Havana are at the Gilcrease Institute, and the more highly finished watercolor in the Roderic H. D. Henderson Collection. William H. Gerdts published the Henderson watercolor in "Americans in Faraway Places, in the Roderic H. D. Henderson Collection," *Antiques* 91, no. 5 (May 1967): 647–649.

Moran arrived at Vera Cruz on February 3 and immediately began to paint the city from the harbor, *Harbor and City of Vera Cruz* (Gilcrease Institute, catalogue no. 203). The striking Castle of San Juan d'Ulúa especially caught his attention and he sketched it on the spot (Gilcrease Institute, catalogue no. 236). From this sketch and from memory, he later completed a highly finished watercolor, *Castle of San Juan d'Ulloa, Vera Cruz, Mexico* (Schweitzer Gallery, catalogue no. 199), an etching, and an oil painting. The cathedral held similar appeal for him, and he painted its richly ornamented surfaces from close by, *Vera Cruz Cathedral*, and far away, *Vera Cruz* (Kennedy Galleries, catalogue nos. 235 and 234). Moran found Vera Cruz, like most Mexican towns, picturesque and suited to his talents: "Vera Cruz is a most interesting and picturesque town as indeed are all the Spanish places I have seen," he wrote to Mollie.[26] His letters to his wife describe Mexico by comparing it with places she had visited or knew through his travels: "The landscape as far as I can see is much like the Green River neighborhood,"[27] and "the country around Vera Cruz reminds me very much of Colorado and Idaho."[28] Although neither of the Morans had seen Venice, Thomas likened Vera Cruz to the Italian city they longed to visit: "The city with its numerous churches, from the ship looked much like Venice."[29]

The artist of western mountain scenery remained attracted to the mountains of Mexico. He traveled by rail toward Orizaba; he finally could see the peak from the base town of Esperanza. He quickly sketched the highest mountain in Mexico while the train stopped, *Mountain Peaks Near Orizaba, Mexico* (Gilcrease Institute, catalogue no. 215), and told Mollie: "It was a grand sight . . . and I think I can do something with it when I get home."[30]

He and his English companion, Arthur G. Renshaw, arrived in Mexico City at Mardi Gras. Moran enjoyed the local color of the celebration and wrote to his wife: ". . . I wandered about the town and found it very interesting and pictorial and as it was a feast day everybody seemed to be out in the streets, bad smelling and dirty but just the thing for pictures."[31] Again the mountains held Moran's attention, as he waited for the clouds to clear and reveal the peaks of Popocatapetl and Iztaccihuatl.

26.   Moran to Mary Nimmo Moran, February 8, 1883, East Hampton Free Library, cited in Bassford and Fryxell, *Home Thoughts*, p. 63.
27.   Ibid., February 4, 1883, p. 62.
28.   Ibid., February 8, 1883, pp. 63–64.
29.   Ibid., p. 63.
30.   Ibid., p. 65.
31.   Ibid.

Among his party was a businessman identified in Moran's correspondence as Mr. Hahn, who was to inspect the Mexican silver mines. They thus traveled west of Mexico City to Maravatio, arriving on February 9, and from there to Acambaro, Morelia, and back again to Maravatio on February 20. Moran's letters to Mollie reveal his confusion over the travel plans and doubling back, but he followed Renshaw and Hahn, pleased to have arrangements made and at least one Spanish speaker in the party. As in Vera Cruz, Maravatio's cathedral appealed to Moran, from near, *Sunday Morning, Maravatio* (Gilcrease Institute, catalogue no. 230), and far, *Maravatio, in Old Mexico* (Parrish Art Museum, catalogue no. 210). The mountainous setting of the Trojes Mine provided the most colorful and impressive subject of the trip for sketches. One finished watercolor, *In the Cañon above Trojes, Mexico* (private collection, catalogue no. 204), is particularly reminiscent of Moran's views of falls plunging into canyons, or of mountain tops suddenly revealed in the American West, or of the wilds of the Glencoe Pass in Scotland for dramatic power and scope.

From Maravatio the party headed north through San Juan Abajo, which Moran painted (Charlotte Moran Rich, catalogue no. 227), San Miguel Allende, and Dolores, which he found "dull and uninteresting."[32] He was ready to be home again, but stopped long enough near San Francisco to paint one of his best watercolors of this or any season, *The Mountain Range on the West Side of the San Louis Valley above San Francisco, March 1st, 1883* (Addison Gallery, catalogue no. 216). Here the penciled skeleton of the watercolor is clear and structured, washed over to define form and suggest color in a sweeping and successful panorama. The party moved along through Saltillo to Monterey, which Moran painted from the hotel roof (Gilcrease Institute, catalogue no. 211), and then to Laredo and home through the States. He would later return to Mexico, but he would never depart with as rich a portfolio of pencil drawings and watercolors.

Grand Tour of the West

In 1892, Thomas Moran was fifty-five years old. He had not traveled West since the 1883 Mexican trip, choosing instead the new challenge of Venice, where he made two notable trips in 1886 and 1890. Thus, twenty-one years after the Yellowstone expedition, the artist revisited the western scenery that had established his reputation. The Santa Fe Railroad in part sponsored this trip, giving Moran and his son, Paul, transportation west in exchange for a canvas the company could use to publicize the route. In May father and son were in Arizona to see the Grand Canyon of the

32. Diary fragment, entry for February 27, 1883, Gilcrease Institute.

Colorado, which the artist painted from several vantage points. *The Grand Cañon of the Colorado* (Gilcrease Institute, catalogue no. 116) and *Looking West from Moran's Point* (East Hampton Free Library, catalogue no. 124) are two of many. Atmospheric changes, clouds and storms, held Moran's attention on this trip, and he captured the eerie, changeable character of the cliffs in *Grand Canyon of the Colorado* (Mr. and Mrs. Michael Coleman, catalogue no. 117).

Preparations for Wyoming's contribution to the World's Columbian Exposition in Chicago included a journey into the state in search of characteristic scenery. W. H. Jackson had joined Thomas and Paul Moran in Arizona for the Grand Canyon foray, and afterward the two artists continued on to Denver to await word about the sponsored trip to Yellowstone. On the way to Denver, Moran sketched in New Mexico at Laguna (East Hampton Free Library, catalogue no. 249, and Mr. and Mrs. Condie Lamb, catalogue no. 250), and San Juan (Gilcrease Institute, catalogue no. 258, and Cooper-Hewitt Museum, catalogue no. 247). In Colorado he had the pleasure of seeing new sights and of returning to paint places he had visited previously, Toltec Gorge, Cascade Twin Lakes, and Glen Eyrie (Cooper-Hewitt Museum, catalogue nos. 157, 158, 139, 144, and Gilcrease Institute, catalogue no. 143), among others. An industrial scene, which Moran had handled well at Communipaw, New Jersey, again became a vehicle for dark, dramatic silhouettes in *Smelting Works at Denver* (The Cleveland Museum of Art, catalogue no. 156).

While Moran and Jackson awaited word about the Wyoming trip, the artist worked on the sketches he had made during the trip. He still relied on his old collaboration with Jackson, for he anxiously awaited development of the photographer's work from the Grand Canyon. He wrote to Mollie: "Jackson's negatives are turning out splendidly and they will furnish me materials for innumerable pictures."[33] Before reaching the Yellowstone, the two old friends shared an adventure akin to that twenty-one years before. Setting off to see Devils Tower, they lost their way, sought in vain for food and lodging and directions, and suffered in a terrible thunder and ice storm before finally tracing the Belle Fourche to Devils Tower. The event proved to be more important and exciting as a story than as a pictorial motif, and Moran had material for his first and only travel story for *Century Magazine*.

The Yellowstone sojourn was a sentimental favorite for Moran, yet he continued to see potential for his career in its imagery. This time he stayed

33. Moran to Mary Nimmo Moran, June 11, 1892, East Hampton Free Library, cited in Bassford and Fryxell, *Home Thoughts*, p. 97.

at the hotel at Mammoth Hot Springs, only one sign of the changes wrought since 1871. Another, sadder change, was a notation at the bottom of *Hot Springs of the Yellowstone Park* (Cooper-Hewitt Museum, catalogue no. 75): "Dead since first visit in -71." The experience of first discovery would never come again to Moran in Yellowstone, yet he seemed undaunted by the passage of time. He described his second reaction to the Grand Canyon to his wife: "It is as glorious in color as ever and I was completely carried away by its magnificence. I think I can paint a better picture of it than the old one after I have made my sketches. I will not attempt to say anything about it as no words can express the faintest notion of it."[34] But new, stronger financial concerns crept into his correspondence with Mollie. He complained of the high prices in Denver, of running short of money, and of business schemes among art supporters. He hoped to benefit from this trip, closing one letter: "I am very well satisfied with the artistic side of the trip so far and I think the financial part will pan out all right when I get some work out. . . . I think I have opened the way to come out again whenever I want to without paying R.R. fares."[35] Moran continued to have financial worries, but he was right to seem assured of his artistic achievements on the trip. *Moran Point, Yellowstone Cañon* (Gilcrease Institute, catalogue no. 79) and *Hot Springs, Yellowstone* (Yellowstone National Park, catalogue no. 76) are fine examples of his draftsmanship and understanding of color.

The 1892 trip was the last of Moran's great, productive trips to the West. He continued to travel there frequently and moved to California, first during the winters and then on a permanent basis. After the death of his wife in 1899, the greatly saddened artist was free to travel anywhere and for as long as he wanted, and he almost threw himself into prolonged journeys, always accompanied by his devoted daughter Ruth. Railroad trips to the Grand Canyon became fashionable, and Thomas and Ruth joined a group of artists on a private excursion on the Santa Fe Railroad in 1910. The published account of the trip summed up the change in Moran's mode of travel: "Instead of long and weary rides over a hitherto unexplored country, he arrived at the door of the luxurious hotel perched upon the rim of the Canyon, in a private car, in the company of four brother artists of a younger generation."[36] The early twentieth century was a period of great productivity in oil for Moran, in which he recalled the many scenes he had

34. Ibid., July 26, 1892, p. 119.
35. Ibid., pp. 121–122.
36. Nina Spalding Stevens, "A Pilgrimage to the Artist's Paradise," *Fine Arts Journal* 34, no. 2 (February 1911): 106.

previously visited and painted in watercolor and oil. But the artist had painted his strongest field and finished watercolors by the first years of the twentieth century. He was capable of beautiful watercolors in the field, *Pike's Peak, Manitou Canyon* (Amon Carter Museum, catalogue no. 155) and *Looking up the Trail at Bright Angel, Grand Canyon of Arizona* (Cooper-Hewitt Museum, catalogue no. 126), and in the studio, *Castle Butte, Green River, Wyoming* (Christopher T. May, Sterling A. May, Meredith May, and Laura May, catalogue no. 263). As the nineteenth century closed, so did Moran's career as a foremost exploration watercolor artist. The character of the West had changed drastically during Moran's adult life and with it the artist's reasons for choosing western travel and art.

The Watercolors

West Spring Creek, Idaho 1871
Yellowstone National Park, Wyoming
Gift of George D. Pratt, Mrs. Henry Strong, Mr. John D. Rockefeller, Jr., Col. Herbert J. Slocum (8524); catalogue no. 22

Cliffs of the Rio Virgin, Southern Utah 1873
Cooper-Hewitt Museum, The Smithsonian Institution's National Museum of Design
Gift of the artist (1917.17.20); catalogue no. 103

From Powell's Plateau 1873
Cooper-Hewitt Museum, The Smithsonian Institution's National Museum of Design
Gift of the artist (1917.17.26); catalogue no. 107

Extinct Craters, Gardiner's River 1871
Yellowstone National Park, Wyoming
Gift of George D. Pratt, Mrs. Henry Strong, Mr. John D. Rockefeller, Jr., Col. Herbert J. Slocum (8532); catalogue no. 6

Liberty Cap and Clematis Gulch 1871
Yellowstone National Park, Wyoming
Gift of George D. Pratt, Mrs. Henry Strong, Mr. John D. Rockefeller, Jr., Col. Herbert J. Slocum (8524); catalogue no. 15

Springs on the Border of Yellowstone Lake 1871
Yellowstone National Park, Wyoming
Gift of George D. Pratt, Mrs. Henry Strong, Mr. John D. Rockefeller, Jr., Col. Herbert J. Slocum (8525); catalogue no. 19

Castle Geyser 1872
Private Collection
catalogue no. 31

The Ruby Range, Nevada 1879
The Cleveland Museum of Art
Bequest of Mrs. Henry A. Everett for the Dorothy Burnham Everett Memorial Collection (38.67); catalogue no. 191

Great Blue Spring of the Lower Geyser Basin, Fire Hole River, Yellowstone 1872
The Dietrich Corporation, Philadelphia, Pennsylvania
catalogue no. 39

Mammoth Hot Springs, Yellowstone 1872
National Collection of Fine Arts, Smithsonian Institution
Gift of Mrs. Armistead Peter, Jr. (1958.5.2); catalogue no. 50

Minerva Terrace, Yellowstone National Park, Wyoming Territory 1872
Private Collection
catalogue no. 51

Pike's Peak, Manitou Canyon 1901
Amon Carter Museum of Western Art, Fort Worth (66.73)
catalogue no. 155

Tower Creek, Yellowstone 1873
Collection, The Pennsylvania State University, Ogontz Campus
catalogue no. 53

South Dome, Yosemite 1873
Cooper-Hewitt Museum, The Smithsonian Institution's National Museum of Design
Gift of the artist (1917.17.32); catalogue no. 94

Shin-Au-Av-Tu-Weap, or "God Land." Cañon of the Colorado, Utah Ter.
National Collection of Fine Arts, Smithsonian Institution
Gift of Dr. William H. Holmes (1930.12.42); catalogue no. 133

Upper Falls, Yellowstone 1874
Philbrook Art Center. Tulsa, Oklahoma
catalogue no. 61

Mammoth Hot Springs 1875
Collection of Robert H. Levis II
catalogue no. 49

Canyon of the Rio Virgen, S. Utah 1873
Cooper-Hewitt Museum, The Smithsonian Institution's National Museum of Design
Gift of the artist (1917.17.27); catalogue no. 101

Mosquito Trail, Rocky Mountains of Colorado 1875
Private Collection in New York
catalogue no. 149

Green River 1879
The George F. McMurray Collection at Trinity College, Hartford, Connecticut
catalogue no. 271

95

Green River, Wyoming 1879
Cooper-Hewitt Museum, the Smithsonian Institution's National Museum of Design
Gift of the artist (1917.17.39); catalogue no. 285

The Upper End of Little Cottonwood Cañon 1879
Cooper-Hewitt Museum, The Smithsonian Institution's National Museum of Design
Gift of the artist (1917.17.79); catalogue no. 195

Green River from the Ferry 1879
Cooper-Hewitt Museum, The Smithsonian Institution's National Museum of Design
Gift of the artist (1917.17.38); catalogue no. 282

Green River Crossing 1880
Courtesy of Mr. and Mrs. William H. Bertsche
catalogue no. 281

Orizaba, Mexico 1883
J. V. Hawn
catalogue no. 221

Tower of Cortez, Mexico 1883
Amherst College, Mead Art Museum
catalogue no. 232

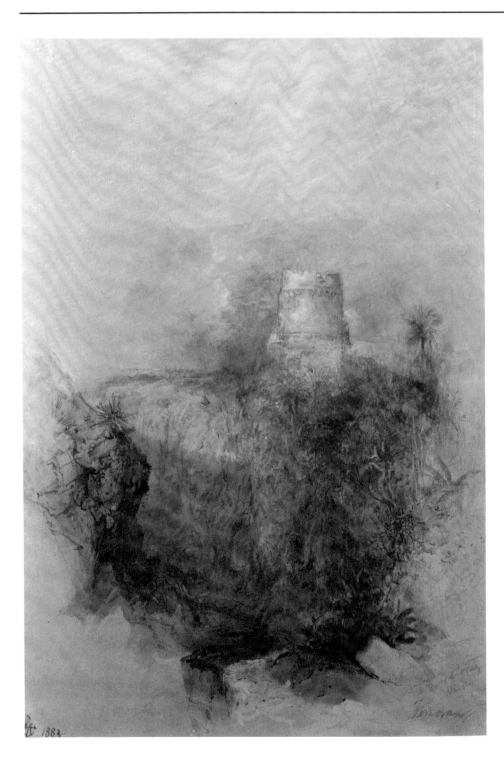

Vera Cruz 1883
Courtesy of Kennedy Galleries, Inc., New York
catalogue no. 234

Acambaro 1883
Charlotte Moran Rich
catalogue no. 197

The Mountain Range on the West Side of the San Louis [Luis] Valley above San Francisco, March 1st, 1883
Addison Gallery of American Art, Phillips Academy, Andover, Massachusetts
catalogue no. 216

The Hacienda of San Juan Mexico 1892
Cooper-Hewitt Museum, The Smithsonian Institution's National Museum of Design
Gift of the artist (1917.17.48); catalogue no. 247

Grand Canyon of the Colorado 1892
Collection of Mr. and Mrs. Michael Coleman
catalogue no. 117

112

Smelting Works at Denver 1892
The Cleveland Museum of Art
Bequest of Mrs. Henry A. Everett for the Dorothy Burnham Everett Memorial Collection (38.56); catalogue no. 156

114

Index-Peak and Clark's Fork, Wyoming 1892
Cooper-Hewitt Museum, The Smithsonian Institution's National Museum of Design
Gift of the artist (1917.17.69); catalogue no. 169

Shoshone Tepee 1892
Peabody Museum of Archaeology and Ethnology, Harvard University
catalogue no. 177

Hot Springs of the Yellowstone Park 1892
Cooper-Hewitt Museum, The Smithsonian Institution's National Museum of Design
Gift of the artist (1917.17.70); catalogue no. 75

Mountain of the Holy Cross 1894
Loaned by the Great Grand-daughter of William A. Bell and the Grand-daughter of Mrs. Harold Pearce
for whom it was painted and gifted by the artist
catalogue no. 153

Hopi House, Grand Canyon, Arizona 1905
Mr. and Mrs. William Belknap
catalogue no. 248

Catalogue Raisonné

Previously accepted titles are cited in parentheses after those currently in use.

All works are on paper support.

In citing dimensions, height precedes width.

Location of inscriptions is indicated by the following abbreviations:

Upper Left u.l.
Upper Center u.c.
Upper Right u.r.
Lower Left l.l.
Lower Center l.c.
Lower Right l.r.

Dates given in parentheses are those established by documentation or stylistic analysis.

Where dates of acquisition or ownership are not commonly known, they are given in parentheses in the provenance.

Abbreviated citations appear in full in the List of Short Titles. See the Bibliography for complete publication data on these titles and on those listed in the literature.

AAA-Ortgies (1886)
New York. American Art Association. *Catalogue of the Oils and Water Colors of Thomas Moran, N.A.*

AAA-Prang (1892)
New York. American Art Association. *Sale of Paintings Belonging to Louis Prang.*

AWCS, *Annual Exhibition* (1867–1902)
New York. American Water-Color Society. *Annual Exhibition.*

Ballinger, *Endless River* (1979)
Phoenix Art Museum. *Beyond the Endless River: Western American Drawings and Watercolors of the Nineteenth Century.*

Bassford and Fryxell, *Home Thoughts*
Bassford, Amy O., and Fritiof Fryxell. *Home Thoughts from Afar: Letters of Thomas Moran to Mary Nimmo Moran.*

Biltmore Salon (LA), *Water Colors* (1927)
Los Angeles. The Biltmore Salon. *Water Colors by Thomas Moran, N.A., 1837–1926.*

CSU, *Moran in Yellowstone* (1972)
Colorado State University. Fort Collins. Student Center Gallery. *Thomas Moran in Yellowstone.*

Century Association (1979)
New York. The Century Association. *Drawings by Centurions Lent by the Cooper-Hewitt Museum.*

Clinton Academy, *Paintings and Etchings* (1928)
East Hampton, New York. Clinton Academy. *Memorial Exhibition, Paintings and Etchings by Thomas Moran, N.A.*

Denver (1892)
The Denver Art League. *Catalogue: The Works of Thomas Moran.*

Fern, "Drawings and Watercolors" (1976)
Fern, Thomas S. "The Drawings and Watercolors of Thomas Moran (1837–1926)."

Fern, *Drawings and Watercolors* (1976)
Notre Dame, Indiana, University. Art Gallery. *The Drawings and Watercolors of Thomas Moran (1837–1926).*

Fryxell, "National Parks Collection"
Fryxell, Fritiof M. "The Thomas Moran Art Collection of the National Parks."

Gerdts, *Thomas Moran* (1963)
California, University at Riverside. Picture Gallery. *Thomas Moran 1837–1926.*

Heckscher Museum, *Moran Family* (1965)
Huntington, New York. Heckscher Museum. *The Moran Family.*

Higgins, *Grand Cañon*
Higgins, Charles A. *Grand Cañon of the Colorado River, Arizona.*

Hirschl & Adler, *Faces and Places* (1972)
New York. Hirschl & Adler Galleries, Inc. *Faces and Places: Changing Images of 19th Century America.*

LA Art Association (1937)
Los Angeles Art Association. Los Angeles Public Library. *Thomas Moran, N.A. Centenary Exhibition.*

MFA, *Frontier America* (1975)
Boston. The Museum of Fine Arts. *Frontier America: The Far West.*

MFA, *Karolik Drawings*
Boston. The Museum of Fine Arts. *M. and M. Karolik Collection of American Water Colors & Drawings, 1800–1875.*

MMA, *Middendorf* (1967)
New York. The Metropolitan Museum of Art. *American Paintings and Historical Prints from the Middendorf Collection.*

MMA, *Watercolor Painting in America* (1966)
New York. The Metropolitan Museum of Art. *Two Hundred Years of Watercolor Painting in America: An Exhibition Commemorating the Centennial of the American Watercolor Society.*

MOMA, *Natural Paradise* (1976)
New York. The Museum of Modern Art. *The Natural Paradise: Painting in America 1800–1950.*

Milch, *Water Color Sketches* (1926)
New York. The Milch Galleries. *Memorial Exhibition: Water Color Sketches by Thomas Moran.*

NCFA, *National Parks* (1972)
Washington, D.C. Smithsonian Institution. National Collection of Fine Arts. *National Parks and the American Landscape.*

Newhouse (1937)
New York. Newhouse Galleries, Inc. *A Loan Exhibition of Paintings by Thomas Moran, N.A., to Commemorate the Centenary of His Birth.*

Parker, "Water-Colors"
Parker, Robert Allerton. "The Water-Colors of Thomas Moran."

Sachs, "Drawings and Watercolors"
Sachs, Samuel I. "Thomas Moran—Drawings and Watercolors."

Santa Barbara (1925)
Santa Barbara, California. Santa Barbara Art Association. Casa de la Guerra. *Exhibition of Water Color Sketches by Thomas Moran.*

Santa Barbara (1937)
Santa Barbara, California. Free Public Library. Faulkner Memorial Art Gallery. *Loan Exhibition: Paintings and Etchings by Thomas Moran.*

Sellin, *Preparatory Studies* (1976)
Sellin, David. *American Art in the Making: Preparatory Studies for Masterpieces of American Painting, 1800–1900.*

Stark Museum, *Western Collection*
Orange, Texas. Stark Museum of Art. *Stark Museum of Art: The Western Collection.*

Truettner, "Scenes of Majesty"
Truettner, William H. "'Scenes of Majesty and Enduring Interest': Thomas Moran Goes West."

UCB, *Turner* (1975)
California, University at Berkeley. University Art Museum. *J. M. W. Turner: Works on Paper from American Collections.*

Washburn, *Cooper-Hewitt Collection* (1974)
New York. Washburn Gallery. *Drawings and Watercolors of the West, Thomas Moran, from the Collection of the Cooper-Hewitt Museum of Design.*

Wilkins, *American Scene*
Wilkins, Thurman. "Moran."

Wilkins, *Moran*
Wilkins, Thurman. *Thomas Moran, Artist of the Mountains.*

Wilson, "Moran"
Wilson, James Benjamin. "The Significance of Thomas Moran as an American Landscape Painter."

1. *Beaver Head Cañon, Montana*
Pencil, watercolor, and opaque color
10⅜ × 14⅛ in. (26.3 × 35.9 cm.)
l.r.: "Beaver Head Canon, Montana / 1871"
u.c.: "City Mon . . . July 4th 1871 TM"
Museum of Fine Arts, Boston, Gift of Maxim Karolik (60.427)
PROVENANCE: Macbeth Gallery, New York (1949); Maxim Karolik
LITERATURE: MFA, *Karolik Drawings*, no. 569; MFA, *Frontier America* (1975), no. 92, illus. p. 73

2. *Cañon Walls, Yellowstone*
Pencil, watercolor, and opaque color
8⅛ × 5⅛ in. (20.6 × 13 cm.)
l.l.: "Canon Walls. Yellowstone / TMoran 1871"
Yellowstone National Park, Wyoming, Gift of George D. Pratt, Mrs. Henry Strong, Mr. John D. Rockefeller, Jr., Col. Herbert J. Slocum (8538)
PROVENANCE: The artist; Ruth B. Moran
LITERATURE: Santa Barbara (1925), no. 14 (as "Canyon Falls"); Milch, *Water Color Sketches* (1926), no. 14 (as "Canyon Falls"); Wilson, "Moran," no. 7; Fern, *Drawings and Watercolors* (1976), no. 18, illus. p. 31

3. *Cinnibar Mountain, Yellowstone River*
Pencil, watercolor, and opaque color
10¼ × 14⅛ in. (26.0 × 35.9 cm.)
u.l.: "Cinnibar Mt. Yellowstone river. July 20th 1871 TM"
l.l.: "TMoran"
Yellowstone National Park, Wyoming, Gift of George D. Pratt, Mrs. Henry Strong, Mr. John D. Rockefeller, Jr., Col. Herbert J. Slocum (8534)
PROVENANCE: The artist; Ruth B. Moran

LITERATURE: Santa Barbara (1925), no. 2; Milch, *Water Color Sketches* (1926), no. 2; Wilson, "Moran," no. 9; CSU, *Moran in Yellowstone* (1972), no. 14; Fern, *Drawings and Watercolors* (1976), no. 7, illus. p. 23

4. *Crystal Fall, Crystal Creek*
Pencil, watercolor, and opaque color
11⅛ × 8⅛ in. (28.2 × 20.6 cm.)
l.l.: "TMoran / Yellowstone"
l.r.: "Crystal Fall Crystal Creek 1871"
Yellowstone National Park, Wyoming, Gift of George D. Pratt, Mrs. Henry Strong, Mr. John D. Rockefeller, Jr., Col. Herbert J. Slocum (8541)
PROVENANCE: The artist; Ruth B. Moran
LITERATURE: Santa Barbara (1925), no. 11; Milch, *Water Color Sketches* (1926), no. 11; Wilson, "Moran," no. 18; Fern, *Drawings and Watercolors* (1976), no. 21, illus. p. 33; Fern, "Drawings and Watercolors" (1976), illus. p. 34

5. *The Devil's Slide, Yellowstone*
Pencil, watercolor, and opaque color
10¼ × 7 in. (26.0 × 17.8 cm.)
u.l.: "at the Devil's Slide / July 21st 71 TM"
l.l.: "The Devil's Slide, Yellowstone TMoran 1871"
Yellowstone National Park, Wyoming, Gift of George D. Pratt, Mrs. Henry Strong, Mr. John D. Rockefeller, Jr., Col. Herbert J. Slocum (8533)
PROVENANCE: The artist; Ruth B. Moran
LITERATURE: Milch, *Water Color Sketches* (1926), unnumbered; Parker, "Water-Colors," illus. p. 68; Wilson, "Moran," no. 12; CSU, *Moran in Yellowstone* (1972), no. 15; Fern, *Drawings and Watercolors* (1976), no. 8, illus. p. 23; Fern, "Drawings and Watercolors" (1976), illus. p. 41

6. *Extinct Craters, Gardiner's River*
Pencil, watercolor, and opaque color
5 × 9½ in. (irreg.) (12.7 × 24.1 cm.)
l.l.: "Extinct Craters, Gardiner's River. Showing manner of formation"
l.r.: "⚕ 1871"
Yellowstone National Park, Wyoming, Gift of George D. Pratt, Mrs. Henry Strong, Mr. John D. Rockefeller, Jr., Col. Herbert J. Slocum (8532)
PROVENANCE: The artist; Ruth B. Moran
LITERATURE: Santa Barbara (1925), no. 12; Milch, *Water Color Sketches* (1926), no. 12; Wilson, "Moran," no. 23; CSU, *Moran in Yellowstone* (1972), no. 20

7. *Gardiner River (Mammoth Hot Springs Showing Liberty Cap)*
Pencil, watercolor, and opaque color
5 × 7¾ in. (12.7 × 19.7 cm.)
u.r.: "Gardiner's River / July 1871"
l.l.: "TMoran"
Yellowstone National Park, Wyoming, Gift of George D. Pratt, Mrs. Henry Strong, Mr. John D. Rockefeller, Jr., Col. Herbert J. Slocum (8526)
PROVENANCE: The artist; Ruth B. Moran
LITERATURE: Santa Barbara (1925), no. 15; Milch, *Water Color Sketches* (1926), no. 15; Wilson, "Moran," no. 5; CSU, *Moran in Yellowstone* (1972), no. 18

8. *The Great Blue Spring of the Lower Geyser Basin of Fire Hole River, Yellowstone*
Pencil and watercolor
10 × 14 in. (25.4 × 35.6 cm.)
u.r.: "The Great Blue spring in the Lower Geyser Basin / of fire Hole River / Yellowstone V. / Aug 7th / 1871 / T.M."
l.r.: "T.M."
Unlocated

PROVENANCE: Mrs. L. B. Sturges, Pleasantville, New York (1946); M. Knoedler & Co., Inc., New York; H. B. Harris (1948)
LITERATURE: Wilson, "Moran," no. 6

9. *The Great Spring on the Firehole River*
Pencil, watercolor, and opaque color
8⅛ × 11⅛ in. (20.6 × 28.2 cm.)
u.l.: "The Great Spring on / the Fire Hole River"
l.r.: "TMoran"
(1871)
Yellowstone National Park, Wyoming, Gift of George D. Pratt, Mrs. Henry Strong, Mr. John D. Rockefeller, Jr., Col. Herbert J. Slocum (8536)
PROVENANCE: The artist; Ruth B. Moran
LITERATURE: Santa Barbara (1925), no. 8 (as "Hot Springs, Fire Hole River"); Milch, *Water Color Sketches* (1926), no. 8 (as "Hot Springs, Fire Hole River"); Wilson, "Moran," no. 8; CSU, *Moran in Yellowstone* (1972), no. 32; Fern, *Drawings and Watercolors* (1976), no. 20, illus. p. 31

10. *The Hot Springs of Gardiner's River*
Pencil, pen and ink, watercolor, and opaque color
12 × 9 in. (30.5 × 22.9 cm.)
l.l.: "❉ ORAN. / 1871"
The Thomas Gilcrease Institute of American History and Art (0236.1367)
PROVENANCE: The artist; William Blackmore, Salisbury, England; Bertram M. Newhouse, New York (1937); George A. Hormel, Los Angeles; M. Knoedler & Co., Inc., New York; Thomas Gilcrease
LITERATURE: New York, Goupil's Gallery (1872); Newhouse (1937); LA Art Association (1937); Santa Barbara (1937), no. 18 (or 24); Wilson, "Moran," no. 79

11. *Hot Springs of Gardiner's River, Yellowstone (Mammoth Hot Springs)*
Pencil, watercolor, and opaque color
10⅜ × 14⅛ in. (26.3 × 35.9 cm.)
l.l.: "❉ 1871 Hot Springs of Gardiners River. Yellowstone Park"
l.r.: "Gardiners river"
Yellowstone National Park, Wyoming, Gift of George D. Pratt, Mrs. Henry Strong, Mr. John D. Rockefeller, Jr., Col. Herbert J. Slocum (8529)
PROVENANCE: The artist; Ruth B. Moran
LITERATURE: Santa Barbara (1925), no. 6; Milch, *Water Color Sketches* (1926), no. 6; Wilson, "Moran," no. 13; Fern, *Drawings and Watercolors* (1976), no. 10, illus. p. 25

12. *In Lower Madison Cañon*
Pencil, watercolor, and opaque color
8 × 5¾ in. (20.3 × 14.6 cm.)
u.r.: "in Lower Madison Canon Aug 8th"
l.r.: "❉"
(1871)
The Thomas Gilcrease Institute of American History and Art, Gift of the Thomas Gilcrease Foundation (0236.1576)
PROVENANCE: The artist; Ruth B. Moran; M. Knoedler & Co., Inc., New York; Thomas Gilcrease

13. *In the Grand Cañon*
Pencil, watercolor, and opaque color
7⅜ × 5 in. (18.7 × 12.7 cm.)
u.l.: "In the Grand Canon of the Yellowstone / July 1871 TM."
l.r.: "TMoran / Tmoran"
Yellowstone National Park, Wyoming, Gift of George D. Pratt, Mrs. Henry Strong, Mr. John D. Rockefeller, Jr., Col. Herbert J. Slocum (8540)

PROVENANCE: The artist; Ruth B. Moran
LITERATURE: Milch, *Water Color Sketches* (1926), unnumbered (as "On the Canyon"); Wilson, "Moran," no. 4; Fern, *Drawings and Watercolors* (1976), no. 51

14. *In the Yellowstone*
Pencil and watercolor
2 × 3 in. (5.1 × 7.6 cm.)
l.r.: "T.Moran"
(1871)
Mr. and Mrs. Horace Marden Albright, Sherman Oaks, California, Gift of Ruth B. Moran
PROVENANCE: The artist; Ruth B. Moran
LITERATURE: Santa Barbara (1925), unnumbered; Milch, *Water Color Sketches* (1926), unnumbered; Wilson, "Moran," no. 25

15. *Liberty Cap and Clematis Gulch*
Pencil, watercolor, and opaque color
10 × 6⅞ in. (25.4 × 17.4 cm.)
l.l.: "❉ 1871"
Yellowstone National Park, Wyoming, Gift of George D. Pratt, Mrs. Henry Strong, Mr. John D. Rockefeller, Jr., Col. Herbert J. Slocum (8524)
PROVENANCE: The artist; Ruth B. Moran
LITERATURE: Santa Barbara (1925), no. 32 (as "A Cone, Yellowstone"); Parker, "Water-Colors," illus. p. 70; Wilson, "Moran," no. 21

16. *Lower Entrance to Madison Cañon, Yellowstone*
Pencil, watercolor, and opaque color
5¼ × 8¼ in. (13.3 × 21.0 cm.)
u.l.: "Lower Entrance to Mad. Canon / Aug. 8th. TMoran."
Jefferson National Expansion Memorial, St. Louis, Missouri (4299)
PROVENANCE: The artist; Ruth B. Moran

LITERATURE: Fryxell, "National Parks Collection," no. TM-53; Wilson, "Moran," no. 26; NCFA, *National Parks* (1972), no. 56, illus. p. 94; Fern, *Drawings and Watercolors* (1976), no. 22, illus. p. 33

17. *Lower Falls, Yellowstone*
Pencil and watercolor
2 × 3 in. (5.1 × 7.6 cm.)
l.r.: "T.Moran"
(1871)
Mr. and Mrs. Horace Marden Albright, Sherman Oaks, California, Gift of Ruth B. Moran
PROVENANCE: The artist; Ruth B. Moran
LITERATURE: Santa Barbara (1925), unnumbered; Milch, *Water Color Sketches* (1926), unnumbered; Wilson, "Moran," no. 24

18. *Sand in the Cañon*
Pencil, watercolor, and opaque color
5⅞ × 10 in. (14.9 × 25.4 cm.)
u.l.: "Sand in the Canon"
l.c.: "TMoran"
Yellowstone National Park, Wyoming, Gift of George D. Pratt, Mrs. Henry Strong, Mr. John D. Rockefeller, Jr., Col. Herbert J. Slocum (8542)
PROVENANCE: The artist; Ruth B. Moran
LITERATURE: Wilson, "Moran," no. 17

19. *Springs on the Border of Yellowstone Lake*
Pencil, watercolor, and opaque color
5 × 10¾ in. (12.7 × 27.3 cm.)
l.l.: "Springs on the border of Yellowstone Lake July 28th TMoran"
l.r.: "⚹ 1871"
Yellowstone National Park, Wyoming, Gift of George D. Pratt, Mrs. Henry Strong, Mr. John D. Rockefeller, Jr., Col. Herbert J. Slocum (8525)
PROVENANCE: The artist; Ruth B. Moran

LITERATURE: Santa Barbara (1925), no. 7; Milch, *Water Color Sketches* (1926), no. 7; Wilson, "Moran," no. 22; CSU, *Moran in Yellowstone* (1972), no. 31

20. *Tower Creek*
Pencil and watercolor
7¾ × 10⅝ in. (19.7 × 27.0 cm.)
u.l.: "Devil's Hoof"
l.l.: "TMoran / Tower Creek"
(1871)
Yellowstone National Park, Wyoming, Gift of George D. Pratt, Mrs. Henry Strong, Mr. John D. Rockefeller, Jr., Col. Herbert J. Slocum (8528)
PROVENANCE: The artist; Ruth B. Moran
LITERATURE: Santa Barbara (1925), no. 10; Milch, *Water Color Sketches* (1926), no. 10; Wilson, "Moran," no. 11; CSU, *Moran in Yellowstone* (1972), no. 25; Fern, *Drawings and Watercolors* (1976), no. 12

21. *Upper Falls, Yellowstone*
Pencil and watercolor
2½ × 4 in. (6.34 × 10.2 cm.)
l.l.: "T.Moran [illeg.]"
(1871)
Mr. and Mrs. Horace Marden Albright, Sherman Oaks, California, Gift of Ruth B. Moran
PROVENANCE: The artist; Ruth B. Moran
LITERATURE: Santa Barbara (1925), unnumbered; Milch, *Water Color Sketches* (1926), unnumbered; Wilson, "Moran," no. 26

22. *West Spring Creek, Idaho*
Watercolor
3⅜ × 7 in. (8.6 × 17.8 cm.)
u.l.: "W. Springs C. July 8 Idaho"
l.l.: "⚹ 1871"
l.r.: "T Moran"
Yellowstone National Park, Wyoming, Gift of George D. Pratt, Mrs. Henry Strong, Mr. John D. Rockefeller, Jr., Col. Herbert J. Slocum (8524)
PROVENANCE: The artist; Ruth B. Moran

LITERATURE: Santa Barbara (1925), no. 13 (as "Warm Springs, Idaho, 1871"); Milch, *Water Color Sketches* (1926), no. 13 (as "Warm Springs, Idaho, 1871"); Parker, "Water-Colors," illus. p. 65 (as "Warm Springs, Idaho, 1871"); Wilson, "Moran," nos. 3 and 19; CSU, *Moran in Yellowstone* (1972), no. 13

23. *Yellowstone Cañon*
Pencil, watercolor, and opaque color
8⅛ × 11⅛ in. (20.6 × 28.2 cm.)
u.l.: "Yellowstone Canon 1871 TMoran."
Yellowstone National Park, Wyoming, Gift of George D. Pratt, Mrs. Henry Strong, Mr. John D. Rockefeller, Jr., Col. Herbert J. Slocum (8539)
PROVENANCE: The artist; Ruth B. Moran
LITERATURE: Santa Barbara (1925), no. 4 (or 6); Milch, *Water Color Sketches* (1926), no. 4 (or 6); Wilson, "Moran," no. 14; Fern, *Drawings and Watercolors* (1976), no. 19, illus. p. 31; Fern, "Drawings and Watercolors" (1976), illus. p. 38; Truettner, "Scenes of Majesty," no. 8, illus. p. 245

24. *Yellowstone Cañon*
Pencil, watercolor, and opaque color
10⅜ × 14⅛ in. (26.3 × 35.9 cm.)
u.r.: "Part of the Great Canon of the Yellowstone looking East / Aug 3rd 1871"
l.l.: "⚶ 1871. Yellowstone Canon"
Yellowstone National Park, Wyoming, Gift of George D. Pratt, Mrs. Henry Strong, Mr. John D. Rockefeller, Jr., Col. Herbert J. Slocum (8544)
PROVENANCE: The artist; Ruth B. Moran

LITERATURE: Denver (1892), no. 50; Santa Barbara (1925), no. 5 (or 4); Milch, *Water Color Sketches* (1926), no. 5 (or 4); Wilson, "Moran," no. 15; Fern, *Drawings and Watercolors* (1976), no. 16, illus. p. 29; Fern, "Drawings and Watercolors" (1976), illus. p. 39; Truettner, "Scenes of Majesty," no. 7, illus. p. 245

25. *Yellowstone from above the Lower Fall (Red Rock)*
Pencil, watercolor, and opaque color
8¼ × 10¾ in. (21.0 × 27.3 cm.)
u.l.: "[illeg.] Yellowstone from above the Lower Fall"
l.l.: "⚶ TMoran"
(1871)
Yellowstone National Park, Wyoming, Gift of George D. Pratt, Mrs. Henry Strong, Mr. John D. Rockefeller, Jr., Col. Herbert J. Slocum (8543)
PROVENANCE: The artist; Ruth B. Moran
LITERATURE: Milch, *Water Color Sketches* (1926), no. 9; Fern, *Drawings and Watercolors* (1976), no. 17, illus. p. 29

26. *Yellowstone Lake*
Pencil and watercolor
5 × 12 in. (12.7 × 30.5 cm.)
l.l.: "Yellowstone Lake / TM. 1871"
Jefferson National Expansion Memorial, St. Louis, Missouri (4295)
PROVENANCE: The artist; Ruth B. Moran
LITERATURE: Denver (1892), no. 49; Milch, *Water Color Sketches* (1926), no. 9; Santa Barbara (1925), no. 9; Fryxell, "National Parks Collection," no. TM-54; Wilson, "Moran," no. 27

27. *The Yellowstone Range from Near Fort Ellis*
Pencil, watercolor, and opaque color
13¾ × 10⅛ in. (34.9 × 25.7 cm.)
u.l.: "The Yellowstone Range from near fort Ellis July 12th 1871 / TM"
l.l.: "Near Fort Ellis. TM. 1871"
Yellowstone National Park, Wyoming, Gift of George D. Pratt, Mrs. Henry Strong, Mr. John D. Rockefeller, Jr., Col. Herbert J. Slocum (8531)
PROVENANCE: The artist; Ruth B. Moran
LITERATURE: Santa Barbara (1925), no. 1; Milch, *Water Color Sketches* (1926), no. 1; Clinton Academy, *Paintings and Etchings* (1928), no. 16 (as "The Yellowstone Range. 1871"); Santa Barbara (1937), no. 23; Wilson, "Moran," no. 10

28. *Yellowstone Sketchbook*
Pencil and watercolor in bound book
Each sheet 8¼ × 11½ in. (21.0 × 29.2 cm.)
(1871)
Jefferson National Expansion Memorial, St. Louis, Missouri (4335)
PROVENANCE: The artist; Ruth B. Moran

29. *Big Springs in Yellowstone Park*
Watercolor
9 × 19 in. (22.9 × 48.3 cm.)
l.r.: "T.Moran. 1872"
Private Collection
PROVENANCE: The artist; Senator
George F. Edmunds, Burlington,
Vermont, Gift of the artist;
Mary M. Edmunds, Pasadena,
California; Ralph M. Dyer, Beverly
Hills, California; [His daughter],
Phoenix, Arizona
LITERATURE: Sotheby Parke Bernet,
Inc., Los Angeles, sale 182, lot
100, illus. (October 20, 1975);
Maurice Bloch, "American
Watercolors," illus. p. 82;
Ballinger, *Endless River* (1979), pl.
26, p. 81

30. *Canyon of the Yellowstone* (*River
Pinnacle*) (*Tower of Tower Falls*)
Pencil, watercolor, and opaque
color
15⅝ × 10¼ in. (39.7 × 26.0 cm.)
l.r.: "✝ ORAN. / 1872"
National Collection of Fine Arts,
Smithsonian Institution, Gift of
Mrs. Armistead Peter, Jr. (1958.5.3)
PROVENANCE: Mrs. Armistead
Peter, Jr.
LITERATURE: Gerdts, *Thomas
Moran* (1963), no. 36; Washington,
D.C., Smithsonian Institution,
National Collection of Fine Arts,
American Landscape; NCFA,
National Parks (1972), no. 49,
illus. p. 90; Fern, *Drawings and
Watercolors* (1976), no. 14, illus.
p. 27

31. *Castle Geyser*
Watercolor and opaque color
13 × 8¾ in. (33.0 × 22.2 cm.)
l.l.: "✝ ORAN 1872"
Private Collection
PROVENANCE: Dr. John A.
Mitchell's aunt (1918–1919); Dr.
John A. Mitchell, Interlaken,
Massachusetts (1919–1970?);
Kennedy Galleries, Inc., New York
LITERATURE: Wilson, "Moran," no.
91; New York, Kennedy Galleries,
Inc., *Kennedy Quarterly* 11, no. 4
(March 1972): no. 153, illus. p. 201

32. *The Castle Geyser, Fire Hole
Basin*
Pencil, watercolor, and opaque
color
7 × 11 in. (17.8 × 27.9 cm.)
l.r.: "✝ ORAN. / 1872"
The Thomas Gilcrease Institute of
American History and Art
(0236.1363)
PROVENANCE: The artist; William
Blackmore, Salisbury, England;
Bertram M. Newhouse, New York
(1937); George A. Hormel, Los
Angeles; M. Knoedler & Co., Inc.,
New York; Thomas Gilcrease
LITERATURE: New York, Goupil's
Gallery (1872); Newhouse (1937);
LA Art Association (1937); Santa
Barbara (1937), no. 15; Wilson,
"Moran," no. 74; "Sketches Which
Went to Congress to Prove a Myth
and Preserve a Park," *American
Scene* 1, no. 1 (Spring 1958): illus.
p. 4; Wilkins, *American Scene*,
illus. p. 32; "Microcosm, the
Northwest Quadrant," *American
Scene* 17, no. 4 (1976): illus. p. 32

33. *The Castle Geyser, Upper Geyser
Basin, Yellowstone National Park*
Pencil, watercolor, and opaque
color
9½ × 14 in. (24.1 × 35.6 cm.)
(ca. 1874–1875)
Unlocated
PROVENANCE: The artist; L. Prang
& Company, Boston

34. *The Devil's Den on Cascade
Creek*
Pencil, watercolor, and opaque
color
13 × 9½ in. (33.0 × 24.1 cm.)
l.l.: "✝ ORAN. / 1872."
The Thomas Gilcrease Institute of
American History and Art
(0236.1453)
PROVENANCE: The artist; William
Blackmore, Salisbury, England;
Bertram M. Newhouse, New York
(1937); George A. Hormel, Los
Angeles; M. Knoedler & Co., Inc.,
New York; Thomas Gilcrease

LITERATURE: New York, Goupil's Gallery (1872); Newhouse (1937); LA Art Association (1937); Santa Barbara (1937), no. 14; Wilson, "Moran," no. 75

35. *Excelsior Geyser, Yellowstone Park (Pines and Pools, Excelsior Geyser)*
Watercolor and opaque color
12¾ × 9¾ in. (32.4 × 24.8 cm.)
l.r.: "✝ ORAN.1873"
National Collection of Fine Arts, Smithsonian Institution, Gift of Mrs. Armistead Peter, Jr. (1958.5.1)
PROVENANCE: Mrs. Armistead Peter, Jr.
LITERATURE: Washington, D.C., Smithsonian Institution, National Collection of Fine Arts, *Prints, Drawings, and Watercolors, Checklist of Opening Exhibition*; NCFA, *National Parks* (1972), no. 51, illus. p. 91

36. *Giant Blue Spring, Yellowstone*
Watercolor
10 × 14 in. (25.4 × 35.6 cm.)
l.l.: "✝ ORAN / 1873"
Private Collection
PROVENANCE: M. Michelotti (1952); M. Knoedler & Co., Inc., New York; Norman B. Woolworth (1957); Mrs. Norman B. Woolworth
LITERATURE: Wilson, "Moran," no. 32; MMA, *Watercolor Painting in America* (1966), no. 86; New York, Coe Kerr Gallery, Inc., *The American Painting Collection of Mrs. Norman B. Woolworth*, no. 80, illus. p. 47

37. *The Grand Canyon of the Yellowstone*
Pencil, watercolor, and opaque color
12 × 9 in. (30.5 × 22.9 cm.)
l.l.: "✝ ORAN.1872"
The Thomas Gilcrease Institute of American History and Art (0226.1619)

PROVENANCE: The artist; William Blackmore, Salisbury, England; Bertram M. Newhouse, New York (1937); George A. Hormel, Los Angeles; M. Knoedler & Co., Inc., New York; Thomas Gilcrease
LITERATURE: New York, Goupil's Gallery (1872); Newhouse (1937); LA Art Association (1937); Santa Barbara (1937), no. 12; Wilson, "Moran," no. 82

38. *The Grand Cañon of the Yellowstone, Yellowstone National Park*
Pencil, watercolor, and opaque color
9½ × 14 in. (24.1 × 35.6 cm.)
(ca. 1874–1875)
Unlocated
PROVENANCE: The artist; L. Prang & Company, Boston
LITERATURE: AAA-Prang (1892), no. 353

39. *Great Blue Spring of the Lower Geyser Basin, Fire Hole River, Yellowstone (Blue Lake, Yellowstone)*
Watercolor and opaque color
9⅛ × 16⅜ in. (23.2 × 41.6 cm.)
l.l.: "✝ ORAN / 1872"
The Dietrich Corporation, Philadelphia, Pennsylvania
PROVENANCE: Ferdinand V. Hayden(?) (1873); Kennedy Galleries, Inc., New York (1965); Mr. and Mrs. J. William Middendorf II, New York (1968); Hirschl & Adler Galleries, Inc., New York (1969)
LITERATURE: MMA, *Watercolor Painting in America* (1966), no. 84; MMA, *Middendorf* (1967), no. 39, illus. pp. 56–57; St. Louis, City Art Museum, *A Collector's Choice*, no. 52; New York, Hirschl & Adler Galleries, Inc., *The American Scene*, no. 71; MOMA, *Natural Paradise* (1976), illus. p. 81

40. *Great Blue Spring of the Lower Geyser Basin, Yellowstone*
Pencil, watercolor, and opaque color
9½ × 13¾ in. (24.1 × 34.9 cm.)
l.r.: "⚑"
(ca. 1873)
Private Collection
PROVENANCE: The artist; L. Prang & Company, Boston; Mrs. J. D. Ratcliffe, Palisades, New York (1962); Mr. and Mrs. J. William Middendorf II, New York (1968); Hirschl & Adler Galleries, Inc., New York (1971)
LITERATURE: AAA-Prang (1892), no. 346; MMA, *Watercolor Painting in America* (1966), no. 85; MMA, *Middendorf* (1967), no. 38, illus. pp. 56–57; Indiana University, Bloomington, Art Museum, *The American Scene, 1820–1900*, no. 65, illus.; New York, Hirschl & Adler Galleries, Inc., *Forty Masterworks of American Art*, no. 26, illus. p. 39; Atlanta, Georgia, High Museum of Art, *The Beckoning Land, Nature and the American Artist*, no. 69, illus. p. 29; Washington, D.C., the National Endowment for the Arts and the Corcoran Gallery of Art, *Wilderness*, no. 138, illus.; NCFA, *National Parks* (1972), no. 54, illus. p. 93; New York, Hirschl & Adler Galleries, Inc., *Retrospective of a Gallery*, illus. no. 69; MOMA, *Natural Paradise* (1976), illus. p. 81; Alan Gussow, *A Sense of Place*, illus. 1:76

41. *The Great Hot Springs, Gardiner's River*
Pencil, watercolor, and opaque color
10 × 14 in. (25.4 × 35.6 cm.)
l.l.: "TMORAN / 1872"
The Thomas Gilcrease Institute of American History and Art
(0236.1359)

PROVENANCE: The artist; William Blackmore, Salisbury, England; Bertram M. Newhouse, New York (1937); George A. Hormel, Los Angeles; M. Knoedler & Co., Inc., New York; Thomas Gilcrease
LITERATURE: New York, Goupil's Gallery (1872); Newhouse (1937); LA Art Association (1937); Santa Barbara (1937), no. 22; Wilson, "Moran," no. 78

42. *The Grotto Geyser, Fire Hole Basin (Liberty Cap)*
Pencil, pen and ink, watercolor, and opaque color
10 × 7 in. (25.4 × 17.8 cm.)
The Thomas Gilcrease Institute of American History and Art
(0236.1360)
PROVENANCE: The artist; William Blackmore, Salisbury, England; Bertram M. Newhouse, New York (1937); George A. Hormel, Los Angeles; M. Knoedler & Co., Inc., New York; Thomas Gilcrease
LITERATURE: New York, Goupil's Gallery (1872); Newhouse (1937); LA Art Association (1937); Santa Barbara (1937), no. 11; Wilson, "Moran," no. 77; Wilkins, *American Scene*, illus. p. 30

43. *Head of Yellowstone River*
Pencil, watercolor, and opaque color
9½ × 14 in. (24.1 × 35.6 cm.)
l.l.: "T. Moran 1874"
Unlocated
PROVENANCE: The artist; L. Prang & Company, Boston
LITERATURE: AAA-Prang (1892), no. 356; Wilson, "Moran," no. 36

44. *The Hot Springs of Gardiner's River, "Diana's Baths"*
Pencil, watercolor, and opaque color
14 × 10 in. (35.6 × 25.4 cm.)
l.r.: "TMORAN. / 1872"
The Thomas Gilcrease Institute of American History and Art
(0236.1454)

PROVENANCE: The artist; William Blackmore, Salisbury, England; Bertram M. Newhouse, New York (1937); George A. Hormel, Los Angeles; M. Knoedler & Co., Inc., New York; Thomas Gilcrease
LITERATURE: New York, Goupil's Gallery (1872); Newhouse (1937); LA Art Association (1937); Santa Barbara (1937), no. 21; Wilson, "Moran," no. 76; "Microcosm, the Northwest Quadrant," *American Scene* 17, no. 4 (1976): illus. p. 30

45. *The Hot Springs of Gardiner's River, Upper Pools*
Pencil, watercolor, and opaque color
10 × 17 in. (25.4 × 43.2 cm.)
l.l.: "⚑ ORAN. / 1872"
The Thomas Gilcrease Institute of American History and Art
(0236.1361)
PROVENANCE: The artist; William Blackmore, Salisbury, England; Bertram M. Newhouse, New York (1937); George A. Hormel, Los Angeles; M. Knoedler & Co., Inc., New York; Thomas Gilcrease
LITERATURE: New York, Goupil's Gallery (1872); Newhouse (1937); LA Art Association (1937); Santa Barbara (1937), no. 18 or 24; Wilson, "Moran," no. 80

46. *Hot Springs of Gardiner's River, Yellowstone National Park, Wyoming Territory*
Watercolor
20¼ × 28⅝ in. (51.3 × 72.7 cm.)
l.r.: "⚑ ORAN. / 1872."
Reynolda House Museum of American Art

PROVENANCE: The artist; A. G. Renshaw, Fellow of the Geological Society of London; Geological Society of London, presented by the artist and A. G. Renshaw (1884–1972); Sotheby's Belgravia Sale on May 31, 1972, lot 40, illus. p. 16; Hirschl & Adler Galleries, Inc., New York
LITERATURE: Washington, D.C., Barlow's (1873); *Official Catalogue of the International Exhibition of 1876* (Philadelphia, 1876), Annex Gallery No. 16, No. 376; Hirschl & Adler, *Faces and Places* (1972), no. 68 (illus.); MOMA, *Natural Paradise* (1976), illus. p. 80; Donelson F. Hoopes, *American Watercolor Painting*, pl. 20, p. 116

47. *Lower Geyser Basin (Blue Spring, Lower Geyser Basin, Yellowstone)*
Pencil, watercolor, and opaque color
10 × 14 in. (25.4 × 35.6 cm.)
l.l.: "⚜ ORAN. / 1873"
The Thomas Gilcrease Institute of American History and Art (0226.1365)
PROVENANCE: The artist; Ruth B. Moran; M. Knoedler & Co., Inc., New York; Thomas Gilcrease
LITERATURE: Clinton Academy, *Paintings and Etchings* (1928), unnumbered; Paul A. Rossi and David C. Hunt, *The Art of the Old West*, illus. pp. 208–209

48. *Lower Yellowstone Range*
Watercolor and opaque color
9½ × 14 in. (24.0 × 35.6 cm.)
l.r.: "⚜ ORAN. / 1874"
Division of Graphic Arts, National Museum of History and Technology, Smithsonian Institution, Gift of L. Prang and Company (1883)
PROVENANCE: The artist; L. Prang & Company, Boston
LITERATURE: Wilson, "Moran," no. 35; Fort Worth, Amon Carter Museum, *The Democratic Art*, no. 54*a*, illus. p. 58; Peter C. Marzio,

Chromolithography, 1840–1900, p. 310, illus. pl. 67

49. *Mammoth Hot Springs (Hot Springs of Gardiner's River)*
Pencil, watercolor, and opaque color
9¼ × 14 in. (23.5 × 35.6 cm.)
l.l.: "⚜ ORAN / 1873"
Collection of Robert H. Levis II
PROVENANCE: The artist; L. Prang & Company, Boston; Dr. John A. Mitchell's aunt (1918–1919); Dr. John A. Mitchell, Interlaken, Massachusetts (1919–1970?); Kennedy Galleries, Inc., New York
LITERATURE: AAA-Prang (1892), no. 352; Los Angeles County, Museum of Art, *The American West*, no. 100, pl. 107; New York, Kennedy Galleries, Inc., *Kennedy Quarterly* 11, no. 4 (March 1972): illus. p. 202

50. *Mammoth Hot Springs, Yellowstone*
Pencil, watercolor, and opaque color
14½ × 10⅜ in. (36.9 × 26.3 cm.)
l.l.: "⚜ ORAN / 1872"
National Collection of Fine Arts, Smithsonian Institution, Gift of Mrs. Armistead Peter, Jr. (1958.5.2)
PROVENANCE: Mrs. Armistead Peter, Jr.
LITERATURE: Gerdts, *Thomas Moran* (1963), no. 36; NCFA, *National Parks* (1972), no. 57, illus. p. 94; MFA, *Frontier America* (1975), no. 96, illus. p. 76; Fern, *Drawings and Watercolors* (1976), no. 9

51. *Minerva Terrace, Yellowstone National Park, Wyoming Territory*
Watercolor and opaque color
11½ × 8⅞ in. (29.2 × 22.5 cm.)
l.l.: "⚜ ORAN. / 1872"
Private Collection
PROVENANCE: General A. B. Nettleson; Jay Cooke, Abington, Pennsylvania; James McGrath (1968); Hirschl & Adler Galleries, Inc., New York (1968–1975);

Private Collection (1975–1978); Coe Kerr Galleries, New York
LITERATURE: New York, Hirschl & Adler Galleries, Inc., *The American Scene*, no. 70, illus.; Washington, D.C., Adams, Davidson Galleries, *100 Years of American Painting, 1840–1940*, p. 12; Brooklyn Museum, *A Century of American Illustration*, no. 5, illus. p. 6; NCFA, *National Parks* (1972), no. 58, illus. p. 95; Hirschl & Adler, *Faces and Places* (1972), no. 66, illus.; Alan Gussow, *A Sense of Place*, illus. 2:24; UCB, *Turner* (1975), no. 75, illus. p. 208

52. *Old Faithful*
Watercolor
14 × 10¼ in. (35.6 × 26.0 cm.)
l.l.: "⚜ ORAN 1873"
Phelan Collection
PROVENANCE: Dr. John A. Mitchell's aunt (1918–1919); Dr. John A. Mitchell, Interlaken, Massachusetts (1919–1970?); Kennedy Galleries, Inc., New York; Berry-Hill Galleries, New York
LITERATURE: Los Angeles County, Museum of Art, *The American West*, no. 101, pl. 13 (as "Castle Geyser, 1872"); Peter Hassrick, *The Way West*, pl. 138, p. 135; Bethesda, Maryland, Government Services Savings and Loan, Inc., *The American West*, no. 21, illus. p. 9; Ballinger, *Endless River* (1979), pl. 27, p. 82

53. *Tower Creek, Yellowstone*
Watercolor
16 × 11 in. (40.6 × 27.9 cm.)
l.l.: "⚜ ORAN / 1873"
Collection, The Pennsylvania State University, Ogontz Campus
PROVENANCE: The artist; Jay Cooke, Abington, Pennsylvania; Ogontz School for Girls, Abington, Pennsylvania
LITERATURE: John P. Driscoll, "Moran Watercolor Found in University Attic," pp. 111–112

54. *Tower Falls*
Pencil, watercolor, and opaque color
12 × 8½ in. (30.5 × 21.6 cm.)
l.l.: "☫ ORAN. / 1872"
The Thomas Gilcrease Institute of American History and Art (0236.1457)
PROVENANCE: The artist; William Blackmore, Salisbury, England; Bertram M. Newhouse, New York (1937); George A. Hormel, Los Angeles; M. Knoedler & Co., Inc., New York; Thomas Gilcrease
LITERATURE: New York, Goupil's Gallery (1872); Newhouse (1937); LA Art Association (1937); Santa Barbara (1937), no. 30; Wilson, "Moran," no. 30; Wilkins, *Moran*, illus. fol. p. 128; Marie Keene, "Moran," illus. p. 9; Helen Comstock, "In Recognition of Thomas Moran," illus. p. 38; Sachs, "Drawings and Watercolors," pl. 14

55. *Tower Falls and Sulphur Mountain, Yellowstone*
Pencil, watercolor, and opaque color
9½ × 13½ in. (24.1 × 34.3 cm.)
l.r.: "☫ ORAN. / 1872"
Collection of Robert H. Levis II
PROVENANCE: The artist; Robert Adams (1878); Kennedy Galleries, Inc., New York
LITERATURE: New York, E. Schenck Auction Rooms (1878); New York, Kennedy Galleries, Inc., *Kennedy Quarterly* 5, no. 1 (October 1964): no. 32, illus. p. 33

56. *Tower Falls and Sulphur Mountain, Yellowstone National Park*
Pencil, watercolor, and opaque color
10 × 14 in. (25.4 × 35.6 cm.)
l.l.: "☫ 1874"
Inscription on verso by Moran: "It is certainly [one] of the most weird and impressive scene[s] in the [Yellowstone] park. The Sulphur Mountain lies across the Yellowstone river which flows at its base. The snowy dome of the Mountain is supported upon a base of columnar basalt of great regularity and formation. The columns of which are about 40 feet in height. Beneath these columns lies a strata of calcerous deposit intermixed with sulphur and iron given the most delicate and beautiful tints of red and yellow. This is again supported upon another mass of columnar structure."
Unlocated
PROVENANCE: The artist; L. Prang & Company, Boston; Private Collection; Kennedy Galleries, Inc., New York
LITERATURE: AAA-Prang (1892), no. 348; Wilson, "Moran," no. 34; New York, Kennedy Galleries, Inc., *Kennedy Quarterly* 3, no. 2 (October 1962): no. 106, illus. p. 74

57. *Tower Falls and Sulfur Rock, Yellowstone*
Watercolor
14½ × 10½ in. (36.8 × 26.7 cm.)
(ca. 1874–1875)
l.r.: "☫ ORAN."
Private Collection
PROVENANCE: The artist; L. Prang & Company, Boston; Private Collection; Kennedy Galleries, Inc., New York
LITERATURE: New York, Kennedy Galleries, Inc., *Kennedy Quarterly* 13, no. 2 (June 1974): no. 90, illus. p. 106

58. *Towering Heights*
Watercolor and opaque color
8 × 6 in. (20.3 × 15.2 cm.)
l.l.: "☫ ORAN / 1873"
Unlocated
PROVENANCE: Edward Eberstadt & Sons, New York
LITERATURE: New York, Edward Eberstadt & Sons, *American Paintings, Historical, Genre, Western*, no. 125, illus.

59. *The Towers of Tower Falls*
Pencil, pen and ink, watercolor, and opaque color
11 × 8 in. (27.9 × 20.3 cm.)
l.r.: "⚹ ORAN / 1872"
The Thomas Gilcrease Institute of American History and Art (0236.1455)
PROVENANCE: The artist; William Blackmore, Salisbury, England; Bertram M. Newhouse, New York (1937); George A. Hormel, Los Angeles; M. Knoedler and Co., Inc., New York; Thomas Gilcrease
LITERATURE: New York, Goupil's Gallery (1872); Newhouse (1937); LA Art Association (1937); Santa Barbara (1937), no. 32; Wilson, "Moran," no. 71; Elizabeth M. Cock, "The Influence of Photography on American Landscape Painting, 1839–1880," pl. 49

60. *Upper Falls, Yellowstone*
Watercolor and opaque color
10 × 8 in. (25.4 × 20.3 cm.)
l.r.: "⚹ ORAN.1872"
The Thomas Gilcrease Institute of American History and Art (0236.1451)
PROVENANCE: The artist; William Blackmore, Salisbury, England; Bertram M. Newhouse, New York (1937); George A. Hormel, Los Angeles; M. Knoedler & Co., Inc., New York; Thomas Gilcrease
LITERATURE: New York, Goupil's Gallery (1872); LA Art Association (1937); Newhouse (1937); Santa Barbara (1937), no. 26; Wilkins, *American Scene*, illus. p. 31; Wilkins, *Moran*, illus. fol. p. 128; Paul A. Rossi and David C. Hunt, *The Art of the Old West*, illus. p. 204

61. *Upper Falls, Yellowstone*
Watercolor and opaque color
14 × 9¾ in. (35.6 × 24.8 cm.)
l.l.: "⚹ / 1874"
Letter accompanying watercolor: "About 25 mi below the Yellowstone Lake the river makes the first grand leap over a Basaltic ledge of rock, a distance of 125′ into a vast black looking cauldron, worn by the waters in their tremendous rush. Unlike the lower Fall (half a mile below) it is broken in its descent by projecting rocks, tearing the waters into clouds of spray ere it reaches the bottom and giving the peculiar rocket-like discharge of water points shown in the picture. This point is the proper head of the Grand Canon and the river makes a fitting entrance into it. A curious fact is that all fish caught in the river below these falls are free from a worm which is found in the flesh of nearly all those caught above."
Philbrook Art Center, Tulsa, Oklahoma
PROVENANCE: Mr. Kirkpatrick, Newark, New Jersey; John Nicholson Gallery, New York (1947); M. Knoedler & Co., Inc., New York (1948); Private Collection
LITERATURE: Wilson, "Moran," no. 89; CSU, *Moran in Yellowstone* (1972), no. 30; Fern, *Drawings and Watercolors* (1976), no. 24

62. *Upper Twin Lake, Colorado*
Pencil, watercolor, and opaque color
9½ × 14 in. (24.1 × 35.6 cm.)
(ca. 1874–1875)
Unlocated
PROVENANCE: The artist; L. Prang & Company, Boston
LITERATURE: AAA-Prang (1892), no. 358

63. *Wyoming Falls, Yellowstone River*
Pencil, watercolor, and opaque color
13½ × 8 in. (34.3 × 20.3 cm.)
l.l.: "TMORAN. / 1872"
The Thomas Gilcrease Institute of American History and Art (0236.1452)

PROVENANCE: The artist; William Blackmore, Salisbury, England; Bertram M. Newhouse, New York (1937); George A. Hormel, Los Angeles; M. Knoedler & Co., Inc., New York; Thomas Gilcrease
LITERATURE: New York, Goupil's Gallery (1872); Newhouse (1937); LA Art Association (1937); Santa Barbara (1937), no. 25; Wilson, "Moran," no. 73; "Sketches Which Went to Congress to Prove a Myth and Preserve a Park," *American Scene* 1, no. 1 (Spring 1958): 5

64. *Yellowstone Canyon* (*In the Yellowstone*)
Watercolor
14½ × 10½ in. (36.8 × 26.7 cm.)
l.r.: "T.Moran 1872"
Collection of Carl Schaefer Dentzel
PROVENANCE: The artist; Carl Oscar Borg
LITERATURE: Gerdts, *Thomas Moran* (1963), no. 7

65. *Yellowstone Cone, Liberty Cap* (*The Cone*)
Pencil, watercolor, and opaque color
11½ × 8½ in. (29.2 × 21.6 cm.)
l.l.: "ORAN. / 1873"
Private Collection
PROVENANCE: Dr. John A. Mitchell's aunt (1918–1919); Dr. John A. Mitchell, Interlaken, Massachusetts (1919–1970?); Kennedy Galleries, Inc., New York; Anschutz Corporation, Denver, Colorado; J. N. Bartfield, Inc., New York
LITERATURE: Denver Art Museum, *Colorado Collects Historic Western Art*, no. 18 (as "Liberty Cap, Yellowstone"); New York, J. N. Bartfield Art Galleries, Inc., *The American West*, no. 50, illus.

66. *The Yellowstone Lake with Hot Springs*
Pencil, pen and ink, watercolor, and opaque color
7 × 14 in. (17.8 × 35.6 cm.)
l.r.: "ORAN.1872"
The Thomas Gilcrease Institute of American History and Art
(0236.1362)
PROVENANCE: The artist; William Blackmore, Salisbury, England; Bertram M. Newhouse, New York (1937); George A. Hormel, Los Angeles; M. Knoedler & Co., Inc., New York; Thomas Gilcrease
LITERATURE: New York, Goupil's Gallery (1872); Newhouse (1937); LA Art Association (1937); Santa Barbara (1937), no. 27; Wilson, "Moran," no. 33

67. *Yellowstone Lake, Yellowstone National Park*
Pencil, watercolor, and opaque color
9½ × 14 in. (24.1 × 35.6 cm.)
(ca. 1874–1875)
Unlocated
PROVENANCE: The artist; L. Prang & Company, Boston
LITERATURE: AAA-Prang (1892), no. 354

68. *Yellowstone Range Near Fort Ellis*
Pencil, watercolor, and opaque color
8 × 11 in. (20.3 × 27.9 cm.)
l.l.: "ORAN. / 1872"
The Thomas Gilcrease Institute of American History and Art
(0236.1358)
PROVENANCE: The artist; William Blackmore, Salisbury, England; Bertram M. Newhouse, New York (1937); George A. Hormel, Los Angeles; M. Knoedler & Co., Inc., New York; Thomas Gilcrease
LITERATURE: New York, Goupil's Gallery (1872); Newhouse (1937); LA Art Association (1937); Santa Barbara (1937), no. 23; Wilson, "Moran," no. 83

69. *The Yellowstone Range; Near the Crow "Mission," Party en Route to the Mountains*
Pencil, watercolor, and opaque color
7 × 14 in. (17.8 × 35.6 cm.)
l.r.: "TMORAN. / 1872"
The Thomas Gilcrease Institute of American History and Art
(0236.1364)
PROVENANCE: The artist; William Blackmore, Salisbury, England; Bertram M. Newhouse, New York (1937); George A. Hormel, Los Angeles; M. Knoedler & Co., Inc., New York; Thomas Gilcrease
LITERATURE: New York, Goupil's Gallery (1872); Newhouse (1937); LA Art Association (1937); Santa Barbara (1937), no. 17

70. *Yellowstone River*
Pencil, watercolor, and opaque color
13 × 9½ in. (33.0 × 24.1 cm.)
l.l.: "TMORAN / 1872"
The Thomas Gilcrease Institute of American History and Art
(0236.1456)
PROVENANCE: The artist; William Blackmore, Salisbury, England; Bertram M. Newhouse, New York (1937); George A. Hormel, Los Angeles; M. Knoedler & Co., Inc., New York; Thomas Gilcrease
LITERATURE: New York, Goupil's Gallery (1872); Newhouse (1937); LA Art Association (1937); Santa Barbara (1937), no. 28; Wilson, "Moran," no. 84

71. *Above Tower Falls, Yellowstone*
(Tower Creek, Yellowstone)
Watercolor
10 × 14 in. (25.4 × 35.6 cm.)
(1893)
Unlocated
PROVENANCE: Mrs. George P.
Cammann, New York (1928)
LITERATURE: AWCS, *Annual
Exhibition* (1894), no. 603;
Clinton Academy, *Paintings and
Etchings* (1928), no. 2

72. *East Wall of the Cañon from
Inspiration Point*
Pencil, watercolor, and opaque
color
12⅝ × 9¾ in. (32.1 × 24.8 cm.)
l.l.: "East Wall of the Cañon from
Inspiration Point. TM. 1892"
Yellowstone National Park,
Wyoming, Gift of George D. Pratt,
Mrs. Henry Strong, Mr. John D.
Rockefeller, Jr., Col. Herbert J.
Slocum (8537)
PROVENANCE: The artist; Ruth B.
Moran
LITERATURE: Milch, *Water Color
Sketches* (1926), unnumbered;
Wilson, "Moran," no. 58; Fern,
Drawings and Watercolors (1976),
no. 101, illus. p. 127; Fern,
"Drawings and Watercolors"
(1976), illus. p. 37

73. *The Grand Canyon of the
Yellowstone*
Watercolor
14 × 20 in. (35.6 × 50.8 cm.)
Unlocated
LITERATURE: AWCS, *Annual
Exhibition* (1902), no. 258;
Philadelphia Art Club, Water
Color Exhibition (1904)

74. *Head Waters of the Yellowstone*
Watercolor
Dimensions unknown
(ca. 1880)
Unlocated
LITERATURE: AWCS, *Annual
Exhibition* (1880), no. 430

75. *Hot Springs of the Yellowstone
Park*
Pencil, black crayon, and
watercolor
9⅝ × 12⅝ in. (24.4 × 32.1 cm.)
l.l.: "July 21st 92 TM. Dead since
first visit in -71"
l.r.: "⚕ 1892"
On mount: "Hot Springs of the
Yellowstone Park. TMoran. 1892"
Cooper-Hewitt Museum, The
Smithsonian Institution's
National Museum of Design, Gift
of the artist (1917.17.70)
PROVENANCE: The artist
LITERATURE: Denver (1892), no. 25
or 26; Wilson, "Moran," no. 137;
Gerdts, *Thomas Moran* (1963), no.
33, illus. p. 45; Bassford and
Fryxell, *Home Thoughts*, illus. p.
116; CSU, *Moran in Yellowstone*
(1972), no. 23, illus.; Century
Association (1979)

76. *Hot Springs, Yellowstone (Main
Terrace, Mammoth Hot Springs)*
Pencil, watercolor, and opaque
color
9⅝ × 12⅝ in. (24.4 × 32.1 cm.)
l.r.: "Hot Springs,
Yellowstone / TMoran. 1892"
Yellowstone National Park,
Wyoming, Gift of George D. Pratt,
Mrs. Henry Strong, Mr. John D.
Rockefeller, Jr., Col. Herbert J.
Slocum (8527)
PROVENANCE: The artist; Ruth B.
Moran
LITERATURE: Denver (1892), no. 25
(or 26); Santa Barbara (1925), no.
36; Milch, *Water Color Sketches*
(1926), no. 40; Biltmore Salon
(LA), *Water Colors* (1927), no. 11;
Wilson, "Moran," no. 60; CSU,
Moran in Yellowstone (1972), no.
22; Fern, *Drawings and
Watercolors* (1976), no. 93, illus. p.
121

77. *Jupiter and Cleopatra,
Yellowstone Hot Springs*
Watercolor
Dimensions unknown
(July 21, 1892)
Unlocated
LITERATURE: Santa Barbara (1925),
no. 50; Milch, *Water Color
Sketches* (1926), no. 54; Biltmore
Salon (LA), *Water Colors* (1927),
no. 7

78. *Lower Geyser Basin of the
Yellowstone*
Pencil and watercolor
7¾ × 10 in. (19.7 × 25.4 cm.)
u.l.: "Lower Geyser Basin July
29th 1892 / TMoran"
The Thomas Gilcrease Institute of
American History and Art
(0236.829)
PROVENANCE: The artist; Ruth B.
Moran; Mrs. Nelson Osborne; M.
Knoedler & Co., Inc., New York;
Thomas Gilcrease
LITERATURE: Santa Barbara (1925),
no. 48; Milch, *Water Color
Sketches* (1926), no. 52; Biltmore
Salon (LA), *Water Colors* (1927),
no. 12; Clinton Academy,
Paintings and Etchings (1928)

79. *Moran Point, Yellowstone Cañon*
Pencil, watercolor, and opaque
color
9½ × 12½ in. (24.1 × 31.8 cm.)
u.l.: "Moran's Point. Yellowstone
Canon / July 31st 1892 TM"
l.l.: "TMoran."
The Thomas Gilcrease Institute of
American History and Art
(0236.830)
PROVENANCE: The artist; Ruth B.
Moran; M. Knoedler & Co., Inc.,
New York; Thomas Gilcrease
LITERATURE: Denver (1892), no. 35;
Milch, *Water Color Sketches*
(1926); Parker, "Water-Colors,"
illus. p. 71; Clinton Academy,
Paintings and Etchings (1928), no.
15; Santa Barbara (1937), no. 29;
Wilson, "Moran," no. 57

80. *Upper Basin of the Yellowstone*
Pencil, watercolor, and opaque
color
9¼ × 12½ in. (23.5 × 31.8 cm.)
l.l.: "July 21st 1892 TM"
l.r.: "TM. 1892"
On mount: "Upper Basins"
The Thomas Gilcrease Institute of
American History and Art
(0236.831)
PROVENANCE: The artist; Ruth B.
Moran; M. Knoedler & Co., Inc.,
New York; Thomas Gilcrease
LITERATURE: Santa Barbara (1925),
no. 51; Milch, *Water Color
Sketches* (1926), no. 55

81. *Upper Falls, Yellowstone*
Pencil and watercolor
12¾ × 9¾ in. (32.4 × 24.8 cm.)
l.r.: "upper Fall of / the
Yellowstone / T.Moran / 1892"
Stark Museum of Art, Orange,
Texas (31.18/3)
PROVENANCE: Joseph Sartor
Galleries, Dallas, Texas (1957);
H. J. Lutcher Stark, Orange, Texas
LITERATURE: Stark Museum,
Western Collection, p. 209

82. *The Yellowstone Range, National
Park, Wyoming*
Watercolor
Dimensions unknown
(ca. 1898)
Unlocated
LITERATURE: AWCS, *Annual
Exhibition* (1898), no. 63

83. *Bridal Vail Fall, Yosemite Valley*
Watercolor, pencil, and opaque
color
6½ × 4⅜ in. (16.5 × 11.1 cm.)
l.l.: "⚹"
On mount: "Bridal Vail Fall,
Yosemite / Valley by Thomas
Moran / Presented to WH Holmes
by W.L. Woods, Washington
1880 / Moran was here at that
time / WH Holmes."
Bound in William H. Holmes's
"Random Records of a Lifetime,"
vol. 8
National Collection of Fine Arts
Library, Smithsonian Institution
PROVENANCE: The artist; Dr.
William H. Holmes, Washington,
D.C.

84. *Coastal Scene, California*
Pencil and watercolor
8¾ × 17¾ in. (22.2 × 45.1 cm.)
Signed
Unlocated
PROVENANCE: Thom-Woodall
families, Whitewell, Whitchurch,
Salop, England; Castellane
Gallery, New York
LITERATURE: Parke-Bernet
Galleries, Inc., sale 2617, lot 11
(November 15, 1967)

85. *Colorado River at Needles,
California*
Watercolor
Dimensions unknown
Unlocated
LITERATURE: Milch, *Water Color
Sketches* (1926), unnumbered;
Biltmore Salon (LA), *Water Colors*
(1927), no. 13

86. *In the High Sierras*
Watercolor
10 × 12½ in. (25.4 × 31.8 cm.)
Unlocated
LITERATURE: Parke-Bernet
Galleries, Inc., sale 1966, lot 81
(April 9, 1960)

87. *Lake Tahoe*
Pencil and watercolor
9 × 12 in. (22.9 × 30.5 cm.)
l.l.: "Lake Tahoe / TM / 1871"
The Thomas Gilcrease Institute of
American History and Art
(0236.881)
PROVENANCE: The artist; Ruth B.
Moran; M. Knoedler & Co., Inc.,
New York; Thomas Gilcrease

88. *Lake Tahoe*
Pencil, watercolor, and opaque
color
10½ × 14½ in. (26.7 × 36.8 cm.)
u.l.: "Tahoe. Aug 8th -79 TM"
l.l.: "TM. TMoran"
The Thomas Gilcrease Institute of
American History and Art
(0236.886)
PROVENANCE: The artist; Ruth B.
Moran; M. Knoedler & Co., Inc.,
New York; Thomas Gilcrease

89. *Lake Tahoe, California*
Watercolor
Dimensions unknown
(1872)
Unlocated
LITERATURE: Santa Barbara (1925),
no. 20; Milch, *Water Color
Sketches* (1926), no. 20; Biltmore
Salon (LA), *Water Colors* (1927),
no. 20

90. *Lake Tahoe, California*
Watercolor and opaque color
Dimensions unknown
l.l.: "Tahoe / Aug 19th 79 T.
Moran"
Unlocated
LITERATURE: Santa Barbara (1925),
no. 58; Milch, *Water Color
Sketches* (1926), no. 23; Biltmore
Salon (LA), *Water Colors* (1927),
no. 21; Parker, "Water-Colors,"
illus. p. 66; Wilson, "Moran," no.
44

91. *The Needles*
Pencil and watercolor
5 × 7 in. (12.7 × 17.8 cm.)
u.r.: "The Needles / June 2, 189
[illeg.] [1892]"
l.r.: "TM"

Cooper-Hewitt Museum, The Smithsonian Institution's National Museum of Design, Gift of the artist (1917.17.18)
PROVENANCE: The artist
LITERATURE: Denver (1892), no. 60; Wilson, "Moran," no. 112

92. *The Sentinel, Yosemite Valley*
Watercolor
4¾ × 3½ in. (12.1 × 8.9 cm.)
l.l.: "The Sentinel, Yosemite Valley"
l.r.: "T Moran"
Unlocated
PROVENANCE: Davis Galleries, New York; Mrs. William H. Bender, Bronxville, New York
LITERATURE: Sotheby Parke-Bernet, Inc., sale 3978, lot 52, illus. (April 21, 1977)

93. *Sierra Nevada Range*
Watercolor
11 × 14 in. (27.9 × 35.6 cm.)
(1898)
Unlocated
PROVENANCE: The artist; Ruth B. Moran; Joe Thirp; Emily Thirp; Emily and Jack Millhisk, Gift of Emily Thirp
LITERATURE: AWCS, *Annual Exhibition* (1898), no. 14 (as "In the Sierra Nevada"); Clinton Academy, *Paintings and Etchings* (1928), unnumbered; New York, Whitney Museum of American Art, *A History of American Watercolor Painting*, no. 103

94. *South Dome, Yosemite*
Pencil, watercolor, and opaque color
16½ × 12¼ in. (42.0 × 31.0 cm.)
l.l.: "⚹ 1873 Yosemite"
l.r.: "South Dome. T.Moran. 1873"
Cooper-Hewitt Museum, The Smithsonian Institution's National Museum of Design, Gift of the artist (1917.17.32)
PROVENANCE: The artist

LITERATURE: Denver (1892), no. 91 (?); New York, The Cooper Union Museum for the Arts of Decoration, *An Exhibition of American Drawings*, no. 83; Wilson, "Moran," no. 73, illus. pl. XIX, p. 247; Gerdts, *Thomas Moran* (1963), no. 25, illus. p. 3a; Heckscher Museum, *Moran Family* (1965), no. 27; Wilkins, *Moran*, illus. fol. p. 48; St. Petersburg, Florida, Museum of Fine Arts, *They Saw the West*, unnumbered; NCFA, *National Parks* (1972), no. 102, illus. p. 128; Massachusetts, University at Amherst, The University Gallery, *Late Nineteenth Century American Drawings and Watercolors*, no. 20

95. *The South Dome, Yosemite Valley*
Pencil, watercolor, and opaque color
15 × 11¼ in. (38.1 × 28.6 cm.)
l.l.: "TMoran, 1872"
Jefferson National Expansion Memorial, St. Louis, Missouri (4300)
PROVENANCE: The artist; Ruth B. Moran
LITERATURE: Denver (1892), no. 91 (?); Fryxell, "National Parks Collection," no. TM-55; Wilson, "Moran," no. 43

96. *A Study from Nature, Yosemite Valley*
Watercolor
14 × 10 in. (35.6 × 25.4 cm.)
Unlocated
LITERATURE: AAA-Ortgies (1886), no. 55

97. *Study of Conifers in Yosemite*
Ink and watercolor
9½ × 14½ in. (24.1 × 36.8 cm.)
l.l.: "Yo Semite / Aug. '71 / TM"
l.r.: "Yo Semite / Aug. '71"
Private Collection
PROVENANCE: The artist; Ruth B. Moran; Chapellier Galleries, New York

98. *Summit of the Sierras, Nevada*
Watercolor and opaque color
14⅕ × 9⅘ in. (36.0 × 25.0 cm.)
l.l.: "⚹ ORAN"
(1874)
The Art Institute of Chicago, Gift of Mrs. Byron Harvey (1965.852)
PROVENANCE: The artist; L. Prang & Company, Boston; Katherine Harvey, Santa Barbara, California; Mrs. Byron Harvey
LITERATURE: AAA-Prang (1892), no. 350; Ruth B. Moran, "Thomas Moran," illus. p. 45; Wilson, "Moran," no. 94; The Arts Club of Chicago, *The American Landscape*, no. 21, illus. p. 17

99. *At the Rock Cabin*
Watercolor
Dimensions unknown
l.l.: "🌿"
Unlocated
LITERATURE: Higgins, *Grand Cañon*, p. 17

100. *Canyon of the Colorado, Arizona*
Watercolor
3½ × 4¾ in. (8.9 × 12.1 cm.)
(ca. 1901)
Cooper-Hewitt Museum, The Smithsonian Institution's National Museum of Design, Gift of the artist (1917.17.89)
PROVENANCE: The artist

101. *Canyon of the Rio Virgen, S. Utah*
Pencil and watercolor
4 × 9 in. (10.2 × 22.9 cm.)
l.l.: "T.M."
On mat: "Canon of the Rio Virgen. S. Utah. 1873"
Cooper-Hewitt Museum, The Smithsonian Institution's National Museum of Design, Gift of the artist (1917.17.27)
PROVENANCE: The artist
LITERATURE: Heckscher Museum, *Moran Family* (1965), no. 23; Bassford and Fryxell, *Home Thoughts*, illus. p. 34; NCFA, *National Parks* (1972), no. 107, illus. p. 132; Washburn, *Cooper-Hewitt Collection* (1974), illus.

102. *Canyon of the Rio Virgin, Utah*
Watercolor
14 × 10 in. (35.6 × 25.4 cm.)
l.r.: "🌿 ORAN. / 1875"
Private Collection
PROVENANCE: Mr. Kirkpatrick, Newark, New Jersey; John Nicholson Gallery, New York (1947); M. Knoedler & Co., Inc., New York (1948)
LITERATURE: Wilson, "Moran," no. 39

103. *Cliffs of the Rio Virgin, Southern Utah*
Pencil, watercolor, and opaque color

8¾ × 14 in. (22.2 × 35.6 cm.)
l.l.: "🌿. 1873 Cliffs of the Rio Virgin / S. Utah"
Cooper-Hewitt Museum, The Smithsonian Institution's National Museum of Design, Gift of the artist (1917.17.20)
PROVENANCE: The artist
LITERATURE: Denver (1892), no. 67; *Art in America* 15, no. 4 (June 1927): illus. p. 156; The Art Institute of Chicago, *The Hudson River School and the Early American Landscape Tradition*, no. 138; Wilson, "Moran," no. 74, illus. pl. XXII, p. 253; New York, The Cooper Union Museum for the Arts of Decoration, *Five Centuries of Drawing*, no. 98; Henri Dorra, *The American Muse*, illus. p. 71; Gerdts, *Thomas Moran* (1963), no. 24, illus. p. 38; Sachs, "Drawings and Watercolors," pl. 18; New York, Gallery of Modern Art, *Major 19th and 20th Century Drawings*; Washington, D.C., Smithsonian Institution, National Collection of Fine Arts, *Treasures from the Cooper Union Museum*, no. 220; Birmingham, Alabama, Museum of Art, *American Watercolors 1850–1972*, illus. p. 13; The Arts Club of Chicago, *The American Landscape*, no. 20, illus. p. 16; Washburn, *Cooper-Hewitt Collection* (1974), illus.; New York, National Academy of Design, *A Century and a Half of American Art*, illus. p. 196; MOMA, *Natural Paradise* (1976), illus. p. 80; Century Association (1979)

104. *Cliffs of the Upper Colorado River*
Pencil, watercolor, and opaque color
11½ × 6½ in. (29.2 × 16.5 cm.)
Unlocated
PROVENANCE: L. Prang & Company, Boston
LITERATURE: AAA-Prang (1892), no. 419

105. *Colburn's Butte, S. Utah*
Watercolor
15 × 10¾ in. (38.1 × 27.3 cm.)
l.c.: "Colburns Butte. Utah. 1873"
Unlocated
PROVENANCE: Mrs. Edith Lord
Winslow, 24 Mercer Street,
Somerville, New Jersey
(descendant of Justin E. Colburn)
LITERATURE: Bassford and Fryxell,
Home Thoughts, illus. p. 32

106. *Colorado Sketchbook*
Pencil and watercolor in bound
book
Each sheet 4 × 8 in. (10.2 × 19.3
cm.)
(1873)
Jefferson National Expansion
Memorial, St. Louis, Missouri
(4336)
PROVENANCE: The artist; Ruth B.
Moran

107. *From Powell's Plateau*
Pencil, watercolor, and opaque
color
7½ × 10½ in. (19.1 × 26.7 cm.)
l.l.: "T.Moran. / 1873"
Cooper-Hewitt Museum, The
Smithsonian Institution's
National Museum of Design, Gift
of the artist (1917.17.26)
PROVENANCE: The artist
LITERATURE: Wilson, "Moran," no.
69; Sachs, "Drawings and
Watercolors," pl. 20; Gerdts,
Thomas Moran (1963), no. 9;
Heckscher Museum, *Moran
Family* (1965), no. 28; Bassford and
Fryxell, *Home Thoughts* (1967),
illus. p. 38; NCFA, *National Parks*
(1972), no. 16, illus. p. 55; J. Gray
Sweeney, "The Artists-Explorers
of the American West, 1860–
1880," no. 10, illus. p. 398; Sellin,
Preparatory Studies (1976), no. 26,
fig. 41; Truettner, "Scenes of
Majesty," no. 12, illus. p. 248;
Peter Hassrick, *The Way West*, p.
127, pl. 139

108. *The Gate Keeper (Mountain), Zion
Valley*
Pencil, watercolor, and chalk
9½ × 6 in. (24.1 × 15.2 cm.)
u.l.: "in the Narrows. Zion
Valley / The Gate Keeper 1873"
The Thomas Gilcrease Institute of
American History and Art
(0236.878)
PROVENANCE: The artist; Ruth B.
Moran; M. Knoedler & Co., Inc.,
New York; Thomas Gilcrease
LITERATURE: Santa Barbara (1925),
no. 17; Milch, *Water Color
Sketches* (1926), no. 17; Biltmore
Salon (LA), *Water Colors* (1927),
no. 14

109. *The Grand Canyon*
Pencil and watercolor
8½ × 6 in. (21.6 × 15.2 cm.)
Verso: "Rare water color / Hayden
1871 / Father's early / watercolor"
[in Ruth Moran's hand]
The Thomas Gilcrease Institute of
American History and Art
(0126.937)
PROVENANCE: The artist; Ruth B.
Moran; M. Knoedler & Co., Inc.,
New York; Thomas Gilcrease

110. *Grand Canyon*
Watercolor
8½ × 6 in. (21.6 × 15.2 cm.)
l.l.: "TMoran"
(1873)
Collection of Mr. and Mrs. Gerald
P. Peters
PROVENANCE: Mr. John Norton,
Pueblo, Colorado

111. *Grand Cañon from Hance's Trail, Ayers Butte in Foreground*
Pencil and watercolor
5 × 7 in. (12.7 × 17.8 cm.)
l.c.: "Grand Canon / from Hances Trail / Ayers Butte in Foreground / T.Moran."
(May, 1892)
East Hampton Free Library, The Thomas Moran Biographical Art Collection
PROVENANCE: The artist; Ruth B. Moran
LITERATURE: Denver (1892), no. 87 (as "Ayer's Butte, Colorado Cañon"); Santa Barbara (1925), no. 54; Milch, *Water Color Sketches* (1926), no. 58

112. *The Grand Canyon in Stormy Weather*
Watercolor
3¼ × 4¾ in. (8.3 × 12.1 cm.)
(ca. 1908)
Cooper-Hewitt Museum, The Smithsonian Institution's National Museum of Design, Gift of the artist (1917.17.89)
PROVENANCE: The artist
LITERATURE: Wilson, "Moran," no. 70

113. *Grand Canyon of Arizona, from "Berrys," May 30, 1901*
Watercolor
Dimensions unknown
Unlocated
PROVENANCE: The artist; Ruth B. Moran; G. Fraser, Gift of Ruth B. Moran
LITERATURE: Santa Barbara (1925), no. 56; Milch, *Water Color Sketches* (1926), no. 60

114. *Grand Canyon of Colorado*
Pencil and watercolor
18 × 30 in. (45.7 × 76.2 cm.)
(ca. 1873)
The Thomas Gilcrease Institute of American History and Art (0236.880)
PROVENANCE: The artist; Ruth B. Moran; M. Knoedler & Co., Inc., New York; Thomas Gilcrease
LITERATURE: Truettner, "Scenes of Majesty," no. 15, illus. p. 249

115. *Grand Canyon of the Colorado*
Watercolor
5 × 8 in. (12.7 × 20.3 cm.)
(May 27, 1892)
Unlocated
PROVENANCE: The artist; J. L. G. Ferris

116. *The Grand Cañon of the Colorado*
Pencil, watercolor, and opaque color
11½ × 24 in. (29.2 × 61.0 cm.)
u.r.: "The Grand Canon of the Colorado. Arizona / TMoran. / Looking West. / May 29th 1892"
l.l.: "The Grand Canon of the Colorado / Looking West from Hance's 1892. May."
The Thomas Gilcrease Institute of American History and Art (0236.931)
PROVENANCE: The artist; Ruth B. Moran; M. Knoedler & Co., Inc., New York; Thomas Gilcrease

117. *Grand Canyon of the Colorado*
Pencil, watercolor, and opaque color
12½ × 19½ in. (31.8 × 49.5 cm.)
l.l.: "Grand Canon of the Colorado May 30th 1892 TMoran"
Collection of Mr. and Mrs. Michael Coleman
PROVENANCE: Burk; C. H. Sage; Gustave H. Buek, Brooklyn and East Hampton, New York; Edward Eberstadt & Sons, Inc., New York; Kennedy Galleries, Inc., New York
LITERATURE: Santa Barbara (1925), no. 25; Milch, *Water Color Sketches* (1926), no. 59; New York, The Anderson Galleries, *American Water Colors*, no. 66; Wilson, "Moran," no. 55, illus. pl. XX, p. 249

118. *The Grand Canyon of the Colorado*
Watercolor
16¼ × 23¼ in. (41.3 × 59.1 cm.)
l.r.: signed and dated 1892
Unlocated

PROVENANCE: The artist; Gustave H. Buek, Brooklyn and East Hampton, New York; LeRoy Ireland
LITERATURE: New York, The Anderson Galleries, *American Water Colors*, no. 58

119. *Hance's Canyon*
Watercolor
9½ × 12¼ in. (24.1 × 31.1 cm.)
Signed and dated (not given) and dedicated to Mr. Buek by the artist
Unlocated
PROVENANCE: The artist; Gustave H. Buek, Brooklyn and East Hampton, New York
LITERATURE: New York, The Anderson Galleries, *American Water Colors*, no. 108

120. *Head of the Hance Trail*
Watercolor
Dimensions unknown
l.r.: "⚹"
Unlocated
LITERATURE: Higgins, *Grand Cañon*, p. 11

121. *In a Side Canyon of the Colorado River*
Watercolor
Dimensions unknown
Unlocated
LITERATURE: AWCS, *Annual Exhibition* (1902), no. 263

122. *In the Granite*
Watercolor
Dimensions unknown
l.r.: "⚹"
Unlocated
LITERATURE: Higgins, *Grand Cañon*, p. 19

123. *In Utah, 1873, Powell Expedition*
Watercolor
Dimensions unknown
Unlocated
LITERATURE: Santa Barbara (1937), no. 20

139

124. *Looking West from Moran's Point*
Pencil and watercolor
5 × 7¾ in. (12.7 × 19.7 cm.)
u.r.: "looking West from Morans
point / Sunday May 29 / 1892"
l.l.: "T.Moran"
East Hampton Free Library, The
Thomas Moran Biographical Art
Collection
PROVENANCE: The artist; Ruth B.
Moran

125. *Looking up the Hance Trail*
Watercolor
Dimensions unknown
l.l.: "⚓ ORAN. / 1893."
l.r.: "The Hance Trail"
Unlocated
LITERATURE: Higgins, *Grand
Cañon*, p. 15

126. *Looking up the Trail at Bright
Angel, Grand Canyon of Arizona*
Pencil, watercolor, and opaque
color
14⅞ × 10⅜ in. (37.8 × 26.3 cm.)
l.l.: "Looking up the trail at Bright
Angel. / Grand Canon of
Arizona / T.Moran May 1901"
Cooper-Hewitt Museum, The
Smithsonian Institution's
National Museum of Design, Gift
of the artist (1917.17.83)
PROVENANCE: The artist
LITERATURE: Evansville, Indiana,
Public Museum, *Homer and
Moran*; Wilson, "Moran," no. 156;
Gerdts, *Thomas Moran* (1963), no.
39, illus. p. 48; NCFA, *National
Parks* (1972), no. 21, illus. p. 58;
Fern, *Drawings and Watercolors*
(1976), no. 118, illus. p. 143

127. *Marble Cañon, Colorado River*
Watercolor
4½ × 3¼ in. (11.4 × 8.3 cm.)
Unlocated
LITERATURE: AAA-Ortgies (1886),
no. 60

128. *Midway Station at Cedar Ranch*
Watercolor
Dimensions unknown
l.r.: "⚓"
Unlocated
LITERATURE: Higgins, *Grand
Cañon*, p. 9

129. *Mu Koon tu Weap Valley*
Pencil, watercolor, and opaque
color
Dimensions unknown
(ca. 1874–1875)
Unlocated
PROVENANCE: The artist; L. Prang
& Company, Boston

130. *On the Bright Angel Trail, Grand
Cañon of Arizona*
Watercolor
20 × 24 in. (50.8 × 61.0 cm.)
(1902)
Unlocated
LITERATURE: Philadelphia Art
Club, Water Color Exhibition,
1902

131. *On the Colorado River, Morning*
Watercolor
10 × 8 in. (25.4 × 20.3 cm.)
Unlocated
LITERATURE: AAA-Ortgies (1886),
no. 54

132. *Rock Tower in the Grand Canyon
of Arizona*
Watercolor
10 × 12 in. (25.4 × 30.5 cm.)
Unlocated
PROVENANCE: Robbin's daughter,
Gift of the artist, 1902
LITERATURE: AWCS, *Annual
Exhibition* (1902), no. 262

133. *Shin-Au-Av-Tu-Weap, or "God
Land." Cañon of the Colorado,
Utah Ter.*
Pencil, watercolor, and opaque
color
4⅞ × 14⅝ in. (12.4 × 37.1 cm.)
l.l.: "T.Moran."
National Collection of Fine Arts,
Smithsonian Institution, Gift of
Dr. William H. Holmes
(1930.12.42)
PROVENANCE: The artist; H. N.
Barlow's Art Store, Washington,
D.C. (1878) or Ruth B. Moran; Dr.
William H. Holmes (1926)
LITERATURE: Wilson, "Moran," no.
87; Sachs, "Drawings and
Watercolors," pl. 17; Fern,
Drawings and Watercolors (1976),
no. 35, illus. p. 47

134. *Shiva's Temple*
Pencil and watercolor
4½ × 7 in. (11.4 × 17.8 cm.)
u.r.: "Shivas Temple / May
31st / 1892"
l.l.: "T.Moran."
East Hampton Free Library, The
Thomas Moran Biographical Art
Collection
PROVENANCE: The artist; Ruth B.
Moran
LITERATURE: Denver (1892), no. 86
(?)

135. *Shiva's Temple, Grand Canyon*
Pencil and watercolor
7¾ × 4¾ in. (19.7 × 12.1 cm.)
u.r.: "Shiva's Temple"
l.l.: "T.Moran"
(1892)
Jefferson National Expansion
Memorial, St. Louis, Missouri
(4296)
PROVENANCE: The artist; Ruth B.
Moran
LITERATURE: Denver (1892), no. 86
(?); Fryxell, "National Parks
Collection," no. TM-52; Wilson,
"Moran," no. 131; NCFA,
National Parks (1972), no. 24,
illus. p. 60

136. *Southern Utah*
Watercolor
5¾ × 9 in. (14.6 × 22.9 cm.)
(1873)
Jefferson National Expansion
Memorial, St. Louis, Missouri
(4294)
PROVENANCE: The artist; Ruth B.
Moran
LITERATURE: Fryxell, "National
Parks Collection," no. TM-56;
Wilson, "Moran," no. 64

137. *Utah Buttes*
Watercolor
Dimensions unknown
Unlocated
LITERATURE: Milch, *Water Color
Sketches* (1926), unnumbered

138. *Valley of Babbling Waters, Southern Utah*
Pencil, watercolor, and opaque color
9½ × 14 in. (24.1 × 35.6 cm.)
l.r.: "⚒"
(ca. 1874–1875)
Unlocated
PROVENANCE: The artist; L. Prang & Company, Boston
LITERATURE: AAA-Prang (1892), no. 344; Wilson, "Moran," no. 95

139. *Alpine Pass at Cascade. Twin Lakes, Colorado*
Pencil, watercolor, and opaque color
9¾ × 12⅝ in. (24.8 × 32.0 cm.)
u.r.: "Alpine Pass at Cascade. Twin Lakes, Colorado."
(ca. 1892)
Cooper-Hewitt Museum, The Smithsonian Institution's National Museum of Design, Gift of the artist (1917.17.71)
PROVENANCE: The artist
LITERATURE: Evansville, Indiana, Public Museum, *Homer and Moran*; Wilson, "Moran," no. 220; Washburn, *Cooper-Hewitt Collection* (1974)

140. *Colorado Landscape*
Watercolor
9½ × 13½ in. (24.1 × 34.3 cm.)
l.l.: "TMoran / 1873."
Unlocated
PROVENANCE: M. Knoedler & Co., Inc., New York
LITERATURE: Wilson, "Moran," no. 31; Parke-Bernet Galleries, Inc., sale 1314, lot 271 (February 15–16, 1952)

141. *Garden of the Gods, Colorado*
Pencil and watercolor
10 × 13¾ in. (25.4 × 34.9 cm.)
l.l.: "Garden of the Gods"
l.r.: "T.Moran."
(1898 or 1900)
The Thomas Gilcrease Institute of American History and Art (0236.844)
PROVENANCE: The artist; Ruth B. Moran; M. Knoedler & Co., Inc., New York; Thomas Gilcrease
LITERATURE: Santa Barbara (1925), no. 42 (or 43); Milch, *Water Color Sketches* (1926), no. 46 (or 47); Biltmore Salon (LA), *Water Colors* (1927), no. 17 (or 18)

142. *Garden of the Gods, Colorado*
Watercolor
Dimensions unknown
(1898 or 1900)
Unlocated

LITERATURE: Santa Barbara (1925), no. 43 (or 42); Milch, *Water Color Sketches* (1926), no. 47 (or 46); Biltmore Salon (LA), *Water Colors* (1927), no. 18 (or 17)

143. *Glen Eyrie*
Pencil and watercolor
10¼ × 14½ in. (26.0 × 36.8 cm.)
u.l.: "Glen Eyrie TM."
The Thomas Gilcrease Institute of American History and Art (0236.781)
PROVENANCE: The artist; Ruth B. Moran; M. Knoedler & Co., Inc., New York; Thomas Gilcrease
LITERATURE: Sachs, "Drawings and Watercolors," pl. 25

144. *Glen Eyrie, Colorado*
Pencil and watercolor
10½ × 14 in. (26.7 × 35.6 cm.)
u.l.: "Glen Eyrie. Col. / T.M."
(1892)
Cooper-Hewitt Museum, The Smithsonian Institution's National Museum of Design, Gift of the artist (1917.17.67)
PROVENANCE: The artist
LITERATURE: Wilson, "Moran," no. 140; Washburn, *Cooper-Hewitt Collection* (1974)

145. *Heywood Hot Springs, Colorado*
Pencil, watercolor, and opaque color
6¼ × 12 in. (15.9 × 30.5 cm.)
u.l.: "Heywood Hot Springs"
l.r.: "TMoran"
(1892)
The Thomas Gilcrease Institute of American History and Art (0236.846)
PROVENANCE: The artist; Ruth B. Moran; M. Knoedler & Co., Inc., New York; Thomas Gilcrease

146. *Hot Springs, Elko*
Pencil and watercolor
5¼ × 9¾ in. (13.3 × 24.8 cm.)
u.l.: "Hot Spring Elko"
The Thomas Gilcrease Institute of American History and Art (0246.842)

PROVENANCE: The artist; Ruth B. Moran; M. Knoedler & Co., Inc., New York; Thomas Gilcrease

147. *Iowa Gulch, Colorado*
Pencil, watercolor, and opaque color
11½ × 18 in. (29.2 × 45.7 cm.)
l.r.: "TMoran 1879 / Iowa Gulch, Colorado"
The Thomas Gilcrease Institute of American History and Art (0236.892)
PROVENANCE: The artist; Ruth B. Moran; M. Knoedler & Co., Inc., New York; Thomas Gilcrease
LITERATURE: Denver (1892), no. 48; Sachs, "Drawings and Watercolors," pl. 26; Paul A. Rossi and David C. Hunt, *The Art of the Old West*, illus. pp. 192–193

148. *Monument Valley Park, Colorado*
Watercolor and opaque color
12⅜ × 8¾ in. (32.4 × 22.2 cm.)
l.r.: "⚹ ORAN / 1872"
Colorado Springs Fine Arts Center
Collection: Dreffein Purchase Funds in Memory of Mr. Henry A. Dreffein
PROVENANCE: Edward Eberstadt & Sons, New York; Kennedy Galleries, Inc., New York
LITERATURE: Wilson, "Moran," no. 67; New York, Edward Eberstadt & Sons, *American Paintings, Historical, Genre, Western*, no. 124, illus.; New York, Kennedy Galleries, Inc., *Kennedy Quarterly* 12, no. 3 (June 1973): no. 146, illus. p. 172, and 13, no. 2 (June 1974): no. 89, illus. p. 105; Ballinger, *Endless River* (1979), pl. 28, p. 83

149. *Mosquito Trail, Rocky Mountains of Colorado*
Pencil, watercolor, and opaque color
9¾ × 14¼ in. (24.8 × 36.2 cm.)
l.r.: "⚹ 1875"
Private Collection in New York
PROVENANCE: The artist; L. Prang & Company, Boston; Mrs. J. D. Ratcliffe, Palisades, New York

(1962); Mr. and Mrs. J. William Middendorf II, New York; Hirschl & Adler Galleries, Inc., New York (1969–1973)
LITERATURE: AAA-Prang (1892), no. 345; Laura Bride Powers, "Early Art of Thomas Moran Shown in Art Club Exhibit"; Wilson, "Moran," no. 40; MMA, *Watercolor Painting in America* (1966), no. 87; Wilkins, *Moran*, p. 97; MMA, *Middendorf* (1967), no. 40, illus. p. 59; Indiana University, Bloomington, Art Museum, *The American Scene, 1820–1900*, no. 66, illus.; Hirschl & Adler, *Faces and Places* (1972), no. 67, illus.; Katherine Morrison McClinton, "L. Prang and Company," illus. no. 9a, p. 104

150. *Mount of the Holy Cross*
Watercolor
Dimensions unknown
(1874)
l.l.: "⚹"
Unlocated
PROVENANCE: William Henry Jackson

151. *The Mount of the Holy Cross*
Pencil, watercolor, and opaque color
14 × 9½ in. (35.6 × 24.1 cm.)
l.r.: signed
Unlocated
PROVENANCE: L. Prang & Company, Boston
LITERATURE: AAA-Prang (1892), no. 349; Gustave H. Buek, "Thomas Moran, N.A.—The Grand Old Man of American Art," illus. p. 37; Wilson, "Moran," no. 93

152. *The Mountain of the Holy Cross*
Watercolor and opaque color
18¼ × 11¼ in. (46.3 × 28.6 cm.)
(ca. 1874)
Private Collection
PROVENANCE: W. H. Jackson, New York; Bruce Wear, Art Investments, Tulsa, Oklahoma (1968)

LITERATURE: AWCS, *Annual Exhibition* (1886), no. 344; Wilson, "Moran," no. 93; *Tulsa World*, April 6, 1969, illus. on cover; *Art News* 68, no. 4 (Summer 1969): illus. p. 15

153. *Mountain of the Holy Cross*
Pencil and watercolor
19½ × 14 in. (49.5 × 35.6 cm.)
l.l.: "⚕ Moran / 1894"
Loaned by the Great Grand-daughter of William A. Bell and the Grand-daughter of Mrs. Harold Pearce for whom it was painted and gifted by the artist
PROVENANCE: The artist; Mrs. Harold Pearce, Gift of the artist; William J. Pearce
LITERATURE: AWCS, *Annual Exhibition* (1894), no. 66

154. *Pike's Peak*
Pencil, watercolor, and opaque color
Dimensions unknown
(ca. 1874–1875)
Unlocated
PROVENANCE: The artist; L. Prang & Company, Boston

155. *Pike's Peak, Camerons Cone, and Manitou Cañon*
Pencil and watercolor
10⅞ × 15⅛ in. (27.6 × 38.4 cm.)
l.l.: "Pikes Peak & / Camerons Cone / & Manitou Cañon / T. Moran. June 7, 1901."
Amon Carter Museum of Western Art, Fort Worth (66.73)
PROVENANCE: Milch Galleries, New York; Charles Moran (1973); J. N. Bartfield Art Galleries, Inc., New York
LITERATURE: Santa Barbara (1925), no. 47; Milch, *Water Color Sketches* (1926), no. 51; Biltmore Salon (LA), *Water Colors* (1927), no. 5; New York, J. N. Bartfield Art Galleries, Inc., *American Paintings and Sculpture*, no. 37, illus.

156. *Smelting Works at Denver*
Watercolor
13¾ × 16⅝ in. (34.9 × 42.2 cm.)
l.l.: "⚕ / TMoran."
l.r.: "Smelting Works at Denver / June 12th 1892 / TMoran."
The Cleveland Museum of Art, Bequest of Mrs. Henry A. Everett for the Dorothy Burnham Everett Memorial Collection (38.56)
PROVENANCE: Biltmore Salon, Los Angeles, California; Mrs. Henry A. Everett (1928–1938)
LITERATURE: Denver (1892), no. 82 (as "The Smelters, Denver"); Santa Barbara (1925), no. 49 (as "The Smelters, Denver, Colorado"); Milch, *Water Color Sketches* (1926), no. 53; Biltmore Salon (LA), *Water Colors* (1927), no. 6 (as "The Smelters, Denver, Colorado"); Wilson, "Moran," no. 56; William S. Talbot, "A Check List, American Paintings and Water Colors of the Eighteenth, Nineteenth, and Early Twentieth Centuries in The Cleveland Museum of Art," *Bulletin of The Cleveland Museum of Art* 40, no. 1 (January 1973): no. 138

157. *Toltec Gorge and Eva Cliff from the West*
Pencil, watercolor, and white crayon
12⅓ × 9⅝ in. (31.8 × 24.4 cm.)
u.l.: "Toltec Gorge and Eva Cliff / from the West."
l.l.: "T.M."
l.r.: "⚕"
On mount: "Toltec Gorge and Eva Cliff, Colorado, 1892"
Cooper-Hewitt Museum, The Smithsonian Institution's National Museum of Design, Gift of the artist (1917.17.31)
PROVENANCE: The artist
LITERATURE: Evansville, Indiana, Public Museum, *Homer and Moran*; Wilson, "Moran," no. 147; Heckscher Museum, *Moran Family* (1965), no. 47; Washburn,

Cooper-Hewitt Collection (1947); Fern, *Drawings and Watercolors* (1976), no. 51, illus. p. 71

158. *Toltec Gorge, Colorado*
Pencil, watercolor, and opaque color
12½ × 9½ in. (31.8 × 24.2 cm.)
u.l.: "Toltec Gorge."
l.r.: "⚕"
(1892)
Cooper-Hewitt Museum, The Smithsonian Institution's National Museum of Design, Gift of the artist (1917.17.68)
PROVENANCE: The artist
LITERATURE: Sachs, "Drawings and Watercolors," pl. 32; Heckscher Museum, *Moran Family* (1965), no. 49; Fern, *Drawings and Watercolors* (1976), no. 52, illus. p. 73; Wilson, "Moran," no. 139

159. *Upper Twin Lake, Colorado*
Pencil, watercolor, and opaque color
9½ × 14 in. (24.1 × 35.6 cm.)
(ca. 1874–1875)
Unlocated
PROVENANCE: The artist; L. Prang & Company, Boston
LITERATURE: AAA-Prang (1892), no. 358

160. *Bitter Creek, Wyoming*
Pencil and watercolor
4¾ × 11 in. (12.1 × 27.9 cm.)
l.l.: "Bitter Creek, Wyoming / 1879
TMoran"
American Heritage Center,
University of Wyoming at
Laramie, Gift of F. M. Fryxell
PROVENANCE: The artist; Ruth B.
Moran; Mr. and Mrs. Fritiof M.
Fryxell, Rock Island, Illinois

161. *Blue Lakes, Idaho*
Pencil and watercolor
10¾ × 15 in. (27.3 × 38.1 cm.)
l.l.: "Blue Lakes, Idaho / T. Moran.
1900"
The Thomas Gilcrease Institute of
American History and Art, Gift of
the Thomas Gilcrease Foundation
(0237.1578)
PROVENANCE: The artist; Ruth B.
Moran; M. Knoedler & Co., Inc.,
New York; Thomas Gilcrease
LITERATURE: Wilson, "Moran," no.
153

162. *Cliffs of the Upper Colorado,
Wyoming*
Watercolor
Dimensions unknown
Unlocated
LITERATURE: AWCS, *Annual
Exhibition* (1897), no. 168

163. *Cloud's Peak, in the Big Horn
Range, Wyoming, July 6, 1892*
Watercolor
Dimensions unknown
Unlocated
LITERATURE: Santa Barbara (1925),
no. 46; Milch, *Water Color
Sketches* (1926), no. 50; Biltmore
Salon (LA), *Water Colors* (1927),
no. 4

164. *Effect of Mirage, Bad Lands,
Wyoming*
Watercolor
Dimensions unknown
Unlocated
LITERATURE: AWCS, *Annual
Exhibition* (1894), no. 65

165. *Fort Hall, Idaho*
Pencil and watercolor
7½ × 11½ in. (19.1 × 29.2 cm.)
l.l.: "Fort Hall, Idaho. T Moran"
(1879)
Grand Teton National Park,
Moose, Wyoming
PROVENANCE: The artist; Ruth B.
Moran
LITERATURE: Santa Barbara (1925),
no. 3; Milch, *Water Color
Sketches* (1926), no. 3; Clinton
Academy, *Paintings and Etchings*
(1928), no. 2; Wilson, "Moran," no.
45; CSU, *Moran in Yellowstone*
(1972), no. 43

166. *Great Blue Lake, Idaho (Blue
Lakes, Idaho)*
Pencil and watercolor
10¾ × 15 in. (27.3 × 38.1 cm.)
l.l.: "Blue Lakes, Idaho / T.Moran. /
1900"
The Thomas Gilcrease Institute of
American History and Art; Gift of
the Thomas Gilcrease Foundation,
1974 (0226.1356)
PROVENANCE: The artist; Ruth B.
Moran; M. Knoedler & Co., Inc.,
New York; Thomas Gilcrease

167. *The Great Tetons, Idaho (The
Teton Range, Idaho)*
Watercolor
14¼ × 19⅞ in. (36.2 × 50.5 cm.)
l.r.: "✝ ORAN / 1898"
Stark Museum of Art, Orange,
Texas (31.18/8)
PROVENANCE: The artist; Gustave
H. Buek, Brooklyn and East
Hampton, New York (1910); Mrs.
Goodman, New York (1939);
Babcock Galleries, New York
(1946); Joseph Sartor Galleries,
Dallas, Texas (1957); H. J. Lutcher
Stark, Orange, Texas
LITERATURE: The Art Institute of
Chicago, *A Collection of Paintings
in Water Color by American
Artists*, no. 112; New York,
Whitney Museum of American
Art, *A History of American
Watercolor Painting*, no. 104;
Stark Museum, *Western
Collection*, p. 208

168. *In the Big Horn Mountains,
Wyoming*
Pencil and watercolor
11½ × 15 in. (29.2 × 38.1 cm.)
l.l.: "✝ ORAN. 1899."
l.r.: "In the Big Horn
Mts. / Wyoming."
Private Collection
PROVENANCE: Mr. and Mrs. George
P. Cammann; Frederic A.
Cammann
LITERATURE: AWCS, *Annual
Exhibition* (1898), no. 281;
Clinton Academy, *Paintings and
Etchings* (1928), no. 3

169. *Index-Peak and Clark's Fork,
Wyoming*
Pencil, watercolor, and opaque
color
9⅝ × 12⅝ in. (24.5 × 32.1 cm.)
l.l.: "✝ 1892 Index peak. Clarks
fork Wyoming"
l.r.: "1892 / Index peak.
Wyoming / Clarks fork. T.M."
Cooper-Hewitt Museum, The
Smithsonian Institution's
National Museum of Design, Gift
of the artist (1917.17.69)
PROVENANCE: The artist
LITERATURE: Denver (1892), no. 34;
Wilson, "Moran," no. 38; Gerdts,
Thomas Moran (1963), no. 32,
illus. p. 44; Bassford and Fryxell,
Home Thoughts, illus. p. 115;
CSU, *Moran in Yellowstone*
(1972), no. 55; Washburn, *Cooper-
Hewitt Collection* (1974), illus.;
Fern, *Drawings and Watercolors*
(1976), no. 92, illus. p. 119

170. *On the Upper Colorado, Wyoming
Territory*
Watercolor
Dimensions unknown
Unlocated
LITERATURE: AWCS, *Annual
Exhibition* (1899), no. 308

171. *Pocatello Station, Idaho*
Pencil and watercolor
2¾ × 5⅛ in. (7 × 13 cm.)
u.r.: "Pocatello station / 1st south
of Ross fork / T.Moran / 1871"
Mr. and Mrs. Horace Marden
Albright, Sherman Oaks,
California, Gift of Ruth B. Moran
PROVENANCE: The artist; Ruth B.
Moran
LITERATURE: Wilson, "Moran," no.
27

172. *Port Neuf Cañon, Idaho*
Pencil and watercolor
2¾ × 5⅛ in. (7 × 13 cm.)
u.r.: "Port Neuf Canon / from 2
stations / T Moran / 1871"
Mr. and Mrs. Horace Marden
Albright, Sherman Oaks,
California, Gift of Ruth B. Moran
PROVENANCE: The artist; Ruth B.
Moran
LITERATURE: Wilson, "Moran," no.
28

173. *Port Neuf Canyon, Idaho*
Pencil and watercolor
3 × 5½ in. (7.6 × 14 cm.)
u.r.: "Port Neuf / between [illeg.]"
On mount l.l.: "in Idaho. Port
Neuf Canon. T. Moran"
(1873)
Cooper-Hewitt Museum, The
Smithsonian Institution's
National Museum of Design, Gift
of the artist (1917.17.25)
PROVENANCE: The artist
LITERATURE: The Art Institute of
Chicago, *The Hudson River
School and the Early American
Landscape Tradition*, no. 139;
Wilson, "Moran," no. 218;
Heckscher Museum, *Moran
Family* (1965), no. 24; Washburn,
Cooper-Hewitt Collection (1974)

174. *Port Neuf Canyon, Idaho*
Pencil and watercolor
12 × 20 in. (30.5 × 50.8 cm.)
l.l.: "TM. Port Neuf Canon Idaho"
(1879)
The Thomas Gilcrease Institute of
American History and Art
(0226.855)

PROVENANCE: The artist; Ruth B.
Moran; M. Knoedler & Co., Inc.,
New York; Thomas Gilcrease
LITERATURE: Sachs, "Drawings and
Watercolors," pl. 19

175. *Round Valley [?], Idaho*
Pencil and watercolor
2¾ × 5⅛ in. (7 × 13 cm.)
u.r.: "Round Valley [?] sw 9 mile"
l.r.: "T. Moran. / 1871"
Mr. and Mrs. Horace Marden
Albright, Sherman Oaks,
California, Gift of Ruth B. Moran
PROVENANCE: The artist; Ruth B.
Moran

176. *Shoshone Falls, Snake River,
Idaho*
Watercolor
10 × 14 in. (25.4 × 35.6 cm.)
l.r.: "⚜"
(ca. 1874–1875)
The Chrysler Museum, Norfolk,
Virginia
PROVENANCE: The artist; L. Prang
& Company, Boston; Hugh
Gordon Miller
LITERATURE: AAA-Prang (1892),
no. 355; Wilson, "Moran," no. 92
(as "The Great Falls of Snake
River, Idaho Territory")

177. *Shoshone Tepee*
Pencil and watercolor
5⅜ × 7½ in. (13.6 × 19.1 cm.)
l.l.: "Shoshone"
(1892)
Peabody Museum of Archaeology
and Ethnology, Harvard University
PROVENANCE: The artist; William
Henry Holmes; David Ives
Bushnell (1927)
LITERATURE: G. Verona Taylor
Whatmough, "The Bushnell
Collection of Paintings and Other
Works by Early American Artists,"
manuscript, n.d., no. 444;
Cambridge, Massachusetts, Fogg
Art Museum, *American Art at
Harvard*, no. 99, illus.

178. *A Study from Nature, Wyoming Territory*
Watercolor
14 × 10 in. (35.6 × 25.4 cm.)
Unlocated
LITERATURE: AAA-Ortgies (1886), no. 56

179. *The Tetons*
Watercolor
9¾ × 13¾ in. (24.8 × 34.9 cm.)
u.l.: "The Tetons. 1879"
l.l.: "⚭ 1879."
Yellowstone National Park, Wyoming, Gift of George D. Pratt, Mrs. Henry Strong, Mr. John D. Rockefeller, Jr., Col. Herbert J. Slocum (8530)
PROVENANCE: The artist; Ruth B. Moran
LITERATURE: Wilson, "Moran," no. 49; CSU, *Moran in Yellowstone* (1972), no. 45, illus.; Fern, *Drawings and Watercolors* (1976), no. 49, illus. p. 67

180. *The Tetons, 1879*
Pencil, watercolor, and opaque color
14 × 9¾ in. (35.5 × 24.7 cm.)
u.l.: "The Tetons, 1879"
l.l.: "⚭"
Grand Teton National Park, Moose, Wyoming
PROVENANCE: The artist; Ruth B. Moran

181. *The Tetons, Idaho*
Pencil, watercolor, and opaque color
8¼ × 14⅜ in. (21.0 × 36.5 cm.)
u.l.: "The Tetons. Idaho" (1879)
Cooper-Hewitt Museum, The Smithsonian Institution's National Museum of Design, Gift of the artist (1917.17.33)
PROVENANCE: The artist
LITERATURE: Wilson, "Moran," no. 221; NCFA, *National Parks* (1972), no. 26, illus. p. 62; Washburn, *Cooper-Hewitt Collection* (1974)

182. *The Three Tetons*
Pencil and watercolor
2¾ × 5⅛ in. (7 × 13 cm.)
l.l.: "T. Moran. The 3 Tetons / 1871"
Mr. and Mrs. Horace Marden Albright, Sherman Oaks, California, Gift of Ruth B. Moran
PROVENANCE: The artist; Ruth B. Moran
LITERATURE: Wilson, "Moran," no. 29

183. *The Three Tetons, Idaho, 18 Miles Distant*
Pencil, watercolor, and opaque color
13½ × 20 in. (34.3 × 50.8 cm.)
l.r.: "The Three Tetons. Idaho. 18 miles distant Aug 26th 1879"
Grand Teton National Park, Moose, Wyoming
PROVENANCE: The artist; Ruth B. Moran
LITERATURE: Denver (1892), no. 42; Wilson, "Moran," no. 48; CSU, *Moran in Yellowstone* (1972), no. 46; Fern, *Drawings and Watercolors* (1976), no. 47, illus. p. 63

184. *Above Alta, American Fork Cañon, Utah*
Pencil and watercolor
9¾ × 13½ in. (24.8 × 34.3 cm.)
u.l.: "Above Alta"
l.l.: "American Fork Canon / 1879 TMoran"
The Thomas Gilcrease Institute of American History and Art (0236.888)
PROVENANCE: The artist; Ruth B. Moran; M. Knoedler & Co., Inc., New York; Thomas Gilcrease

185. *The Desert in Southern Utah*
Watercolor
14 × 20 in. (35.6 × 50.8 cm.)
Unlocated
PROVENANCE: The artist; William Bell's daughter, gift of the artist, 1906
LITERATURE: AWCS, *Annual Exhibition* (1902), no. 260; Philadelphia Art Club, Water Color Exhibition, 1904

186. *The Great Salt Lake of Utah*
Pencil, watercolor, and opaque color
9½ × 14 in. (24.1 × 35.6 cm.)
l.r.: "TMoran / 1874."
Unlocated
PROVENANCE: The artist; L. Prang & Company, Boston
LITERATURE: AAA-Prang (1892), no. 347; Wilson, "Moran," no. 37

187. *In Little Cottonwood Cañon*
Pencil and watercolor
9¾ × 14¼ in. (24.8 × 36.2 cm.)
u.l.: "In Little Cottonwood Canon Aug 13–79 TM"
The Thomas Gilcrease Institute of American History and Art (0236.887)
PROVENANCE: The artist; Ruth B. Moran; M. Knoedler & Co., Inc., New York; Thomas Gilcrease

188. *Lake Donner, Nevada*
Pencil, watercolor, and opaque color
9½ × 14 in. (24.1 × 35.6 cm.)
(ca. 1874–1875)
Unlocated

PROVENANCE: The artist; L. Prang & Company, Boston
LITERATURE: AAA-Prang (1892), no. 359; Santa Barbara (1925), no. 16; Milch, *Water Color Sketches* (1926), no. 16; Biltmore Salon (LA), *Water Colors* (1927), no. 1

189. *Land of Standing Rocks*
Watercolor
4 × 13⅛ in. (10.2 × 33.3 cm.)
Stark Museum of Art, Orange, Texas (31.18/5)
PROVENANCE: Joseph Sartor Galleries, Dallas, Texas (1957); H. J. Lutcher Stark, Orange, Texas
LITERATURE: Stark Museum, *Western Collection*, p. 208

190. *Near the Summit of Cottonwood Cañon*
Pencil, watercolor, and opaque color
10¼ × 14¼ in. (26.0 × 36.2 cm.)
u.l.: "Near the Summit of Cottonwood Canon Aug 13th 79"
l.r.: "T.Moran"
The Thomas Gilcrease Institute of American History and Art (0236.890)
PROVENANCE: The artist; Ruth B. Moran; M. Knoedler & Co., Inc., New York; Thomas Gilcrease

191. *The Ruby Range, Nevada*
Pencil, watercolor, and opaque color
8½ × 14⅜ in. (21.6 × 36.5 cm.)
l.l.: "TM / The Ruby Range / Nevada / Aug. 8th-79. TMoran."
The Cleveland Museum of Art, Bequest of Mrs. Henry A. Everett for the Dorothy Burnham Everett Memorial Collection (38.67)
PROVENANCE: The artist; Ruth B. Moran; Milch Galleries, New York; Biltmore Salon, Los Angeles, California; Mrs. Henry A. Everett (1928–1938)
LITERATURE: Denver (1892), no. 53; Santa Barbara (1925), no. 21; Milch, *Water Color Sketches* (1926), no. 21; Biltmore Salon (LA), *Water Colors* (1927), no. 22;

Parker, "Water-Colors," illus. p. 72; Wilson, "Moran," no. 43; William S. Talbot, "A Check List, American Paintings and Water Colors of the Eighteenth, Nineteenth, and Early Twentieth Centuries in The Cleveland Museum of Art," *Bulletin of The Cleveland Museum of Art* 40, no. 1 (January 1973): no. 137, illus. p. 31

192. *Toledo Mine, Cottonwood Cañon, Utah*
Pencil and watercolor
7½ × 11½ in. (19.0 × 29.2 cm.)
u.r.: "Toledo Mine Cottonwood Canon / TMoran Utah 1879"
The Thomas Gilcrease Institute of American History and Art (0236.889)
PROVENANCE: The artist; Ruth B. Moran; M. Knoedler & Co., Inc., New York; Thomas Gilcrease

193. *Upper End of Cottonwood Cañon*
Pencil, watercolor, and opaque color
9¾ × 14¼ in. (24.7 × 36.2 cm.)
u.l.: "Upper end of Cottonwood Canon Aug 13-79 TMoran"
The Thomas Gilcrease Institute of American History and Art (0236.884)
PROVENANCE: The artist; Ruth B. Moran; M. Knoedler & Co., Inc., New York; Thomas Gilcrease

194. *Upper End of Cottonwood Cañon, Wasatch Range, Utah*
Pencil, watercolor, and opaque color
12¾ × 19½ in. (32.4 × 49.5 cm.)
l.l.: "Upper End of / Cottonwood Canon / Wasatch Range / Utah / T.M. 1879."
Jefferson National Expansion Memorial, St. Louis, Missouri (4258)
PROVENANCE: The artist; Ruth B. Moran
LITERATURE: Wilson, "Moran," no. 102; Fern, *Drawings and Watercolors* (1976), no. 45

195. *The Upper End of Little
Cottonwood Cañon*
Pencil, black crayon, watercolor,
and opaque color
10 × 14⅝ in. (25.4 × 37.1 cm.)
u.l.: "The Upper End of Little
Cottonwood Canon. Aug. 13-79."
Cooper-Hewitt Museum, The
Smithsonian Institution's
National Museum of Design, Gift
of the artist (1917.17.79)
PROVENANCE: The artist
LITERATURE: Santa Barbara (1925),
no. 57 (as "Near the Summit at
Cotton Wood Canyon. Aug. 13,
1879"); Milch, *Water Color
Sketches* (1926), no. 57 (as "Near
the Summit at Cotton Wood
Canyon. Aug. 13, 1879"); Biltmore
Salon (LA), *Water Colors* (1927),
no. 10 (as "Cottonwood Canyon");
Evansville, Indiana, Public
Museum, *Homer and Moran*;
Wilson, "Moran," no. 98; Gerdts,
Thomas Moran (1963), no. 26,
illus. p. 40; Washburn, *Cooper-
Hewitt Collection* (1974); Fern,
Drawings and Watercolors (1976),
no. 44, illus. p. 61

196. *The Upper End of Little
Cottonwood Canyon, Wasatch
Range, Utah (Mountain Peaks)*
Pencil, watercolor, and opaque
color
6 × 13½ in. (15.2 × 34.3 cm.)
l.r.: "🕇"
(August, 1879)
Dr. and Mrs. John F. McGonigle,
on extended loan to the Art
Gallery, University of Notre Dame
PROVENANCE: Edward Eberstadt &
Sons, Inc., New York; Kennedy
Galleries, Inc., New York; Thomas
Davies, Tokyo; Hamilton Gallery,
New York; Coe Kerr Gallery, Inc.,
New York

LITERATURE: Washington, D.C.,
Adams, Davidson Galleries, Inc.,
*100 Years of American Drawings
and Watercolors, 1870–1970*; New
York, M. Knoedler & Co., Inc.,
American Western Art (1976), no.
42; Sotheby Parke Bernet, Inc.,
sale 4112, lot 32, illus. (April 22,
1978)

197. *Acambaro*
Pencil and watercolor
10 × 15 in. (25.4 × 38.1 cm.)
u.r.: "Acambaro / Feb 12th 1883 /
T.M."
l.l.: "Acambaro 1883"
l.r.: "🕇. 1883"
Charlotte Moran Rich
PROVENANCE: The artist; by
descent to Charlotte Moran Rich

198. *Calderon, Mexico*
Pencil, watercolor, and opaque
color
10⅛ × 14⅜ in. (25.7 × 36.5 cm.)
u.r.: "Calderon Mex / Feb 25th
1883 / TM"
The Thomas Gilcrease Institute of
American History and Art
(0246.808)
PROVENANCE: The artist; Ruth B.
Moran; M. Knoedler & Co., Inc.,
New York; Thomas Gilcrease

199. *Castle of San Juan d'Ulloa, Vera
Cruz, Mexico*
Pencil, watercolor, and opaque
color
14 × 9⅛ in. (35.6 × 23.2 cm.)
l.l.: "Vera Cruz / 🕇 ORAN 1883"
Lent by Schweitzer Gallery, New
York
PROVENANCE: Patricia A. Marquis,
Florida
LITERATURE: AWCS, *Annual
Exhibition* (1884), no. 196 (as "The
Castle of San Juan d'Ulloa, Harbor
of Vera Cruz, Mexico"); Denver
(1892), no. 79

200. *Cathedral at Maravatio*
Pencil and watercolor
5⅞ × 8½ in. (14.9 × 21.6 cm.)
l.l.: "Maravatio / Feb 13 1883"
The Thomas Gilcrease Institute of
American History and Art
(0246.811)
PROVENANCE: The artist; Ruth B.
Moran; M. Knoedler & Co., Inc.,
New York; Thomas Gilcrease

201. *Chioggia*
Watercolor
Dimensions unknown
Unlocated
PROVENANCE: Feragil Galleries,
New York (?)
LITERATURE: Wilson, "Moran," no.
86

202. *Cordova*
Pencil and watercolor
3½ × 10 in. (8.9 × 25.4 cm.)
u.l.: "Cordova. Feb 4th"
l.l.: "T.M."
(1883)
East Hampton Free Library, The
Thomas Moran Biographical Art
Collection
PROVENANCE: The artist; Ruth B.
Moran

203. *Harbor and City of Vera Cruz*
Pencil, watercolor, and opaque
color
10⅛ × 14¼ in. (25.7 × 36.2 cm.)
l.l.: "Vera Cruz. Feb 3rd 1883 T.
Moran"
The Thomas Gilcrease Institute of
American History and Art
(0246.815)
PROVENANCE: The artist; Ruth B.
Moran; M. Knoedler & Co., Inc.,
New York; Thomas Gilcrease
LITERATURE: AAA-Ortgies (1886),
no. 53; Santa Barbara (1925), no.
32; Parker, "Water-Colors," illus.
p. 70; Wilson, "Moran," no. 51

204. *In the Cañon above Trojes,
Mexico (Moonrise in the Canyon)*
Pencil and watercolor
11 × 21¼ in. (27.9 × 54 cm.)
l.l.: "In the Cañon above Trojes
Mexico /☆ ORAN. / 1883"
Private Collection
PROVENANCE: Michael Kottka,
London; Hirschl & Adler
Galleries, Inc., New York;
Fowler's Period Gallery West,
Scottsdale, Arizona
LITERATURE: *Antiques* 111, no. 6
(June 1977): illus. p. 1084;
Scottsdale, Arizona, Jim Fowler's
Period Gallery West, *The Alluring
West*, p. 10

205. *Jaral*
Watercolor
Dimensions unknown
(March 1, 1883)
Unlocated
LITERATURE: Santa Barbara (1925),
no. 26; Milch, *Water Color
Sketches* (1926), no. 29; Biltmore
Salon (LA), *Water Colors* (1927),
no. 25

206. *A Lagoon [or Canal] in Mexico*
Pencil, watercolor, and opaque
color
6⅛ × 11¾ in. (15.5 × 29.8 cm.)
l.r.: "Mexico Feb 8th 1883 / TM"
The Thomas Gilcrease Institute of
American History and Art
(0246.813)
PROVENANCE: The artist; Ruth B.
Moran; M. Knoedler & Co., Inc.,
New York; Thomas Gilcrease
LITERATURE: Santa Barbara (1925),
no. 31; Milch, *Water Color
Sketches* (1926), no. 34; Biltmore
Salon (LA), *Water Colors* (1927),
no. 28

207. *Landscape in Mexico*
Pencil and watercolor
5¾ × 8¼ in. (14.6 × 20.9 cm.)
u.r.: "from Acambaro. West. 1883 /
TM Feb 12"
The Thomas Gilcrease Institute of
American History and Art
(0246.821)
PROVENANCE: The artist; Ruth B.
Moran; M. Knoedler & Co., Inc.,
New York; Thomas Gilcrease

208. *Maravatio*
Pencil and watercolor
10⅛ × 14¼ in. (25.7 × 36.2 cm.)
u.r.: "Maravatio. / Feb 9th 1883.
TMoran."
The Thomas Gilcrease Institute of
American History and Art
(0246.809)
PROVENANCE: The artist; Ruth B.
Moran; M. Knoedler & Co., Inc.,
New York; Thomas Gilcrease
LITERATURE: Santa Barbara (1937),
no. 10

209. *Maravatio*
Pencil and watercolor
5⅞ × 8⅜ in. (14.9 × 21.3 cm.)
l.l.: "Maravatio Feb 13th / 1883
T.M."
East Hampton Free Library, The
Thomas Moran Biographical Art
Collection
PROVENANCE: The artist; Ruth B.
Moran
LITERATURE: AWCS, *Annual
Exhibition* (1884), no. 189; Santa
Barbara (1925), no. 25; Milch,
Water Color Sketches (1926), no.
28 (or 30); Biltmore Salon (LA),
Water Colors (1927), no. 2(?)

210. *Maravatio, in Old Mexico*
Pencil, watercolor, and opaque
color
10 × 14 in. (25.4 × 35.6 cm.)
u.r.: "Maravatio / Feb 12th 1883"
l.l.: "Maravatio. 1883"
The Parrish Art Museum,
Southampton, New York,
Littlejohn Collection
PROVENANCE: Arthur U. Newton
Gallery, New York; Mrs. Robert
Malcolm Littlejohn
LITERATURE: Milch, *Water Color
Sketches* (1926), no. 30 (or 28);
Biltmore Salon (LA), *Water Colors*
(1927), no. 2(?)

211. *Monterey from the Hotel Roof*
Pencil, watercolor, and opaque
color
9¾ × 14 in. (24.8 × 35.6 cm.)
u.l.: "Monterey from / the Hotel
Roof / TM"
l.l.: "TMoran"
(1883)
The Thomas Gilcrease Institute of
American History and Art
(0246.819)
PROVENANCE: The artist; Ruth B.
Moran; M. Knoedler & Co., Inc.,
New York; Thomas Gilcrease

212. *Monterey, Mexico*
Watercolor
Dimensions unknown
(1883)
Unlocated
LITERATURE: Santa Barbara (1925),
no. 33; Milch, *Water Color
Sketches* (1926), no. 36; Biltmore
Salon (LA), *Water Colors* (1927),
no. 29

213. *Morelia, Mexico*
Pencil, watercolor, and opaque
color
10¾ × 14 in. (27.3 × 35.6 cm.)
u.l.: "Morelia, Mexico TMoran
1883"
The Thomas Gilcrease Institute of
American History and Art
(0246.824)
PROVENANCE: The artist; Ruth B.
Moran; M. Knoedler & Co., Inc.,
New York; Thomas Gilcrease

214. *Morelia, Mexico*
Pencil, watercolor, and opaque
color
10 × 14¼ in. (25.4 × 36.2 cm.)
u.l.: "Morelia, Mexico ½"
Museum of Fine Arts, Boston, Gift
of Maxim Karolik (56.733)
PROVENANCE: Victor Spark, New
York (1950); Maxim Karolik
LITERATURE: Milch, *Water Color
Sketches* (1926), unnumbered;
Biltmore Salon (LA), *Water Colors*
(1927), no. 37; MFA, *Karolik
Drawings*, no. 574

215. *Mountain Peaks Near Orizaba,
Mexico*
Pencil, watercolor, and opaque
color
8½ × 11½ in. (21.6 × 29.2 cm.)
u.l.: "the peak of Orizaba from
Esperanza"
l.l.: "1883 / TMoran"
The Thomas Gilcrease Institute of
American History and Art
(0246.827)
PROVENANCE: The artist; Ruth B.
Moran; M. Knoedler & Co., Inc.,
New York; Thomas Gilcrease

216. *The Mountain Range on the West
Side of the San Louis [Luis] Valley
above San Francisco, March 1st,
1883*
Pencil and watercolor
9 × 13¾ in. (22.9 × 34.9 cm.)
l.r.: "The Mountain Range on the
West side of the San Louis Valley /
above San Francisco. March 1st.
1883 / T.M."
Addison Gallery of American Art,
Phillips Academy, Andover,
Massachusetts
PROVENANCE: The artist; Ruth B.
Moran; Macbeth Gallery, New
York
LITERATURE: AAA-Ortgies (1886),
no. 57 (as "San Luis Potosi,
Mexico"); Santa Barbara (1925), no.
60; Milch, *Water Color Sketches*
(1926), no. 38; Biltmore Salon
(LA), *Water Colors* (1927), no. 31;
Bartlett H. Hayes, Jr., *American
Drawings*, pl. 31, illus. p. 63

217. *Near Saltillo, Mexico*
Pencil, watercolor, and opaque
color
9¾ × 14 in. (24.8 × 35.6 cm.)
u.l.: "Ojo de Agua, Saltillo March
8th 1883 TMoran"
The Thomas Gilcrease Institute of
American History and Art
(0246.818)
PROVENANCE: The artist; Ruth B.
Moran; M. Knoedler & Co., Inc.,
New York; Thomas Gilcrease
LITERATURE: Santa Barbara (1925),
no. 28; Milch, *Water Color
Sketches* (1926), no. 31; Biltmore
Salon (LA), *Water Colors* (1927),
no. 26

218. *Near San Francisco, Mexico*
Pencil, watercolor, and opaque
color
10 × 13⅞ in. (25.4 × 35.2 cm.)
u.r.: "Near San Francisco. March
1st 1883. T.M."
l.l.: "✠ 1883"
On mount: "Near San Francisco,
Mexico. TMoran 1883"
Cooper-Hewitt Museum, The
Smithsonian Institution's

National Museum of Design, Gift
of the artist (1917.17.45)
PROVENANCE: The artist
LITERATURE: Denver (1892), no. 69;
Wilson, "Moran," no. 110; Gerdts,
Thomas Moran (1963), no. 28,
illus. p. 41; Heckscher Museum,
Moran Family (1965), no. 40;
Century Association (1979)

219. *Near Vera Cruz*
Pencil and watercolor
5⅞ × 8⅜ in. (14.9 × 21.3 cm.)
u.l.: "near Vera Cruz Feb 6th 1883
TM"
The Thomas Gilcrease Institute of
American History and Art
(0246.810)
PROVENANCE: The artist; Ruth B.
Moran; M. Knoedler & Co., Inc.,
New York; Thomas Gilcrease

220. *On the Plateau above Dolores*
Pencil, watercolor, and opaque
color
10 × 14¼ in. (25.4 × 36.2 cm.)
u.l.: "on the plateau above Dolores
Feb 28th 1883. TM"
The Thomas Gilcrease Institute of
American History and Art
(0246.816)
PROVENANCE: The artist; Ruth B.
Moran; M. Knoedler & Co., Inc.,
New York; Thomas Gilcrease
LITERATURE: Santa Barbara (1925),
no. 23; Milch, *Water Color
Sketches* (1926), no. 26; Biltmore
Salon (LA), *Water Colors* (1927),
no. 36

221. *Orizaba, Mexico*
Pencil, watercolor, and opaque
color
9½ × 13¾ in. (24.13 × 34.9 cm.)
u.l.: "Orizaba, Feb 5th 1883,
T.Moran"
J. V. Hawn
PROVENANCE: The artist; Ruth B.
Moran; The Milch Galleries, New
York; J. N. Bartfield Art Galleries,
Inc., New York

LITERATURE: AWCS, *Annual Exhibition* (1884), no. 188 (as "The City of Orizaba, Mexico"); Denver (1892), no. 96; Santa Barbara (1925), unnumbered; Wilson, "Moran," no. 50; New York, J. N. Bartfield Art Galleries, Inc., *American Paintings and Sculpture*, no. 38, illus.

222. *Pila Saltillo, Mexico*
Watercolor
10 × 7½ in. (25.4 × 19 cm.)
l.l.: "Pila Saltillo. Mexico"
l.r.: "⚸ ORAN"
(ca. 1883)
Mills College Collection, Gift of Miss M. L. Coffin (1928.15)
PROVENANCE: Miss M. L. Coffin
LITERATURE: Santa Barbara (1925), unnumbered (as "Saltillo"); Oakland, California, Mills College Art Gallery, *Selections from the Drawings and Watercolor Collections*, no. 85, illus. p. 66

223. *Ravine Near Trojes Mines, Mexico*
Pencil, watercolor, and opaque color
10 × 14 in. (25.4 × 35.6 cm.)
u.l.: "Ravine near the Trojes Mine Mexico / TM. 1883"
The Thomas Gilcrease Institute of American History and Art (0246.823)
PROVENANCE: The artist; Ruth B. Moran; M. Knoedler & Co., Inc., New York; Thomas Gilcrease
LITERATURE: Santa Barbara (1925), unnumbered; Milch, *Water Color Sketches* (1926), unnumbered; Biltmore Salon (LA), *Water Colors* (1927), no. 38

224. *San Francisco Mountains*
Watercolor
Dimensions unknown
l.r.: "T.Moran"
(1883)
Unlocated
LITERATURE: Higgins, *Grand Cañon*, p. 7

225. *San José (Maravatio)*
Watercolor
Dimensions unknown
(February 13, 1883)
Unlocated
LITERATURE: Denver (1892), no. 95 (or 46); Santa Barbara (1925), no. 29 (?); Milch, *Water Color Sketches* (1926), no. 32 (?); Biltmore Salon (LA), *Water Colors* (1927), no. 27 (?)

226. *San José beyond Maravatio, Mexico*
Pencil, watercolor, and opaque color
9¾ × 14 in. (24.8 × 35.6 cm.)
l.r.: "San José beyond Maravatio / Feb 13th 1883 / TMoran"
l.l.: "⚸ 1883"
The Thomas Gilcrease Institute of American History and Art (0246.822)
PROVENANCE: The artist; Ruth B. Moran; M. Knoedler & Co., Inc., New York; Thomas Gilcrease
LITERATURE: Denver (1892), no. 46 (or 95); Santa Barbara (1925), no. 29 (?); Milch, *Water Color Sketches* (1926), no. 32 (?); Biltmore Salon (LA), *Water Colors* (1927), no. 27 (?)

227. *San Juan Abajo*
Pencil, watercolor, and opaque color
10 × 15 in. (25.4 × 38.1 cm.)
u.r.: "San Juan Abajo / Feb 25th 1883 / T.Moran"
l.l.: "⚸.1883 San Juan Abajo"
Charlotte Moran Rich
PROVENANCE: The artist; by descent to Charlotte Moran Rich

228. *San Miguel Allende*
Pencil and watercolor
10 × 14½ in. (25.4 × 36.8 cm.)
Signed and dated February 26, 1883
Collection of Carl Schaefer Dentzel
PROVENANCE: The artist; Carl Oscar Borg
LITERATURE: Gerdts, *Thomas Moran* (1963), no. 34

229. *A Street in Maravatio, Mexico*
Watercolor
Dimensions unknown
Unlocated
LITERATURE: AWCS, *Annual Exhibition* (1884), no. 194

230. *Sunday Morning, Maravatio (Cathedral)*
Pencil, watercolor, and opaque color
10 × 7⅜ in. (25.4 × 18.7 cm.)
u.l.: "Sunday Morning / Maravatio. / Feb 11th / 1883 / TM"
l.r.: "⚜ 1883"
The Thomas Gilcrease Institute of American History and Art (0246.812)
PROVENANCE: The artist; Ruth B. Moran; M. Knoedler & Co., Inc., New York; Thomas Gilcrease
LITERATURE: Milch, *Water Color Sketches* (1926), unnumbered; Parker, "Water-Colors," illus. p. 69; Wilson, "Moran," no. 52

231. *Sunset, Gulf of Mexico*
Pencil and watercolor
10⅛ × 14⅛ in. (25.7 × 35.9 cm.)
l.r.: "TMoran. 1883 Sunset. Gulf of Mexico"
The Thomas Gilcrease Institute of American History and Art (0246.814)
PROVENANCE: The artist; Ruth B. Moran; M. Knoedler & Co., Inc., New York; Thomas Gilcrease

232. *Tower of Cortez, Mexico*
Pencil and watercolor
14 × 9½ in. (35.6 × 24.2 cm.)
l.l.: "⚜ 1883"
l.r.: "Tower of Cortez / Mexico / T. Moran"
Amherst College, Mead Art Museum (1953.11)
PROVENANCE: The artist; Ruth B. Moran; The Milch Galleries, New York; Harold C. Milch, New York (1950–1953); Macbeth Gallery, New York

LITERATURE: AWCS, *Annual Exhibition* (1884), no. 197; AAA-Ortgies (1886), no. 50; Denver (1892), no. 33; Wilson, "Moran," no. 53; Deerfield (Massachusetts) Academy (1965); Amherst, Massachusetts, College, Mead Art Gallery, *American Art at Amherst*, illus. p. 145

233. *The Trojes Mine*
Pencil and watercolor
10 × 14½ in. (25.4 × 36.8 cm.)
l.l.: "Mexico / The Trojes Mine / above Angangueo / T Moran / 1883"
l.r.: "⚜ ORAN / 1883"
Private Collection
PROVENANCE: Michael Kottka, London; Hirschl & Adler Galleries, Inc., New York; Fowler's Period Gallery West, Scottsdale, Arizona
LITERATURE: AWCS, *Annual Exhibition* (1884), no. 195 (as "The Silver Mine of Trojes, Mexico"); Denver (1892), no. 97; Santa Barbara (1925), no. 24; Milch, *Water Color Sketches* (1926), no. 27; Biltmore Salon (LA), *Water Colors* (1927), no. 24; Wilson, "Moran," no. 111; Scottsdale, Arizona, Jim Fowler's Period Gallery West, *The Alluring West*, p. 12

234. *Vera Cruz*
Pencil and watercolor
12 × 18 in. (30.5 × 45.7 cm.)
l.r.: "Vera Cruz Mexico Feb. 6th 1883 / T.Moran"
Courtesy of Kennedy Galleries, Inc., New York
PROVENANCE: Private collection
LITERATURE: Milch, *Water Color Sketches* (1926), no. 35 (or 37); Clinton Academy, *Paintings and Etchings* (1928), no. 11; New York, Kennedy Galleries, Inc., *The American View*, no. 21, illus.

235. *Vera Cruz Cathedral*
Pencil, watercolor, and opaque color
14 × 9¾ in. (35.6 × 24.8 cm.)
u.l.: "Vera Cruz Cathedral Feb 4 1883"
u.r.: "Body, yellow gray / trimmings white / Dome pale pink glazed tile / with Blue ornaments"
l.l.: "TMoran"
Courtesy of Kennedy Galleries, Inc., New York
PROVENANCE: The artist; Ruth B. Moran; Samuel Scotten Collection, Chicago; Thurber Art Galleries, Chicago (1924–1928); Private collection
LITERATURE: Santa Barbara (1925), no. 22; Milch, *Water Color Sketches* (1926), no. 25; Clinton Academy, *Paintings and Etchings* (1928), no. 10; Lincoln, Massachusetts, De Cordova and Dana Museum, *Homer to Hopper*, unnumbered

236. *Vera Cruz, Harbor Scene*
Pencil, watercolor, and opaque color
9¾ × 14 in. (24.8 × 35.6 cm.)
u.r.: "Building a [illeg.] white stained by weather. / San Juan D'Ullua / Vera Cruz / Feb 4th 1883 / TMoran"
The Thomas Gilcrease Institute of American History and Art (0246.826)
PROVENANCE: The artist; Ruth B. Moran; M. Knoedler & Co., Inc., New York; Thomas Gilcrease

237. *Wash Day in Maravatio, Mexico*
Pencil and watercolor
5½ × 7 in. (14 × 17.8 cm.)
u.l.: "Maravatio / Feb 13-83 / TMoran"
l.l.: "Washing day"
The Thomas Gilcrease Institute of American History and Art (0246.820)
PROVENANCE: The artist; Ruth B. Moran; M. Knoedler & Co., Inc., New York; Thomas Gilcrease

238. *Butte Near Gallup, New Mexico*
Watercolor
Dimensions unknown
(1892)
Unlocated
LITERATURE: Santa Barbara (1925),
no. 37; Milch, *Water Color
Sketches* (1926), no. 41; Clinton
Academy, *Paintings and Etchings*
(1928), no. 14

239. *Cathedral Rock*
Watercolor
10½ × 14⅞ in. (26.7 × 37.8 cm.)
l.r.: "⚓ ORAN.NA / 1902"
Stark Museum of Art, Orange,
Texas (31.18/1)
PROVENANCE: Joseph Sartor
Galleries, Dallas, Texas (1949);
H. J. Lutcher Stark, Orange, Texas
LITERATURE: Stark Museum,
Western Collection, p. 208

240. *Cave Dwelling, Near Flagstaff*
Watercolor
Dimensions unknown
l.r.: "⚓"
Unlocated
LITERATURE: Higgins, *Grand
Cañon*, p. 26

241. *Chamma below the Summit*
Pencil and watercolor
8⅝ × 11⅞ in. (22.0 × 30.2 cm.)
u.l.: "Chamma Below Summit,
TM 1892."
Cooper-Hewitt Museum, The
Smithsonian Institution's
National Museum of Design, Gift
of the artist (1917.17.50)
PROVENANCE: The artist
LITERATURE: Wilson, "Moran," no.
135; Washburn, *Cooper-Hewitt
Collection* (1974)

242. *Cliff Dwellings, Near Flagstaff*
Watercolor
Dimensions unknown
l.r.: "⚓"
Unlocated
LITERATURE: Higgins, *Grand
Cañon*, p. 27

243. *Cliff Dwellings—Point Moran*
Watercolor
Dimensions unknown
l.r.: "⚓"
Unlocated
LITERATURE: Higgins, *Grand
Cañon*, p. 25

244. *Desert Scene*
Pencil, watercolor, and opaque
color
5 × 11 in. (12.7 × 27.9 cm.)
(ca. late 1890s)
The Thomas Gilcrease Institute of
American History and Art
(0236.849)
PROVENANCE: The artist; Ruth B.
Moran; M. Knoedler & Co., Inc.,
New York; Thomas Gilcrease

245. *Desert Scene*
Pencil, watercolor, and opaque
color
7 × 11 in. (17.8 × 27.9 cm.)
(ca. late 1890s)
The Thomas Gilcrease Institute of
American History and Art
(0236.850)
PROVENANCE: The artist; Ruth B.
Moran; M. Knoedler & Co., Inc.,
New York; Thomas Gilcrease

246. *Española, New Mexico*
Pencil and watercolor on
Baltimore and Ohio Railroad Co. /
Passenger Department stationery
(with imprinted date 1881)
5½ × 7¼ in. (14.0 × 18.4 cm.)
u.l.: "Espanola, New Mexico" /
The Rio Grande, New Mexico."
l.l.: "TMoran"
The Thomas Gilcrease Institute of
American History and Art
(0236.848)
PROVENANCE: The artist; Ruth B.
Moran; M. Knoedler & Co., Inc.,
New York; Thomas Gilcrease

247. *The Hacienda of San Juan Mexico*
Pencil, pen and ink, and
watercolor
8¼ × 11 in. (21.0 × 28.0 cm.)
l.l.: "⚓ oran. 1892"
l.r.: "San Juan, Mexico"

On mount: "The Hacienda of San Juan Mexico TMoran 1892" Cooper-Hewitt Museum, The Smithsonian Institution's National Museum of Design, Gift of the artist (1917.17.48)
PROVENANCE: The artist
LITERATURE: Wilson, "Moran," no. 59; Gerdts, *Thomas Moran* (1963), no. 35, illus. p. 46; Sachs, "Drawings and Watercolors," pl. 29; New York, Gallery of Modern Art, *Major 19th and 20th Century Drawings*; Heckscher Museum, *Moran Family* (1965), no. 48; Century Association (1979)

248. *Hopi House, Grand Canyon, Arizona*
Pencil, watercolor, and opaque color
11½ × 7¼ in. (29.2 × 18.4 cm.)
l.l.: "T.Moran. 1905"
Mr. and Mrs. William Belknap
PROVENANCE: The artist; Mr. and Mrs. Frank Spencer, Gift of the artist

249. *Laguna from the East*
Pencil and watercolor
4⅞ × 6⅞ in. (12.4 × 17.5 cm.)
u.r.: "Laguna from east / Saturday June 4th / 1892"
l.l.: "T.M."
East Hampton Free Library, The Thomas Moran Biographical Art Collection
PROVENANCE: The artist; Ruth B. Moran
LITERATURE: Denver (1892), no. 81 (?); Santa Barbara (1925), no. 41 (?); Milch, *Water Color Sketches* (1926), no. 45 (?); Clinton Academy, *Paintings and Etchings* (1928), no. 8 (?); Santa Barbara (1937), no. 33 (?)

250. *Laguna, New Mexico*
Pencil and watercolor
9¾ × 12½ in. (24.8 × 31.8 cm.)
l.l.: "Laguna, New Mexico. from the East / June 4th 1892. T.Moran."
Mr. and Mrs. Condie Lamb
PROVENANCE: The artist; James Preston

LITERATURE: Denver (1892), no. 81 (?); Santa Barbara (1925), no. 41 (?); Milch, *Water Color Sketches* (1926), no. 45 (?); Clinton Academy, *Paintings and Etchings* (1928), no. 8 (?); Santa Barbara (1937), no. 33 (?); Fern, *Drawings and Watercolors* (1976), no. 83

251. *Morning in Arizona*
Watercolor
Dimensions unknown
Unlocated
LITERATURE: Philadelphia Art Club, Water Color Exhibition, 1904

252. *Ojo Caliente, 3rd Oldest City in U.S.*
Pencil and watercolor
7 × 10¾ in. (17.8 × 27.3 cm.)
u.l.: "Ojo Caliente / 3rd oldest city in US / from the Springs Hotel TMoran"
(1892)
The Thomas Gilcrease Institute of American History and Art (0236.845)
PROVENANCE: The artist; Ruth B. Moran; M. Knoedler & Co., Inc., New York; Thomas Gilcrease
LITERATURE: Santa Barbara (1925), no. 30; Milch, *Water Color Sketches* (1926), no. 33; Biltmore Salon (LA), *Water Colors* (1927), no. 15

253. *On the Lookout*
Pencil, watercolor, and opaque color
20 × 15 in. (50.8 × 38.1 cm.)
l.l.: "⚕ ORAN"
On mat: "To Mrs. Alma Calder Johnston / from Mr. and Mrs. Thomas Moran / May 21st 1878"
The Thomas Gilcrease Institute of American History and Art (0226.1366)
PROVENANCE: The artist; Ruth B. Moran; M. Knoedler & Co., Inc., New York; Thomas Gilcrease
LITERATURE: Wilson, "Moran," no. 38

254. *On the Lookout*
Watercolor
11½ × 6½ in. (29.2 × 16.5 cm.)
Unlocated
PROVENANCE: The artist; L. Prang
& Company, Boston
LITERATURE: AAA-Prang (1892),
no. 418

255. *The Rock of Acoma, New Mexico*
Watercolor
14 × 20 in. (35.6 × 50.8 cm.)
Private Collection
PROVENANCE: The artist; Albert
Gallatin, Gift of the artist (1906);
by descent to his family
LITERATURE: AWCS, *Annual
Exhibition* (1902), no. 259;
Philadelphia Art Club, Water
Color Exhibition, 1904; Clinton
Academy, *Paintings and Etchings*
(1928), no. 1

256. *Sandstorm, Acoma, New Mexico*
Pencil and watercolor
8 × 10 in. (20.3 × 25.4 cm.)
u.l.: "A Sandstorm at Acoma /
May 31st 1901 / T.Moran"
Stark Museum of Art, Orange,
Texas (31.18/2)
PROVENANCE: Joseph Sartor
Galleries, Dallas, Texas (1957);
H. J. Lutcher Stark, Orange, Texas
LITERATURE: Milch, *Water Color
Sketches* (1926), no. 49; Santa
Barbara (1937), no. 16; Stark
Museum, *Western Collection*, p.
209

257. *Sand Storm at Acoma*
Watercolor
Dimensions unknown
(May 31, 1901)
Unlocated
LITERATURE: Santa Barbara (1925),
no. 45; Clinton Academy,
Paintings and Etchings (1928),
unnumbered

258. *San Juan, New Mexico*
Pencil and watercolor
7 × 10¾ in. (17.8 × 27.3 cm.)
u.l.: "San Juan, Pueblo, New
Mexico / T. Moran."
(1892)
The Thomas Gilcrease Institute of
American History and Art
(0236.843)
PROVENANCE: The artist; Ruth B.
Moran; M. Knoedler & Co., Inc.,
New York; Thomas Gilcrease
LITERATURE: Santa Barbara (1925),
no. 39; Milch, *Water Color
Sketches* (1926), no. 43; Biltmore
Salon (LA), *Water Colors* (1927),
no. 41

259. *Ship Rock, Arizona*
Pencil and watercolor
9⅜ × 16¾ in. (23.8 × 42.5 cm.)
l.l.: " ORAN / 1892"
Stark Museum of Art, Orange,
Texas (31.18/13)
PROVENANCE: Joseph Sartor
Galleries, Dallas, Texas (1957);
H. J. Lutcher Stark, Orange, Texas
LITERATURE: Clinton Academy,
Paintings and Etchings (1928),
unnumbered; Stark Museum,
Western Collection, p. 209, illus.
p. 70

260. *Buttes, Green River, Wyoming*
Pencil and watercolor
9½ × 13¾ in. (24.1 × 34.9 cm.)
u.l.: "Green River / Sep 20th 1881 /
T.Moran."
The Thomas Gilcrease Institute of
American History and Art
(0236.898)
PROVENANCE: The artist; Ruth B.
Moran; M. Knoedler & Co., Inc.,
New York; Thomas Gilcrease
LITERATURE: Denver (1892), no. 85
(?)

261. *Buttes on Green River, Wyoming*
Pencil, watercolor, and opaque
color
9 × 12½ in. (22.9 × 31.8 cm.)
l.l.: " 1879 Green River"
The Thomas Gilcrease Institute of
American History and Art
(0236.891)
PROVENANCE: The artist; Ruth B.
Moran; M. Knoedler & Co., Inc.,
New York; Thomas Gilcrease
LITERATURE: Parker, "Water-
Colors," illus. p. 67

262. *Castellated Cliffs, Morning*
Watercolor
14 × 10 in. (35.6 × 25.4 cm.)
Unlocated
LITERATURE: AAA-Ortgies (1886),
no. 59

263. *Castle Butte, Green River,
Wyoming*
Watercolor
26 × 19¾ in. (66 × 50.2 cm.)
l.r.: " ORAN 1902"
Collection of Christopher T. May,
Sterling A. May, Meredith May,
and Laura May
PROVENANCE: Bertram M.
Newhouse, New York (1926);
Stendahl Gallery, Los Angeles
(1927); Mr. and Mrs. Frank Meline,
Beverly Hills, California (1937);
Newhouse Galleries, New York;
Hirschl & Adler Galleries, Inc.,
New York; Meredith Long and
Co., Houston, Texas

LITERATURE: LA Art Association (1937), no. 2 (as "Castle Rock, Green River, Wyoming"); Wilson, "Moran," no. 69; Parke-Bernet Galleries, Inc., sale 3255, lot 47, illus. (as "Western Landscape") (October 27–28, 1971)

264. *Castle Butte, Green River, Wyoming (Castle Rock—On the Columbia*[?])
Pencil, watercolor, and opaque color
7⅝ × 10¼ in. (19.4 × 26 cm.)
l.l.: "⚶ ORAN / 1892"
The Bancroft Library, University of California at Berkeley
PROVENANCE: Robert B. Honeyman, Jr.
LITERATURE: Joseph Armstrong Baird, Jr., comp., *Catalogue of Original Paintings, Drawings and Watercolors in the Robert B. Honeyman, Jr., Collection*, no. 401

265. *"The Castle," Green River*
Watercolor
Dimensions unknown
Unlocated
LITERATURE: AAA-Ortgies (1886), no. 49

266. *Cliffs, Green River, Utah, 1872*
Watercolor and opaque color
6¼ × 12 in. (15.9 × 30.4 cm.)
l.r.: "⚶ ORAN. / 1872"
Museum of Fine Arts, Boston, Gift of Maxim Karolik (60.428)
PROVENANCE: The artist; John Duff; Shore Galleries, Boston; Maxim Karolik
LITERATURE: Clinton Academy, *Paintings and Etchings* (1928), no. 12; MFA, *Karolik Drawings*, no. 570, illus. p. 243; Wilkins, *Moran*, illus. fol. p. 48; Sachs, "Drawings and Watercolors," pl. 13; MFA, *Frontier America* (1975), no. 101; Donelson F. Hoopes, *American Watercolor Painting*, illus. p. 89

267. *The Cliffs of Green River, Wyoming*
Pencil, watercolor, and opaque color
9½ × 22 in. (24.1 × 55.9 cm.)
l.l.: "The Cliffs of Green River, Wyoming Tery. / T.M. 1879 / TMoran."
The Thomas Gilcrease Institute of American History and Art (0236.930)
PROVENANCE: The artist; Ruth B. Moran; M. Knoedler & Co., Inc., New York; Thomas Gilcrease
LITERATURE: New York, Whitney Museum of American Art, *A History of American Watercolor Painting*, no. 102

268. *The Cliffs of Green River, Wyoming*
Watercolor
28 × 24 in. (71.1 × 61 cm.)
(ca. 1900)
Unlocated
PROVENANCE: The artist; Goelet Gallatin, Big Horn, Wyoming, Gift of the artist

269. *Cliffs of Green River, Wyoming*
Watercolor
Dimensions unknown
Unlocated
LITERATURE: AWCS, *Annual Exhibition* (1894), no. 61 (?); Philadelphia Art Club, Water Color Exhibition (1904); Milch, *Water Color Sketches* (1926), no. 24; Biltmore Salon (LA), *Water Colors* (1927), no. 23

270. *Green River*
Watercolor
3 × 5⅛ in. (7.6 × 13 cm.)
l.l.: "T. Moran. 1888"
Collection of Carl Schaefer Dentzel
PROVENANCE: The artist; Carl Oscar Borg

271. *Green River*
Pencil, watercolor, and opaque color
8 × 13 in. (20.3 × 33 cm.)
l.l.: "T. Moran. / Green River. Sep 12th-79"
The George F. McMurray Collection at Trinity College, Hartford, Connecticut
LITERATURE: Santa Barbara (1925), no. 18

272. *Green River*
Pencil and watercolor
4¾ × 8¼ in. (12.1 × 21 cm.)
u.r.: "Green River. w / 1879 / Moran TM"
American Heritage Center, University of Wyoming at Laramie, Gift of F. M. Fryxell
PROVENANCE: The artist; Ruth B. Moran; Mr. and Mrs. Fritiof M. Fryxell, Rock Island, Illinois

273. *Green River*
Watercolor
Dimensions unknown
Unlocated
LITERATURE: Milch, *Water Color Sketches* (1926), no. 18

274. *Green River*
Watercolor
Dimensions unknown
Unlocated
LITERATURE: Milch, *Water Color Sketches* (1926)

275. *Green River Buttes (Chimney Rock)*
Pencil and watercolor
6 × 9½ in. (15.2 × 24.1 cm.)
(1879)
American Heritage Center, University of Wyoming at Laramie, Gift of F. M. Fryxell
PROVENANCE: The artist; Ruth B. Moran; Mr. and Mrs. Fritiof M. Fryxell, Rock Island, Illinois

276. *Green River Buttes, Wyoming*
Pencil, watercolor, and opaque color
10 × 13 in. (25.4 × 33 cm.)
l.l.: "Green River Buttes. Wyoming / TMoran 1879"
The Thomas Gilcrease Institute of American History and Art (0236.885)
PROVENANCE: The artist; Ruth B. Moran; M. Knoedler & Co., Inc., New York; Thomas Gilcrease

277. *Green River Buttes, Wyoming*
Pencil and watercolor
10⅜ × 19⅛ in. (26.3 × 48.6 cm.)
l.l.: "Green River Buttes Wyoming Tery Sep 20th 1881 T.Moran."
Stark Museum of Art, Orange, Texas (31.18/6)
PROVENANCE: Joseph Sartor Galleries, Dallas, Texas (1957); H. J. Lutcher Stark, Orange, Texas
LITERATURE: Denver (1892), no. 85 (?); Santa Barbara (1925), no. 53; Milch, *Water Color Sketches* (1926), no. 57; Biltmore Salon (LA), *Water Colors* (1927), no. 35; Stark Museum, *Western Collection*, p. 208

278. *Green River Cliffs*
Pencil and watercolor
10 × 11⅞ in. (25 × 30.1 cm.)
l.l.: "A Sketch of / Green River Cliffs / T.Moran. / 1923"
Bound in Charles Lummis' Home-Book
Southwest Museum, Los Angeles, California
PROVENANCE: The artist; Charles Lummis, Highland Park, California

279. *Green River Cliffs, Wyoming*
Watercolor
14 × 23 in. (35.6 × 58.4 cm.)
l.l.: signed
Unlocated
PROVENANCE: Mrs. Page, Arcade Gallery, Santa Barbara, California; Gene Record, Gallery "21," Goleta, California
LITERATURE: Santa Barbara (1925), no. 52

280. *Green River Cliffs, Wyoming*
Watercolor
Dimensions unknown
Unlocated
LITERATURE: Milch, *Water Color Sketches* (1926), no. 56; Biltmore Salon (LA), *Water Colors* (1927), no. 34

281. *Green River Crossing*
Watercolor and opaque color
13⅜ × 14¼ in. (33.9 × 36.2 cm.)
l.l.: "TM 1880"
Courtesy of Mr. and Mrs. William H. Bertsche
PROVENANCE: Mr. Fred Rosenstock, Denver, Colorado

282. *Green River from the Ferry*
Pencil, watercolor, and opaque color
8⅝ × 14⅜ in. (21.9 × 36.5 cm.)
u.r.: "Green River from the Ferry. Sep 11th 79"
l.l.: "Hazy morning Red yellow gray Horizon TM. 1880"
Cooper-Hewitt Museum, The Smithsonian Institution's National Museum of Design, Gift of the artist (1917.17.38)
PROVENANCE: The artist
LITERATURE: Wilson, "Moran," no. 101; Gerdts, *Thomas Moran* (1963), no. 27, illus. p. 40; Heckscher Museum, *Moran Family* (1965), no. 36; Washburn, *Cooper-Hewitt Collection* (1974); Ballinger, *Endless River* (1979), pl. 125, illus. p. 80

283. *Green River, Utah*
Watercolor
5¾ × 8½ in. (14.6 × 21.6 cm.)
l.l.: signed and dated March 24, 1879
Private Collection
PROVENANCE: Private collection; Kennedy Galleries, Inc., New York

284. *Green River of Wyoming*
Watercolor
Dimensions unknown
Unlocated
PROVENANCE: Mrs. W. E. Wrather, Washington, D.C.

285. *Green River, Wyoming*
Pencil, watercolor, and opaque color
12⅝ × 18 in. (32.1 × 45.7 cm.)
l.l.: "Green River, Wyoming / 1879"
Cooper-Hewitt Museum, The Smithsonian Institution's National Museum of Design, Gift of the artist (1917.17.39)
PROVENANCE: The artist
LITERATURE: Clinton Academy, *Paintings and Etchings* (1928), no. 6 (or 9); Wilson, "Moran," no. 47, illus. pl. XXIII, p. 255; Sachs, "Drawings and Watercolors," pl. 27; Washburn, *Cooper-Hewitt Collection* (1974); Fern, *Drawings and Watercolors* (1976), no. 61, illus. p. 85

286. *Green River, Wyoming*
Watercolor
Dimensions unknown
(1879)
Unlocated
LITERATURE: Milch, *Water Color Sketches* (1926), unnumbered; Biltmore Salon (LA), *Water Colors* (1927), no. 40

287. *Green River, Wyoming*
Pencil and watercolor
5 × 11½ in. (12.7 × 29.2 cm.)
u.l.: "TMoran"
l.r.: "Green River, W. 1892"
American Heritage Center, University of Wyoming at Laramie, Gift of F. M. Fryxell
PROVENANCE: The artist; Ruth B. Moran; Mr. and Mrs. Fritiof M. Fryxell, Rock Island, Illinois

288. *Green River, Wyoming*
Watercolor
Dimensions unknown
Unlocated
LITERATURE: Milch, *Water Color Sketches* (1926), no. 19

289. *Green River, Wyoming, First Sketch Made in the West*
Pencil, watercolor, and opaque color
3½ × 7¾ in. (8.9 × 19.7 cm.)
l.l.: "TMoran 1871"
On mount: "First sketch made in the West at Green River, Wyoming 1871"
The Thomas Gilcrease Institute of American History and Art (0236.882)
PROVENANCE: The artist; Ruth B. Moran; M. Knoedler & Co., Inc., New York; Thomas Gilcrease
LITERATURE: Sachs, "Drawings and Watercolors," pl. 12; Wilkins, *American Scene*, illus. p. 24

290. *Green River, Wyoming Territory*
Pencil, watercolor, and opaque color
10 × 14½ in. (25.4 × 36.8 cm.)
l.l.: "⚏ 1879"
l.r.: "Sep 10th 1879 / Green River Wyoming Ter. T.M."
Jefferson National Expansion Memorial, St. Louis, Missouri (4297)
PROVENANCE: The artist; Ruth B. Moran
LITERATURE: Fryxell, "National Parks Collection," no. TM-51; Wilson, "Moran," no. 105; Fern, *Drawings and Watercolors* (1976), no. 62, illus. p. 87

291. *Gunnison's Butte, Azure Cliffs at Green River, Utah*
Watercolor
9½ × 14 in. (24.1 × 35.6 cm.)
(ca. 1874–1875)
Unlocated
PROVENANCE: L. Prang & Company, Boston
LITERATURE: AAA-Prang (1892), no. 357

292. *Lake in the Mountains*
Pencil, watercolor, and opaque color
8 × 13¾ in. (20.3 × 34.9 cm.)
The Thomas Gilcrease Institute of American History and Art (0236.851)
PROVENANCE: The artist; Ruth B. Moran; M. Knoedler & Co., Inc., New York; Thomas Gilcrease

293. *Mountain Landscape*
Pencil, watercolor, and opaque color
13 × 9 in. (33.0 × 22.9 cm.)
The Thomas Gilcrease Institute of American History and Art (0216.853)
PROVENANCE: The artist; Ruth B. Moran; M. Knoedler & Co., Inc., New York; Thomas Gilcrease

294. *A Mountain Pass*
Watercolor
19⅛ × 13¼ in. (48.6 × 33.7 cm.)
l.l.: signed
Private Collection
PROVENANCE: Closson (1972); Hirschl & Adler Galleries, Inc., New York; Closson Co. (1973); Hirschl & Adler Galleries, Inc., New York

295. Untitled (Clouds and Mountains)
Pencil and watercolor
7¼ × 5 in. (18.4 × 12.7 cm.)
East Hampton Free Library, The Thomas Moran Biographical Art Collection
PROVENANCE: The artist; Ruth B. Moran

Bibliography

ARCHIVAL SOURCES

Records maintained by museums, libraries, and private collectors are most important in reconstructing the provenance and exhibition history of each watercolor.

Sketchbooks and annotated drawings and watercolors provide information on Moran's trips and insight into his artistic methods. The largest and most important collections are:

Cooper-Hewitt Museum, The Smithsonian Institution's National Museum of Design, New York (gifts of the artist).

East Hampton Free Library, The Thomas Moran Biographical Art Collection, East Hampton, New York (gifts of Ruth B. Moran).

Jefferson National Expansion Memorial, St. Louis, Missouri (gifts of Ruth B. Moran, previously held at Yosemite National Park).

National Collection of Fine Arts, Smithsonian Institution, Washington, D.C. (primarily gifts of William H. Holmes).

The Thomas Gilcrease Institute of American History and Art, Tulsa, Oklahoma (purchase of Ruth B. Moran's estate).

Yellowstone National Park (gifts of George D. Pratt et al.).

Diaries, record books, scrapbooks, annotated catalogues, photographs, correspondence, and biographical and autobiographical manuscripts are held at:

Archives of American Art, Washington, D.C. (Milch Gallery scrapbooks, available on microfilm through the Archives).

Bushnell Collection, Peabody Museum of Archaeology and Ethnology, Harvard University, Cambridge, Massachusetts.

Department of the Interior Library, Washington, D.C.

East Hampton Free Library, The Thomas Moran Biographical Art Collection, East Hampton, New York (gift of Ruth B. Moran; available in part on microfilm through the Archives of American Art).

Frick Art Reference Library, New York.

Grand Teton National Park, Moose, Wyoming.

Hallmark Cards, Inc., Creative Research Library, Hallmark Historical Collection, Kansas City, Missouri.

Jefferson National Expansion Memorial, St. Louis, Missouri (gifts of Ruth B. Moran, previously held at Yosemite National Park).

National Collection of Fine Arts Library (William H. Holmes scrapbooks, "Random Records of a Lifetime").

The New York Public Library.

Office of the Architect of the Capitol, Washington, D.C.

The Thomas Gilcrease Institute of American History and Art, Tulsa, Oklahoma (purchase of Ruth B. Moran's estate).

United States National Archives, United States Geological Survey Records, Washington, D.C.

OTHER SOURCES

Amherst College, Massachusetts. Mead Art Gallery. *American Art at Amherst.* 1978.

Atlanta, Georgia. High Museum of Art. *The Beckoning Land, Nature and the American Artist: A Selection of Nineteenth Century Paintings.* Text by Donelson F. Hoopes. April 17–June 13, 1971.

Baird, Joseph Armstrong, Jr., comp. *Catalogue of Original Paintings, Drawings and Watercolors in the Robert B. Honeyman, Jr., Collection.* Berkeley, Calif.: Friends of the Bancroft Library, 1968.

Bartlett, Richard A. *Great Surveys of the American West.* Norman: University of Oklahoma Press, 1962.

———. *Nature's Yellowstone: The Story of an American Wilderness That Became Yellowstone National Park in 1872.* Albuquerque: University of New Mexico Press, 1974.

Bassford, Amy O., and Fritiof Fryxell. *Home Thoughts from Afar: Letters of Thomas Moran to Mary Nimmo Moran.* East Hampton, N.Y.: East Hampton Free Library, 1967.

Baur, John I. H. "A Romantic Impressionist: James Hamilton." *Brooklyn Museum Bulletin* 13, no. 3 (Spring 1951): 1–9.

Benjamin, Samuel G. W. "American Painters: Thomas Moran and Joseph R. Meeker." *Art Journal* 5 (1879): 41–45.

———. "American Water-Colour Society: Thirteenth Annual Exhibition." *Art Journal* 6 (1880): 91–93.

———. *Art in America: A Critical and Historical Sketch.* 1880. Reprinted in The Art Experience in Late Nineteenth-Century America Series, edited by H. Barbara Weinberg. New York: Garland Publishing, 1976.

———. "A Pioneer of the Palette: Thomas Moran." *Magazine of Art* 5 (February 1882): 89–93.

———. *Our American Artists, 1879* and *Our American Artists, Second Series, 1881*. Reprinted (2 vols. in 1) in The Art Experience in Late Nineteenth-Century America Series, edited by H. Barbara Weinberg. New York: Garland Publishing, 1977.

Benson, Frances M. "The Moran Family." *Quarterly Illustrator* 1, no. 2 (April–June 1893): 67–84.

Berg, Steven F. "The Influence of Art and Photography on the Formation of the United States National Park System." Master's thesis, University of Washington, 1974.

Bethesda, Maryland. Government Services Savings and Loan, Inc. *The American West: Selected Works*. March 29–June 2, 1978.

Billington, Ray Allen. *The American Frontier*. Washington, D.C.: Service Center for Teachers of History, American Historical Association, 1958.

———. *America's Frontier Culture: Three Essays*. College Station: Texas A&M University Press, 1977.

———. *The Far Western Frontier, 1830–1860*. New York: Harper & Row, 1956.

———. *The Genesis of the Frontier Thesis: A Study in Historical Creativity*. San Marino, Calif.: The Huntington Library, 1971.

Birmingham, Alabama. Museum of Art. *American Watercolors, 1850–1972*. January 6–February 13, 1972.

Bloch, Maurice. "American Watercolors." *Architectural Digest* 34, no. 2 (April 1977): illus. p. 82.

Boime, Albert. *The Academy and French Painting in the Nineteenth Century*. London: Phaidon Press, 1971.

Born, Wolfgang. *American Landscape Painting: An Interpretation*. New Haven, Conn.: Yale University Press, 1948.

Boston. The Museum of Fine Arts. *Frontier America: The Far West*. January 23–March 16, 1975.

———. ———. *M. and M. Karolik Collection of American Water Colors & Drawings, 1800–1875*. 2 vols. Boston: Museum of Fine Arts, 1962.

Breuning, Margaret. "Thomas Moran." *Magazine of Art* 30, no. 2 (February 1937): 114–115.

Bromley, Isaac H. "The Wonders of the West—I: The Big Trees and the Yosemite." *Scribner's Monthly* 3, no. 3 (January 1872): 261–277.

Brooklyn Museum. *A Century of American Illustration*. March 22–May 14, 1972.

———. *Drawings of the Hudson River School, 1825–1875*. Text by Jo Miller. November 25, 1969–February 22, 1970.

———. *James Hamilton, 1819–1878: American Marine Painter*. Text by Arlene Jacobowitz. March 28–May 22, 1966.

Bryant, William Cullen, ed. *Picturesque America; or, The Land We Live In*. 2 vols. New York: D. Appleton and Company, [1872–1874].

Buckley, Edmund. "Thomas Moran: A Splendid Example of American Achievement in Art." *Fine Arts Journal* 20, no. 1 (January 1909): 8–17.

Buek, Gustave H. "Thomas Moran." *American Magazine* 75, no. 3 (January 1913): 30–32.

———. "Thomas Moran, N.A.—The Grand Old Man of American Art." *Mentor* 12, no. 7 (August 1924): 29–37. Reprinted in part in *Thomas Moran: Explorer in Search of Beauty*, ed. Fritiof Fryxell, pp. 63–71.

Butler, Howard Russell. "Thomas Moran, N.A.—An Appreciation." *American Magazine of Art* 17, no. 11 (November 1926): 558–560.

California, University at Berkeley. University Art Museum. *J. M. W. Turner: Works on Paper from American Collections*. Text by Joseph R. Goldyne. September 30–November 23, 1975.

California, University at Riverside. Picture Gallery. *Thomas Moran 1873–1926*. Text by William H. Gerdts. April 17–June 7, 1963.

Cambridge, Massachusetts. Harvard University. Fogg Art Museum. *American Art at Harvard*. April 19–June 18, 1972.

———. ———. *Luminous Landscape: The American Study of Light, 1860–1875*. April 18–May 11, 1966.

Chicago. The Art Institute of Chicago. *A Collection of Paintings in Water Color by American Artists, Lent by Gustave H. Buek of Brooklyn, New York*. July 26–August 28, 1910.

———. ———. *The Hudson River School and the Early American Landscape Tradition*. Text by Arnold Sweet. February 15–March 25, 1945.

———. The Arts Club of Chicago. *The American Landscape*. November 14–December 29, 1973.

Chittenden, Hiram Martin. *The Yellowstone National Park*. Cincinnati: Robert Clark Co., 1905.

Clark, Eliot C. *History of the National Academy of Design, 1825–1953*. New York: Columbia University Press, 1954.

———. "Studies by American Masters at Cooper Union." *Art in America* 15, no. 4 (June 1927): 180–188.

Clement, Clara, and Laurence Hutton, eds. *Artists of the Nineteenth Century and Their Works*. 2 vols. 3d rev. ed. Boston: J. R. Osgood, 1885.

Cock, Elizabeth M. "The Influence of Photography on American Landscape Painting, 1839–1880." Ph.D. dissertation, New York University, 1967.

Coen, Rena Neumann. "The Indian as the Noble Savage in Nineteenth Century American Art." Ph.D. dissertation, University of Minnesota, 1969.

Cohn, Marjorie B. *Wash and Gouache: A Study of the Development of the Materials of Watercolor*. Cambridge, Mass.: Fogg Art Museum, Harvard University, 1977.

Coke, Van Deren. *The Painter and the Photograph, from Delacroix to Warhol*. Rev. and enl. ed. Albuquerque: University of New Mexico Press, 1972.

Colburn, J. E. "The Cañons of the Colorado." In *Picturesque America*, ed. William Cullen Bryant, 2: 503–511.

Colorado State University, Fort Collins. Student Center Gallery. *Thomas Moran in Yellowstone*. Text by Robert J. Forsyth. July 31–October 6, 1972.

Comstock, Helen. "In Recognition of Thomas Moran." *Connoisseur* 99, no. 425 (January 1937): 38–39.

Conant, S. S. "Fine Arts." *Putnam's Magazine* n.s. 1, no. 1 (January 1868): 131–132.

———. "Fine Arts." *Putnam's Magazine* n.s. 1, no. 2 (February 1868): 257–259.

———. "Fine Arts: The Winter Exhibition." *Putnam's Magazine* n.s. 3, no. 13 (January 1869): 121–123.

———. "Fine Arts." *Putnam's Magazine* n.s. 3, no. 15 (March 1869): 376–380.

Cook, Clarence. "Fine Arts: Mr. Thomas Moran's Great Cañon of the Yellowstone." *New York Times*, May 5, 1872, p. 4, col. 5.

Cooke, Hereward Lester. "The Development of Winslow Homer's Water-Color Technique." *Art Quarterly* 24, no. 2 (Summer 1961): 169–194.

Cortissoz, Royal. "Moran, a Pioneer in Our Landscape Art." *New York Herald Tribune*, March 14, 1937.

Craven, Wayne. "Samuel Colman (1832–1920): Rediscovered Painter of Far-Away Places." *American Art Journal* 8, no. 1 (May 1976): 16–37.

"Current Opinion on Landscapes and Water-Colours." *Art Journal* 4 (1878): 94.

Darrah, William Culp. "Beaman, Fennemore, Hillers, Dellenbaugh, Johnson, and Hattan." *Utah Historical Quarterly* 16–17 (1948–49): 491–503.

———. *Powell of the Colorado*. Princeton: Princeton University Press, 1951.

Denver. The Turner Museum. *Turner and Moran*. Text by Douglas J. M. Graham. April–May 1977.

Denver Art League. *Catalogue: The Works of Thomas Moran*. Christmas 1892.

Denver Art Museum. *Colorado Collects Historic Western Art: The Nostalgia of the Vanishing West*. January 13–April 15, 1973.

Detroit Institute of Arts. *Travelers in Arcadia: American Artists in Italy, 1830–1875*. Text by E. P. Richardson and Otto Wittmann, Jr. 1951.

DeVoto, Bernard. *Across the Wide Missouri*. New York: Bonanza Books, 1947.

Dickason, David Howard. *The Daring Young Men: The Story of the American Pre-Raphaelites*. Bloomington: Indiana University Press, 1953.

Dorra, Henri. *The American Muse: Parallel Trends in Literature and Art*. New York: Viking Press, 1961.

Downes, William Howe. "American Painters of Mountains." *American Magazine of Art* 25, no. 4 (October 1932): 193–202.

Draper, Benjamin P. "Alfred Edward Mathews: Soldier, Pioneer and Delineator." *Antiques* 35, no. 3 (March 1939): 127–129.

———. "Thomas Moran, Painter, Adventurer and Pioneer." *Art in America* 29, no. 2 (April 1941): 82–87.

Driscoll, John P. "Moran Watercolor Found in University Attic." *American Art Journal* 10, no. 1 (May 1978): 111–112.

Dudley, C. Howard. "Exhibition of the American Water-Color Society." *Brush and Pencil* 10, no. 3 (June 1902): 140–151.

East Hampton, New York. Clinton Academy. *Memorial Exhibition, Paintings and Etchings by Thomas Moran, N.A.* July 18–August 7, 1928.

Eddy, Frederick W. "Thomas Moran's Color Notes Helped Make Yellowstone a National Park." *New York World*, January 9, 1927, p. 14.

Evansville, Indiana. Public Museum. *Homer and Moran.* February 1948.

Ewers, John C. *Artists of the Old West.* Garden City, N.Y.: Doubleday and Co., 1965.

——. "Fact and Fiction in the Documentary Art of the American West." In *The Frontier Re-examined*, ed. John Francis McDermott, pp. 79–95. Urbana: University of Illinois Press, 1967.

"Exhibition of Paintings in Bolton." *Bolton* [England] *Weekly Guardian*, June 9, 1882.

Fabri, Ralph. *History of the American Watercolor Society: The First Hundred Years.* New York: American Watercolor Society, 1969.

[Falconer, J. M.] "The Art of Landscape Painting in Water Colors." *Bulletin of the American Art Union* 4 (November–December 1851): 119–123, 139–143.

Fern, Thomas S. "The Drawings and Watercolors of Thomas Moran (1837–1926)." *Artists of the Rockies and the Golden West* 3, no. 3 (Summer 1976): 34–41.

"Fine Arts." *Nation*, February 15, 1877, pp. 107–108.

"Fine Arts: The Yellowstone Landscape at Washington." *Nation*, September 5, 1872, pp. 157–158.

Fort Worth, Texas. Amon Carter Museum. *The Democratic Art: An Exhibition on the History of Chromolithography in America, 1840–1900.* Text by Peter C. Marzio. September 6–October 21, 1979.

Fryxell, Fritiof M. "The Mount of the Holy Cross." *Trail and Timberline*, no. 183 (January 1934), pp. 3–9, 14.

——. "The Thomas Moran Art Collection of the National Parks." *Yosemite Nature Notes* 15, no. 8 (August 1936): 57–60.

——. "Thomas Moran's Journey to the Tetons in 1879." *Augustana Historical Society Publications*, no. 2 (1932), pp. 3–12.

——, ed. *Thomas Moran: Explorer in Search of Beauty.* East Hampton, N.Y.: East Hampton Free Library, 1958.

——, ed. *The Thomas Moran Art Collection of the National Parks.* 2 vols. Berkeley, Calif., 1936.

Gardner, Albert TenEyck. *History of Water Color Painting in America.* New York: Reinhold Publishing Corp., 1966.

Gerdts, William H. "Americans in Faraway Places, in the Roderic H. D. Henderson Collection." *Antiques* 91, no. 5 (May 1967): 647–649.

——. "The Paintings of Thomas Moran: Sources and Style." *Antiques* 85, no. 2 (February 1964): 202–205.

Gillespie, Harriet Sisson. "Thomas Moran, Dean of Our Painters." *International Studio* 79, no. 327 (August 1924): 361–366.

Goetzmann, William H. *Army Exploration in the American West, 1803–1863.* New Haven, Conn.: Yale University Press, 1957.

——. *Exploration and Empire: The Explorer and the Scientist in the Winning of the American West.* New York: Alfred A. Knopf, 1966.

Goodrich, Lloyd. *American Watercolor and Winslow Homer.* Minneapolis: Walker Art Center, 1945.

Gordon, Dudley. *Charles F. Lummis: Crusader in Corduroy.* [Los Angeles]: Cultural Assets Press, 1972.

Greeley, Horace. *An Overland Journey from New York to San Francisco, in the Summer of 1859.* New York: C. M. Saxton, Barker and Co., 1860.

Gussow, Alan. *A Sense of Place: The Artist and the American Land.* 2 vols. New York: Saturday Review Press for Friends of the Earth, [1973].

Haines, Aubrey L. *Yellowstone National Park: Its Exploration and Establishment.* Washington, D.C.: U.S. National Park Service, 1974.

Hardie, Martin. *Water-Colour Painting in Britain.* 3 vols. London: Batsford, [1967–1968].

Hassrick, Peter. *The Way West: Art of Frontier America.* New York: Harry N. Abrams, 1977.

Haverstock, Mary S. "Can Nature Imitate Art? Landscape of the American West." *Art in America* 54, no. 1 (January–February 1966): 73–80.

Hayden, Ferdinand V. "The Wonders of the West—II: More about the Yellowstone." *Scribner's Monthly* 3, no. 4 (February 1872): 388–396.

——. *The Yellowstone National Park, and the Mountain Regions of Portions of Idaho, Nevada, Colorado and Utah.* Boston: L. Prang & Company, 1876. Review of Ferdinand V. Hayden's *The Yellowstone National Park . . . American Journal of Science and Arts* 13, no. 75 (March 1877): 229–230.

Hayes, Bartlett H., Jr. *American Drawings.* New York: Shorewood Publishers, 1965.

Hendricks, Gordon. *Albert Bierstadt, Painter of the American West.* New York: Harry N. Abrams, 1974.

——. "The First Three Western Journeys of Albert Bierstadt." *Art Bulletin* 46, no. 3 (September 1964): 333–365.

Herbert, Robert, ed. *The Art Criticism of John Ruskin.* Garden City, N.Y.: Doubleday, 1964.

Higgins, Charles A. *Grand Cañon of the Colorado River, Arizona.* Chicago: Passenger Department of the Santa Fe Railroad, 1892.

Hillers, John K. *"Photographed All the Best Scenery": Jack Hillers's Diary of the Powell Expeditions, 1871–1875*. Edited by Don D. Fowler. Salt Lake City: University of Utah Press, 1972.

Hine, Robert V. *The American West: An Interpretive History*. Boston: Little, Brown and Company, 1973.

Holmes, William H. "Random Records of a Lifetime, 1846–1931." [Approximately 20 volumes of typescript and clippings in the Library of the National Collection of Fine Arts, Washington, D.C.]

Hoopes, Donelson F. *American Watercolor Painting*. New York: Watson-Guptill, 1977.

Humboldt, Alexander, freiherr von. *Cosmos: A Sketch of a Physical Description of the Universe*. 5 vols. London: H. G. Bohn, 1848–1852.

Huntington, David C. "Landscape and Diaries: The South American Trips of F. E. Church." *Brooklyn Museum Annual* 5 (1963–64): 65–98.

———. *The Landscapes of Frederic Edwin Church: Vision of an American Era*. New York: George Braziller, 1966.

Huntington, New York. Heckscher Museum. *The Moran Family*. June 5–July 25, 1965.

Hussey, Christopher. *The Picturesque: Studies in a Point of View*. New York: G. P. Putnam's Sons, 1927.

Huth, Hans. *Nature and the American: Three Centuries of Changing Attitudes*. Berkeley and Los Angeles: University of California Press, 1957.

Indiana University, Bloomington. Art Museum. *The American Scene, 1820–1900*. Organized by Louis Hawes. January 18–February 28, 1970.

Ingersoll, Ernest. *The Crest of the Continent: A Record of a Summer's Ramble in the Rocky Mountains and Beyond*. Chicago: R. R. Donnelley and Sons, 1885.

Jackson, Clarence S. *Picture Maker of the Old West, William H. Jackson*. New York: Scribner's Sons, 1947.

Jackson, John Brinckerhoff. *American Space: The Centennial Years, 1865–1876*. New York: W. W. Norton and Co., 1972.

———. "Jefferson, Thoreau and After: The Life and Death of American Landscapes." *Landscape* 15, no. 2 (Winter 1965–66): 25–27.

Jackson, William Henry. *The Pioneer Photographer, Rocky Mountain Adventures with a Camera*. Yonkers-on-Hudson, N.Y.: World Book Company, 1929.

———. *Time Exposure: The Autobiography of William Henry Jackson*. New York: G. P. Putnam's Sons, 1940.

———. "With Moran in Yellowstone." *Appalachia* 21, no. 82 (December 1936): 149–158. Reprinted in *Thomas Moran: Explorer in Search of Beauty*, ed. Fritiof Fryxell, pp. 49–61.

Jarves, James Jackson. *Art Thoughts*. New York: Hurd and Houghton, 1871.

Kansas, University at Lawrence. Museum of Art. *The Arcadian Landscape: Nineteenth Century American Painters in Italy*. Text by Charles C. Eldridge. November 4–December 3, 1972.

Keene, Marie. "Moran." *American Scene* 14, no. 1 (1973).

Ladegast, Richard. "Thomas Moran, N.A." *Truth* 19, no. 9 (September 1900): 209–212.

Laffan, W. Mackay. "The Material of American Landscape." *American Art Review* 1, no. 1 (1880): 29–32.

Langford, Nathaniel P. "The Wonders of the Yellowstone." *Scribner's Monthly* 2, nos. 1–2 (May–June 1871): 1–17, 113–128.

Lee, Sherman E. "A Critical Survey of American Watercolor Painting." Ph.D. dissertation, Case Western Reserve University, 1941.

Lincoln, Massachusetts. De Cordova and Dana Museum. *Homer to Hopper: Sixty Years of American Watercolor Painting.* December 12, 1976–February 6, 1977.

Lindquist-Cock, Elizabeth. "Stereoscopic Photography and the Western Paintings of Albert Bierstadt." *Art Quarterly* 33, no. 4 (Winter 1970): 361–378.

Lockington, W. P. "Philadelphia Water-Color Exhibition." *Brush and Pencil* 8, no. 2 (May 1901): 65–72.

Los Angeles. The Biltmore Salon. *Water Colors by Thomas Moran, N.A., 1837–1926.* January 2–29, 1927.

Los Angeles Art Association. Los Angeles Public Library. *Thomas Moran, N.A.: Centenary Exhibition.* May 1937.

Los Angeles County. Museum of Art. *The American West: Painters from Catlin to Russell.* Text by Larry Curry. March 21–May 28, 1972.

Ludlow, Fitz Hugh. *The Heart of the Continent: A Record of Travel across the Plains and in Oregon.* New York: Hurd and Houghton, 1870.

Lynes, Russell. *The Art-Makers of 19th Century America.* New York: Atheneum, 1970.

McClinton, Katherine Morrison. *The Chromolithographs of Louis Prang.* New York: Clarkson N. Potter, 1973.

———. "L. Prang and Company." *Connoisseur* 191, no. 768 (February 1976): 97–105.

McDermott, John Francis, ed. *Travelers on the Western Frontier.* Urbana: University of Illinois Press, 1970.

Maryland, University at College Park. Art Gallery. *From Delacroix to Cézanne: French Watercolor Landscapes of the Nineteenth Century.* Text by Alain de Leiris. Catalogue by Carol Hynning Smith. October 26–December 4, 1977.

Marzio, Peter C. *Chromolithography, 1840–1900: The Democratic Art; Pictures for a 19th-Century America.* Boston: David R. Godine, 1979.

Massachusetts, University at Amherst. The University Gallery. *Late Nineteenth Century American Drawings and Watercolors.* Edited by Martha J. Hoppin. May 14–June 5, 1977.

Mather, Stephen Tyng. "The Work of Thomas Moran." *New York Times*, January 27, 1927, sec. 7, p. 10.

Michigan, University at Ann Arbor. Museum of Art. *Art and the Excited Spirit: America in the Romantic Period.* Text by David C. Huntington. March 19–May 14, 1972.

Monk, Samuel H. *The Sublime: A Study of Critical Theories in XVIII-Century England.* New York: Modern Language Association of America, 1935.

Montgomery, Walter, ed. *American Art and American Art Collections.* 2 vols. 1889. Reprint, New York: Garland Publishing Co., 1978.

Moran, Ruth B. "The Real Life of Thomas Moran." *American Magazine of Art* 17, no. 12 (December 1926): 645–646.

———. "Thomas Moran: An Impression." *Mentor* 12, no. 7 (August 1924): 38–52. Reprinted in *Thomas Moran: Explorer in Search of Beauty*, ed. Fritiof Fryxell, pp. 37–40.

Moran, Thomas. "American Art and American Scenery." In *The Grand Canyon of Arizona.* Chicago: Passenger Department of the Santa Fe Railroad, 1902.

———. "A Journey to the Devil's Tower in Wyoming (Artists' Adventures)." *Century Magazine* 47, no. 3 (January 1894): 450–455.

———. "Knowledge a Prime Requisite in Art." *Brush and Pencil* 12, no. 1 (April 1903): 14–16.

"Moran's Mountain of the Holy Cross." *Aldine* 7, no. 19 (July 1875): 379–380.

Morton, Frederick W. "Thomas Moran, Painter-Etcher." *Brush and Pencil* 7, no. 1 (October 1900): 1–16.

Moure, Nancy Dustin Wall. "Five Eastern Artists Out West." *American Art Journal* 5, no. 2 (November 1973): 15–31.

Muir, John. *Our National Parks*. Boston: Houghton Mifflin, 1909.

———, ed. *Picturesque California: The Rocky Mountains and the Pacific Slope*. 2 vols. New York and San Francisco: J. Dewing Co., 1888.

Murdza, Susan Ellen. "The Influence of J. M. W. Turner on Four American Artists of the Nineteenth Century." Master's thesis, Tufts University, 1975.

Naef, Weston J. *Era of Exploration: The Rise of Landscape Photography in the American West, 1860–1885*. Boston: New York Graphic Society, 1975.

Nash, Roderick. *Wilderness and the American Mind*. New Haven, Conn.: Yale University Press, 1967.

New Haven, Connecticut. Yale University Art Gallery. *Pictures from an Expedition*. Text by Martha A. Sandweiss. September 20, 1978–January 6, 1979.

New York. American Art Association. *Catalogue of the Oils and Watercolors of Thomas Moran, N.A. 1886*. [Sold on Wednesday, February 24, at the Galleries of Messrs. Ortgies and Co.]

———. ———. *Sale of Paintings Belonging to Louis Prang*. February 16–18, 1892. [Catalogue of an unusual collection of watercolor and oil paintings purchased from time to time for reproduction by Louis Prang and Co.]

———. American Water-Color Society. *Annual Exhibition*. [1867–1902].

———. The Anderson Galleries. *American Water Colors: The Collection Formed by the Late G. H. Buek, Easthampton, L.I.* November 4, 1927.

———. J. N. Bartfield Art Galleries, Inc. *American Paintings and Sculpture: Historical-Western*. 1973.

———. ———. *The American West: Paintings and Sculpture*. Catalogue 150. 1978.

———. The Century Association. *Drawings by Centurions Lent by the Cooper-Hewitt Museum*. February 14–March 4, 1979.

———. Coe Kerr Gallery, Inc. *The American Painting Collection of Mrs. Norman B. Woolworth*. Essay by William H. Gerdts. November 10–28, 1970.

———. The Cooper Union Museum for the Arts of Decoration. *An Exhibition of American Drawings*. Assembled for the United States Information Agency by the Smithsonian Institution Traveling Exhibition Service. January 29–March 6, 1954.

———. ———. *Five Centuries of Drawing: The Cooper Union Centennial Exhibition*. 1959–1961.

———. Edward Eberstadt & Sons. *American Paintings, Historical, Genre, Western*. Catalogue 146, Golden Anniversary. 1958.

———. ———. *A Distinguished Collection of Western Paintings Offered for Sale by Edward Eberstadt & Sons*. Catalogue 139. [1956?].

———. Gallery of Modern Art. *Major 19th and 20th Century Drawings*. 1965.

———. Hirschl & Adler Galleries, Inc. *The American Scene: A Survey of Life and Landscape of the 19th Century*. October 29–November 22, 1969.

———. ———. *Faces and Places: Changing Images of 19th Century America*. December 5, 1972–January 6, 1973.

———. ———. *Forty Masterworks of American Art*. October 28–November 14, 1970.

———. ———. *Retrospective of a Gallery*. November 8–December 1, 1973.

———. Kennedy Galleries, Inc. *The American View: Art from 1770 to 1978*. December 6, 1978–January 6, 1979.

———. C. W. Kraushaar Art Galleries. *Catalogue of Pictures by Thomas Moran, N.A., with Original Verses by Edith M. Thomas*. February 8, 1897.

———. The Macbeth Gallery. *First Annual Exhibition by the Painters of the Far West*. November 19–30, 1912.

———. The Metropolitan Museum of Art. *American Paintings and Historical Prints from the Middendorf Collection*. October 4–November 26, 1967.

———. ———. *19th Century America: Paintings and Sculpture*. Text by John K. Howat, Natalie Spassky, and John Wilmerding. April 16–September 7, 1970.

———. ———. *Two Hundred Years of Watercolor Painting in America: An Exhibition Commemorating the Centennial of the American Watercolor Society*. December 8, 1966–January 29, 1967.

———. The Milch Galleries. *Memorial Exhibition: Water Color Sketches by Thomas Moran*. December 20, 1926–January 8, 1927.

———. The Museum of Modern Art. *The Natural Paradise: Painting in America, 1800–1950*. Edited by Kynaston McShine. September 29–November 30, 1976.

———. National Academy of Design. *A Century and a Half of American Art*. October 10–November 16, 1975.

———. Newhouse Galleries, Inc. *A Loan Exhibition of Paintings by Thomas Moran, N.A., to Commemorate the Centenary of His Birth*. January 12–30, 1937.

———. Washburn Gallery. *Drawings and Watercolors of the West, Thomas Moran, from the Collection of the Cooper-Hewitt Museum of Design*. October 1–19, 1974.

————. Whitney Museum of American Art. *The American Frontier: Images and Myths*. Text by Patricia Hills. June 26–September 16, 1973.

————. ————. *A Century of American Landscape Painting, 1800–1900*. Text by Lloyd Goodrich. January 19–February 25, 1938.

————. ————. *A History of American Watercolor Painting*. January 27–February 25, 1942.

Nicholson, Marjorie Hope. *Mountain Gloom and Mountain Glory: The Development of the Aesthetics of the Infinite*. Ithaca, N.Y.: Cornell University Press, 1959.

Noble, R. P. *A Guide to Water Colour Painting*. London: George Rowney & Co., [1850].

Notre Dame, Indiana, University. Art Gallery. *The Drawings and Watercolors of Thomas Moran (1837–1926)*. Text by Thomas S. Fern. April 14–May 30, 1976.

Novak, Barbara. *American Painting of the Nineteenth Century: Realism, Idealism and the American Experience*. New York: Praeger, 1969.

————. "Thomas Moran and the Grand Canyon of the Yellowstone." *Honolulu Academy of Arts Journal* 1 (1974): 30–35.

Oakland, California. Mills College Art Gallery. *Selections from the Drawings and Watercolor Collections*. February 1972.

Orange, Texas. Stark Museum of Art. *Stark Museum of Art: The Western Collection*. Text by Julie Schimmel with the assistance of Gilbert Tapley Vincent. Orange, Texas: Stark Museum of Art, 1978.

"Painter of the Western Scene." *Antiques* 31, no. 3 (March 1937): 136.

Parker, Robert Allerton. "The Water-Colors of Thomas Moran." *International Studio* 86 (March 1927): 65–72. Excerpts reprinted in *Thomas Moran: Explorer in Search of Beauty*, ed. Fritiof Fryxell, pp. 77–84.

Patrick, Darryl. "The Iconographical Significance in Selected Western Subjects Painted by Thomas Moran." Ph.D. dissertation, North Texas State University, 1978.

Philadelphia Museum of Art. *Philadelphia: Three Centuries of American Art*. April 11–October 10, 1976.

Phoenix Art Museum. *Beyond the Endless River: Western American Drawings and Watercolors of the Nineteenth Century*. Text by James K. Ballinger. January 12–February 18, 1979.

Powell, John Wesley. "The Cañons of the Colorado." *Scribner's Monthly* 9, nos. 3–5 (January–March 1875): 293–310, 394–409, 523–537.

————. *Canyons of the Colorado*. 1895. Reprint, New York: Dover Publications, 1961.

Powers, Laura Bride. "Early Art of Thomas Moran Shown in Art Club Exhibit." *Santa Barbara Morning Press*, June 16, 1925.

Rasmussen, William M. S. "Art of the Nineteenth Century Government Explorations in the West: Changing Concepts of the Western Landscape." Master's thesis, University of Delaware, 1975.

Rees, Ronald. "The Scenery Cult: Changing Landscape Tastes over Three Centuries." *Landscape* 19, no. 3 (May 1975): 39–47.

Richardson, Edgar P. *American Romantic Painting*. Edited by Robert Freund. New York: E. Weyhe, 1944.

Richardson, James, ed. *Wonders of the Yellowstone*. New York: Scribner, Armstrong and Company, 1873.

Ross, Marvin C. *The West of Alfred Jacob Miller*. Norman: University of Oklahoma Press, 1951.

Rossi, Paul A., and David C. Hunt. *The Art of the Old West*. New York: Alfred A. Knopf, 1971.

Ruskin, John. *Modern Painters*. 5 vols. 4th ed. Boston: Dana Estes and Company, 1873.

Sachs, Samuel, II. "Thomas Moran—Drawings and Watercolors." Master's thesis, New York University, 1963.

St. Louis. City Art Museum. *A Collector's Choice*. March 1–16, 1969.

St. Petersburg, Florida. Museum of Fine Arts. *They Saw the West*. October 1–November 10, 1968.

Santa Barbara, California. Free Public Library. Faulkner Memorial Art Gallery. *Loan Exhibition: Paintings and Etchings by Thomas Moran*. July 2–20, 1937.

———. Santa Barbara Art Association. Casa de la Guerra. *Exhibition of Water Color Sketches by Thomas Moran*. December 20, 1925–January 8, 1926.

Scottsdale, Arizona. Jim Fowler's Period Gallery West. *The Alluring West*. 1978.

Sellin, David. *American Art in the Making: Preparatory Studies for Masterpieces of American Painting, 1800–1900*. Washington, D.C.: Smithsonian Institution Press, 1976.

Sheldon, G. W. *American Painters*. Enl. ed. New York: D. Appleton and Company, 1881.

Simpson, William H. "Thomas Moran—The Man." *Fine Arts Journal* 20, no. 1 (January 1909): 18–25.

Slatkins, Charles E., and Regina L. Shoolman. *Treasury of American Drawings*. New York: Oxford University Press, 1947.

Steadman, David. "Oil Sketches by Frederic E. Church." *American Art Review* 3, no. 1 (January–February 1976): 116–122.

Stebbins, Theodore E., Jr. *American Master Drawings and Watercolors*. New York: Harper and Row, 1976.

———. *Close Observation: Selected Oil Sketches by Frederic E. Church*. Washington, D.C.: Smithsonian Institution Press, 1978.

———. *The Life and Works of Martin Johnson Heade*. New Haven, Conn.: Yale University Press, 1975.

Stegner, Wallace E. *Beyond the Hundredth Meridian: John Wesley Powell and the Second Opening of the West*. Boston: Houghton Mifflin, 1954.

Stein, Roger B. *John Ruskin and Aesthetic Thought in America, 1840–1900*. Cambridge, Mass.: Harvard University Press, 1967.

———. *Seascape and the American Imagination*. New York: Clarkson N. Potter, 1975.

Stevens, Nina Spalding. "A Notable Collection of American Paintings." *Fine Arts Journal* 22, no. 3 (March 1910): 146–164.

———. "A Pilgrimage to the Artist's Paradise." *Fine Arts Journal* 34, no. 2 (February 1911): 105–113.

Sutherland, Abby. *One Hundred Years of Ogontz*. Abington, Pa., 1958.

Sweeney, J. Gray. "The Artist-Explorers of the American West, 1860–1880." Ph.D. dissertation, Indiana University, 1975.

Sweet, Frederick A. "Painters of the Hudson River School." *Antiques* 47, no. 3 (March 1945): 158–161.

Taft, Robert. *Artists and Illustrators of the Old West: 1850–1900*. New York: C. Scribner's Sons, 1953.

———. *Photography and the American Scene: A Social History, 1839–1889*. New York: Macmillan Co., 1938.

Talbot, William S. "A Check List: American Paintings and Water Colors of the Eighteenth, Nineteenth, and Early Twentieth Century in The Cleveland Museum of Art." *Bulletin of The Cleveland Museum of Art* 60, no. 1 (January 1973): 21–35.

Thomas, Davis, and Karin Ronnefeldt, eds. *People of the First Man*. New York: E. P. Dutton, [1976].

"Thomas Moran Art in Milch Galleries an Amazing Record." *New York American*, December 26, 1926.

"Thomas Moran Memorial." *Brooklyn Eagle*, December 26, 1926.

"Thomas Moran's Grand Cañon of the Yellowstone." *Scribner's Monthly* 4, no. 2 (June 1872): 251–252.

"Thomas Moran's Water-Color Drawings." *Scribner's Monthly* 5, no. 3 (January 1873): 394.

[Thompson, Almon Harris.] "Diary of Almon Harris Thompson." Introduction by Herbert E. Gregory. *Utah Historical Quarterly* 7, nos. 1, 2, 3 (January, April, July 1939).

Trenton, Patricia. *Harvey Otis Young, the Lost Genius, 1840–1901.* Denver: Denver Art Museum, 1975.

Truettner, William H. *The Natural Man Observed: A Study of Catlin's Indian Gallery.* Washington, D.C.: Smithsonian Institution Press, 1979.

———. "'Scenes of Majesty and Enduring Interest': Thomas Moran Goes West." *Art Bulletin* 58, no. 2 (June 1976): 241–259.

Vaughn, Malcolm. "Moran Centennial Heads Art Shows Opened This Week." *New York American,* January 16, 1937.

Washington, D.C. Adams, Davidson Galleries, Inc. *100 Years of American Drawings and Watercolors, 1870–1970.* September–October 1974.

———. ———. *100 Years of American Painting, 1840–1940.* March 19–April 22, 1972.

———. The National Endowment for the Arts and the Corcoran Gallery of Art. *Wilderness.* October 9–November 14, 1971.

———. Smithsonian Institution, National Collection of Fine Arts. *Academy: The Academic Tradition in American Art, an Exhibition Organized on the Occasion of the One Hundred and Fiftieth Anniversary of the National Academy of Design: 1825–1975.* Text by Lois Marie Fink and Joshua C. Taylor. June 6–September 1, 1975.

———. ———. *American Landscape: A Changing Frontier.* Text by David W. Scott. April 28–June 19, 1966.

———. ———. *National Parks and the American Landscape.* Text by William H. Truettner and Robin Bolton-Smith. June 23–August 27, 1972.

———. ———. *Prints, Drawings, and Watercolors, Checklist of Opening Exhibition.* May–June 1968.

———. ———. *Treasures from the Cooper Union Museum.* July 13–September 24, 1967.

Weiss, Ila Joyce Solomon. "Sanford Robinson Gifford, 1823–1880." Ph.D. dissertation, Columbia University, 1968.

Wilkins, Thurman. "Moran." *American Scene* 5, no. 1 (1963): 22–37, 57–58.

———. *Thomas Moran, Artist of the Mountains.* Norman: University of Oklahoma Press, 1966.

Williams, Talcott. "The Philadelphia Watercolor Exhibition." *International Studio* 22 (June 1904): 230.

Wilson, James Benjamin. "The Significance of Thomas Moran as an American Landscape Painter." Ph.D. dissertation, Ohio State University, 1955.

Exhibition Checklist

1. *Beaver Head Cañon, Montana*
   CATALOGUE NO. 1
   Museum of Fine Arts, Boston, Gift of Maxim Karolik (60.427)
2. *Lower Entrance to Madison Cañon, Yellowstone*
   CATALOGUE NO. 16
   Jefferson National Expansion Memorial, St. Louis, Missouri (4299)
3. *Big Springs in Yellowstone Park*
   CATALOGUE NO. 29
   Private Collection
4. *Castle Geyser*
   CATALOGUE NO. 31
   Private Collection
5. *Giant Blue Spring, Yellowstone*
   CATALOGUE NO. 36
   Private Collection
6. *Great Blue Spring of the Lower Geyser Basin, Fire Hole River, Yellowstone*
   CATALOGUE NO. 39
   The Dietrich Corporation, Philadelphia, Pennsylvania
7. *Hot Springs of Gardiners River, Yellowstone National Park, Wyoming Territory*
   CATALOGUE NO. 46
   Reynolda House Museum of American Art
8. *Mammoth Hot Springs*
   CATALOGUE NO. 49
   Collection of Robert H. Levis II
9. *Mammoth Hot Springs, Yellowstone*
   CATALOGUE NO. 50
   National Collection of Fine Arts, Smithsonian Institution, Gift of Mrs. Armistead Peter, Jr. (1958.52)
10. *Minerva Terrace, Yellowstone National Park, Wyoming Territory*
    CATALOGUE NO. 51
    Private Collection
11. *Old Faithful*
    CATALOGUE NO. 52
    Phelan Collection
12. *Tower Creek, Yellowstone*
    CATALOGUE NO. 53
    The Pennsylvania State University, Ogontz Campus
13. *Tower Falls and Sulphur Mountain, Yellowstone*
    CATALOGUE NO. 55
    Collection of Robert H. Levis II
14. *Tower Falls and Sulfur Rock, Yellowstone*
    CATALOGUE NO. 57
    Private Collection

15. *Upper Falls, Yellowstone*
    CATALOGUE NO. 61
    Philbrook Art Center, Tulsa, Oklahoma

16. *Yellowstone Canyon*
    CATALOGUE NO. 64
    Collection of Carl Schaefer Dentzel

17. *Yellowstone Cone, Liberty Cap*
    CATALOGUE NO. 65
    Private Collection

18. *Hot Springs of the Yellowstone Park*
    CATALOGUE NO. 75
    Cooper-Hewitt Museum, The Smithsonian Institution's National Museum of
    Design, Gift of the artist (1917.17.70)

19. *The Needles*
    CATALOGUE NO. 91
    Cooper-Hewitt Museum, The Smithsonian Institution's National Museum of
    Design, Gift of the artist (1917.17.18)

20. *South Dome, Yosemite*
    CATALOGUE NO. 94
    Cooper-Hewitt Museum, The Smithsonian Institution's National Museum of
    Design, Gift of the artist (1917.17.32)

21. *The South Dome, Yosemite Valley*
    CATALOGUE NO. 95
    Jefferson National Expansion Memorial, St. Louis, Missouri (4300)

22. *Study of Conifers in Yosemite*
    CATALOGUE NO. 97
    Private Collection

23. *Summit of the Sierras, Nevada*
    CATALOGUE NO. 98
    The Art Institute of Chicago, Gift of Mrs. Byron Harvey (1965.852)

24. *Canyon of the Rio Virgin, Utah*
    CATALOGUE NO. 102
    Private Collection

25. *Cliffs of the Rio Virgin, Southern Utah*
    CATALOGUE NO. 103
    Cooper-Hewitt Museum, The Smithsonian Institution's National Museum of
    Design, Gift of the artist (1917.17.20)

26. *From Powell's Plateau*
    CATALOGUE NO. 107
    Cooper-Hewitt Museum, The Smithsonian Institution's National Museum of
    Design, Gift of the artist (1917.17.26)

27. *Grand Canyon*
    CATALOGUE NO. 110
    Collection of Mr. and Mrs. Gerald P. Peters

28. *Grand Cañon from Hance's Trail, Ayers Butte in Foreground*
    CATALOGUE NO. 111
    East Hampton Free Library, The Thomas Moran Biographical Art Collection

29. *Grand Canyon of the Colorado*
   CATALOGUE NO. 117
   Collection of Mr. and Mrs. Michael Coleman

30. *Looking West from Moran's Point*
   CATALOGUE NO. 124
   East Hampton Free Library, The Thomas Moran Biographical Art Collection

31. *Looking up the Trail at Bright Angel, Grand Canyon of Arizona*
   CATALOGUE NO. 126
   Cooper-Hewitt Museum, The Smithsonian Institution's National Museum of Design, Gift of the artist (1917.17.83)

32. *Shin-Au-Av-Tu-Weap, or "God Land." Cañon of the Colorado, Utah Ter.*
   CATALOGUE NO. 133
   National Collection of Fine Arts, Smithsonian Institution, Gift of Dr. William H. Holmes (1930.12.42)

33. *Shiva's Temple*
   CATALOGUE NO. 134
   East Hampton Free Library, The Thomas Moran Biographical Art Collection

34. *Shiva's Temple, Grand Canyon*
   CATALOGUE NO. 135
   Jefferson National Expansion Memorial, St. Louis, Missouri (4296)

35. *Glen Eyrie, Colorado*
   CATALOGUE NO. 144
   Cooper-Hewitt Museum, The Smithsonian Institution's National Museum of Design, Gift of the artist (1917.17.67)

36. *Monument Valley Park, Colorado*
   CATALOGUE NO. 148
   Colorado Springs Fine Arts Center Collection: Dreffein Purchase Funds in Memory of Mr. Henry A. Dreffein

37. *Mosquito Trail, Rocky Mountains of Colorado*
   CATALOGUE NO. 149
   Private Collection in New York

38. *The Mountain of the Holy Cross*
   CATALOGUE NO. 152
   Private Collection

39. *Mountain of the Holy Cross*
   CATALOGUE NO. 153
   Loaned by the Great Grand-daughter of William A. Bell and the Grand-daughter of Mrs. Harold Pearce for whom it was painted and gifted by the artist

40. *Pike's Peak, Manitou Canyon*
   CATALOGUE NO. 155
   Amon Carter Museum of Western Art, Fort Worth (66.73)

41. *Smelting Works at Denver*
   CATALOGUE NO. 156
   The Cleveland Museum of Art, Bequest of Mrs. Henry A. Everett for the Dorothy Burnham Everett Memorial Collection (38.56)

69. *The Hacienda of San Juan Mexico*
   CATALOGUE NO. 247
   Cooper-Hewitt Museum, The Smithsonian Institution's National Museum of
   Design, Gift of the artist (1917.17.48)
70. *Hopi House, Grand Canyon, Arizona*
   CATALOGUE NO. 248
   Mr. and Mrs. William Belknap
71. *Laguna from the East*
   CATALOGUE NO. 249
   East Hampton Free Library, The Thomas Moran Biographical Art Collection
72. *Castle Butte, Green River, Wyoming*
   CATALOGUE NO. 263
   Collection of Christopher T. May, Sterling A. May, Meredith May, and Laura
   May
73. *Castle Butte, Green River, Wyoming*
   CATALOGUE NO. 264
   The Bancroft Library, University of California at Berkeley
74. *Green River*
   CATALOGUE NO. 270
   Collection of Carl Schaefer Dentzel
75. *Green River*
   CATALOGUE NO. 271
   The George F. McMurray Collection at Trinity College, Hartford, Connecticut
76. *Green River Buttes*
   CATALOGUE NO. 275
   American Heritage Center, University of Wyoming at Laramie, Gift of F. M.
   Fryxell
77. *Green River Crossing*
   CATALOGUE NO. 281
   Courtesy of Mr. and Mrs. William H. Bertsche
78. *Green River from the Ferry*
   CATALOGUE NO. 282
   Cooper-Hewitt Museum, The Smithsonian Institution's National Museum of
   Design, Gift of the artist (1917.17.38)
79. *Green River, Wyoming*
   CATALOGUE NO. 285
   Cooper-Hewitt Museum, The Smithsonian Institution's National Museum of
   Design, Gift of the artist (1917.17.39)
80. *Green River, Wyoming Territory*
   CATALOGUE NO. 290
   Jefferson National Expansion Memorial, St. Louis, Missouri (4297)

Index

COLLECTORS, DONORS, AND COLLECTIONS